Population and Society

Population and Society

An Introduction

Gregg Lee Carter

polity

First published in 2016 by Polity Press

Polity Press
65 Bridge Street
Cambridge CB2 1UR, UK

Polity Press
350 Main Street
Malden, MA 02148, USA

ISBN-13: 978-0-7456-6837-6
ISBN-13: 978-0-7456-6838-3 (pb)

A catalogue record for this book is available from the British Library.

Library of Congress Cataloging-in-Publication Data

Carter, Gregg Lee, 1951- author.
    Population and society : an introduction / Gregg Lee Carter.
       pages   cm
    Includes bibliographical references and index.
    ISBN 978-0-7456-6837-6 (hardback : alk. paper) – ISBN 978-0-7456-6838-3
(pbk. : alk. paper) 1. Population–Social aspects. I. Title.
    HB849.44.C37 2016
    304.2–dc23
                        2015031295

Typeset in 10 on 12 pt Sabon
by Toppan Best-set Premedia Limited

Printed and bound in the US by RR Donnelley

For further information on Polity, visit our website: politybooks.com

Contents

For Jack, Betsy, and Lisa,
for their love, joy, peace, patience, and kindness...

Acknowledgments

The following individuals carefully reviewed *Population and Society: An Introduction*, for which I am greatly appreciative: Drs Walter F. Carroll (Bridgewater State University), William Egelman (Iona College), and Thomas W. Ramsbey (*Emeritus*, Rhode Island College). Dr William H. Kory (University of Pittsburgh at Johnstown) also reviewed Chapter 1, while Drs Paul Lokken and Antoine Joseph (Bryant University) reviewed parts of Chapter 5. Of course none of them bears responsibility for any errors of omission or commission that might have crept into my final manuscript.

The staff of Bryant University is cheery and always accommodating: Administrative assistants Joanne Socci and Sue Wandyes performed many valued support services. Bryant has a first-rate university library, with a uniformly excellent staff. Head reference librarian Laura Kohl was very helpful, as were her associates Jenifer Bond, Erica Cataldi-Roberts, and Cheryl Richardson. Extra special thanks to Ms Kohl's associates Mackenzie Dunn and Allison Papini, both of whom consistently assisted me in locating my most arcane reference materials.

Regarding translations and interpretations of selected details about Chinese society, I would like to thank my bilingual Bryant University colleagues Professors Yun Xiao, Hong Yang, and Chen Zhang, as well as Mr. Kongli Liu (Associate Director of Bryant's US–China Institute). I am grateful to additional Bryant colleagues Professors David Lux and Michael Bryant for their support in helping me receive a research sabbatical, a critical resource for allowing me to complete this book in a timely manner.

Lindsey A. Bailey and *Pamela* Wasserman at the nonprofit organization Population Connection (http://www.populationconnection.org) graciously helped me gain approval for my use in Chapter 2 of still images from the organization's highly respected video entitled *World Population Growth*. Pastor Matt Kottman of Disciples Church (Leatherhead, UK) graciously granted permission to use the photo of Mumbai in Chapter 2. The epigraph by Castles, de Hass, and Miller at the start of Chapter 5 has been reprinted with permission of Guilford Press.

At Polity Press, senior commissioning editor Jonathan Skerrett was enthusiastic and encouraging of this project from the start. Moreover, his editorial advice was measured and consistently helpful. Justin Dyer served as an excellent copyeditor.

Finally, on a personal note, I want to thank my wife, Lisa, for her unending encouragement, and my children – Travis, Kurtis, Alexis, and Davis – for their love and forbearance.

Gregg Lee Carter
Bryant University
Smithfield, Rhode Island

Introduction

This book presents the field of demography from the perspective of social demography. In this approach, the classic concepts of demography are imparted – including theories and measurements of population size, distribution, composition, and change – while at the same time a stronger emphasis is placed than in a standard demography textbook on their connections to the culture, the economy, the polity, the society, and, ultimately, the choices individuals make in their everyday lives.

The present volume offers the basics, animates the sociological imagination, and throughout gives multiple demonstrations on how taking a demographic perspective can give us a better understanding of phenomena once thought to be largely the products of the culture, the polity, or the economy. Demography does not explain everything, of course, but there is a demographic component to the explanation of virtually all contemporary social problems, as well as in the genesis of many individual-level attitudes and behaviors. Many observers, many students, are unaware of this component and are often surprised at its power when it is brought into the discussion.

For example, what accounts for the rise and vitality of a women's movement in a particular society at a particular time in history? To wit, why the rise of the women's movement in the United States in the late 1960s? Why not the late 1940s or, say, the 1950s? There are volumes written on this topic, but a key part of the explanation resides in the demographic concept of the *marriage squeeze*. Women typically marry men of their age or a few years older – at least for their first marriages.

The US baby boom after World War II produced some 5 million women in their 20s without traditional marriage partners (men of their age or slightly older) by 1970. How? Each year between 1946 and 1957, the number of births increased. When the women born in a particular year got out of high school or college and started looking around for good marriage material, they would have been searching for partners born a few years before them – when a smaller number of men had been born. Thus, starting in the mid-1960s, each year the pool of unmarried women began to grow. The applicable *sex ratios* (number of men per 100 women) for people in their 20s changed dramatically during the late 1960s. For example, in 1960, there were 111 men in the 22–6 age bracket for every 100 women in the 20–4 age bracket; by 1970, the comparable sex ratio had fallen to 84. Traditional female gender role aspirations (wife, mother, homemaker, and working only part-time to supplement the family's income) became unattainable for some 5 million young women – providing a key seed from which the modern women's movement sprouted.

This kind of analysis, bringing the demographic perspective to bear on a variety of contemporary social issues, appears throughout this volume. What gives these analyses coherence is how each emphasizes the ways in which demographic forces both reflect and limit individual choices. Although virtually no contemporary social issue can be truly understood without taking demography into consideration, the topics receiving the most attention in the present volume are (1) the social and individual determinants of fertility, mortality, and migration; (2) the social and individual impacts of changing levels of fertility, mortality, and migration; and (3) the impacts of overpopulation on the environment, and how changes in the environment, in turn, impact the human condition, especially regarding migration.

The sociological perspective and how major social institutions interact with demographic processes are central to the field of social demography and to this book. For example, the institution of the family has undergone dramatic transformations in the past half-century and these transformations are closely entwined with fertility, mortality, and migration. As developed in Chapters 2 and 4 during discussions of *demographic transition theory*, for most of human history, high death rates encouraged human cultures worldwide to have a "be fruitful and multiply" value orientation – with the clan, tribe, or society at risk of extinction if it did not adopt this orientation. This created a very long period, actually most of human history, of traditional gender roles – with women spending the bulk of their fertile years either pregnant or breast-feeding, and thus restricting their food-generating and economic productive activities to the home or very close to it (e.g., foraging nearby plants or tending nearby gardens). After a society brought down its death rate, during the nineteenth and first half of the twentieth centuries in Europe and northern America, and during a much shorter period after World War II in the developing areas of Asia, Africa, and Latin America, cultural norms regarding keeping fertility rates high and women constrained to traditional gender roles could be relaxed. Lower birth rates freed women to increase their levels of education and to enter the paid labor force in large numbers. This both encouraged and was encouraged by couples viewing small families as advantageous, both for themselves, in being able to fulfill their own potential, and for their children, in that fewer children allowed for increased investments (e.g., educationally) in each individual child whom the couple did have. Eventually, a balance of low death rates and low birth rates was achieved. However, in recent decades the cultural emphasis on individual development has intensified and spread both geographically and socially to the point where large numbers of individuals have begun (a) delaying marriage; (b) delaying the age at which they have their first child; (c) reconceptualizing family size, such that having few children – and even no children – is seen as beneficial both to themselves as individuals and to the greater society (e.g., not contributing to "overpopulation" and its attendant problems); and (d) creating and accepting new family forms, including cohabitation without marriage, same-sex unions/marriages, single-parent families, and blended families (with divorced individuals and children from prior unions and marriages coming together to form new families via remarriage or cohabitation). These four trends have become known as the *second demographic transition* and have resulted in birth rates falling below death rates in an increasing number of societies (see Chapters 2 and 4). The upside has been the increased chances of each individual realizing his or her full potential. But the downside is the creation of new social problems affecting an increasing number of countries: When the average woman in a society has fewer than two children in her lifetime, one to replace herself and one to replace a male, the younger generation becomes smaller relative to prior generations. As longevity has increased dramatically in both the developed and developing worlds (see Chapter 3), the burdens on the young generation to support the healthcare and related needs of their aging parents and grandparents rise dramatically. One solution is to encourage immigration, such that the younger generation is bulked up in size by the immigrant population (who tend to be young working adults and thereby can add substantial resources to the younger native generation). In sum, we see the intimate interplay between the changing social institution of the family and how it is impacted by, and in turn impacts, changing rates of mortality, fertility, and migration.

Population and Society is comprised of five main chapters, plus a substantial References section, and a detailed Index. Each chapter ends with a *Main Points and Key Terms* section, a set of *Review Questions*, and an annotated list of *Suggested Readings and Online Sources*. The ultimate goal is to stimulate the reader to better understand how his or her life has been, is, and will continue to be influenced by large and powerful demographic forces; and how, despite being a daunting undertaking, these forces can be reined in and controlled by the choices we make – as individuals, as well as by the group-level decisions we make in our families, neighborhoods, communities, nations, and international bodies.

1

Overview of Population Study

Population trends significantly influence individual experience and national policies; they may cause, or provide necessary conditions for, the occurrence of major social, economic, and cultural changes. ... Some knowledge of population is therefore essential to the rational understanding of the world we live in.

Dennis H. Wrong (1990)

Classic Demography: Population Size, Distribution, Composition, and Change

Demography is the formal study of human populations. In practice, *classic demography* studies the *size* of a population in a given geographic area (e.g., how many hundreds, thousands, or millions of people live in it); the *distribution* of the population within the area (e.g., the percentage living in rural areas, in small towns, in suburbs, in cities); the *composition* of the population (most commonly, breakdowns by age and sex); and the *change* of the population (growth or decline) between specific time points (e.g., 2016 to 2017) – as determined by the number of births (*fertility*), deaths (*mortality*), and migrants to and from the area (*migration*).

Table 1.1 and Figure 1.1 illustrate how three nations – India, the United Kingdom , and the United States – would be described from the approach of classic demography. Figure 1.1 displays the *population*

Table 1.1: *Classic demographic characteristics of India, the United Kingdom, and the United States*

Characteristic	India	UK	US
Size	1,220,800,359	63,395,574	316,668,567
Age composition			
% 0–14 years	28.9	17.3	20.0
% 15–24 years	18.2	12.8	13.7
% 25–54 years	40.4	41.1	40.2
% 55–64 years	6.9	11.5	12.3
% 65 and over	5.7	17.3	13.9
Median male age	26.1	39.1	35.9
Median female age	27.4	41.4	38.5
Sex composition			
0–14 years			
Male	187,236,677	5,625,040	32,344,207
Female	165,219,615	5,346,815	31,006,688
15–24 years			
Male	117,385,009	4,158,813	22,082,128
Female	104,516,448	3,986,831	21,157,025
25–54 years			
Male	253,642,261	13,250,434	63,802,736
Female	239,219,931	12,807,328	63,581,749
55–64 years			
Male	42,307,170	3,589,345	18,699,338
Female	41,785,413	3,680,392	20,097,791
65 years and over			
Male	32,992,850	4,877,079	19,122,853
Female	36,494,985	6,073,497	24,774,052
Overall			
% Male	51.9	49.7	49.2
% Female	48.1	50.3	50.8
	108.0	99.0	97.0
Sex ratio			
(Number of men per 100 women)			
Total fertility rate	2.5	2.0	1.9
(Expected number of children a woman will have in her lifetime)			
Infant mortality rate	44.6	5.9	4.5
(Number of deaths of infants under 1 year of age per 1,000 live births)			
Net migration rate	–0.1	2.6	3.6
(Annual population increase or decrease due to migration)			
Distribution (% Urban)	31.3	80.0	82.0
(Percentage of total population living in an urban area)			

Data sources: Population Reference Bureau (2012); *World Factbook* (2013).

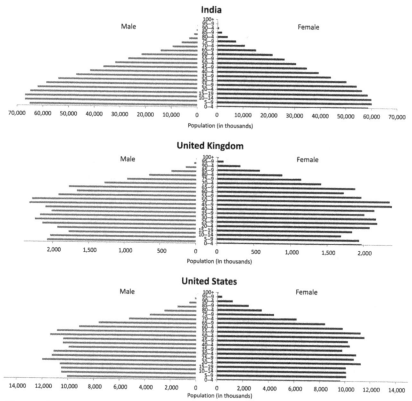

Figure 1.1: Population pyramids for India, the United Kingdom, and the United States
Source: Raw data from United Nations (2016a, 2016b)

pyramid for each nation, a heuristic device to help us get a better grasp of a specific population through a graphic representation of the size, age, and sex information in Table 1.1.

Notice how different the pyramids look, with the United Kingdom and the United States being shaped somewhat like a beehive, while India appears more like a standard pyramid. The narrow bases of the United Kingdom and the United States reveal that they have, relative to India, small populations of youths, while India has a much wider base – revealing a much higher percentage of its population under 40. Moving upward on these pyramids, the United Kingdom and the United States reveal broader middle and broader top sections, indicating that they have, proportionally speaking, many more middle-aged and older individuals.

These two shapes are typical throughout the 267 political states and territories of the world, with those that are economically developed usually having more beehive-shaped pyramids, those that are developing revealing more standard-looking pyramids (bases tend to be wide, while tops tend to be narrow), and those that are the least developed displaying very standard-looking pyramids (very wide bases and very narrow tops). Finally, notice how the male and female age groups tend to be of equal horizontal length until the very oldest groups (70 and over) for the United Kingdom and United States, while for India, the younger ages favor males – revealing a skewed *sex ratio*. (The biological expectation for a human population is close to an even split between the sexes: At birth, about 51% male and about 49% female; male infants naturally have a higher mortality rate during the first year of life, so after very early childhood, a 50–50 split is expected until very old age, when females again have a biological edge and their proportion increases.)

An important observation regarding the preceding paragraph needs to be made here as the level of *socioeconomic development* is a critical variable in cross-national social demographic analysis. The United Nations labels as *more developed* the nations of Europe, plus Australia, Canada, Japan, New Zealand, and the United States – all prosperous by world standards. It labels as *less developed* all the nations of Asia (save for Japan), as well as most of those in Latin America, the Caribbean, and Oceania (the South Pacific); in addition, about 40% of African nations have the "less developed" label ("less developed" nations are on the road to prosperity, but still have a long way to go – examples include both China and India). Finally, the UN labels as *least developed* those nations that are extremely poor – where malnutrition, infectious disease, and early death are common; the majority of these countries are in Africa (34 of its 55 nations); nine are in Asia, one in the Caribbean (Haiti), and four in Oceania (see United Nations 2010, 2013a). Throughout this book, "more developed" and "economically developed" will be used interchangeably, while "less developed" and "least developed" will often be labeled "developing."

Classic demographic analysis tries to build models that both describe and predict variations in a key demographic variable. The variable being predicted in all sciences, including demography, is labeled the *dependent variable* (in everyday English, we say the *outcome*, the *effect*, the *consequence*), and a variable used to predict a dependent variable (again, in all sciences) is called an *independent variable* (synonyms in everyday English include *cause of*, *reason for*). For example, why do fertility rates tend to be higher in poorer societies? In the case of Table 1.1, why do women in the United Kingdom and the United States tend to have fewer children than women in India? *Demographic transition theory*, which will be more fully developed later in this chapter and in Chapter 2, quite logically predicts that if a society has a high death rate and is to survive into the future, then it must develop a culture that emphasizes "be fruitful and multiply" – that is, it must have a high birth rate. Indeed, we can see that India's infant mortality rate is much higher than the rate in either the United Kingdom or the United States, just as predicted. More generally, Figure 1.2 reveals that there is a strong and consistent pattern across the nations of the world for infant mortality and fertility to be *positively* related – a greater level of mortality is associated with a greater probability of having a high fertility rate.

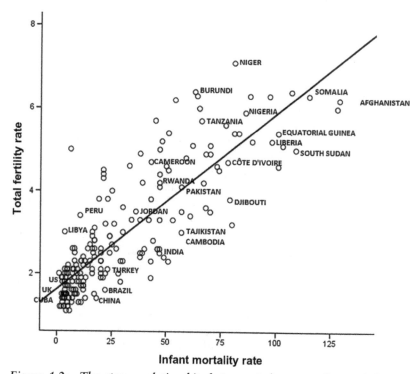

Figure 1.2: The strong relationship between infant mortality and fertility (with selected countries identified)
Source: Raw data from Population Reference Bureau (2012); N = 210 countries

Social Demography: The Interplay between Population Characteristics and Culture, Economy, Polity, Society, and Individual Choice

A social scientist examining Figure 1.1 immediately begins wondering what the implications of these shapes are for the people living in each country, and, further, wonders why the shapes developed as they did (e.g., Why so many young people in India when compared to the United Kingdom and United States? Why so many males versus females in India compared to the other two nations, where the numbers tend to be more equal?). This kind of curiosity spawned the field of *social demography*, which extends classic demographic concepts of population size, distribution, composition, and change into the realms of the culture, the economy, the polity, the society, and the constraints on and opportunities for the choices individuals make. The constructs from this new realm serve as both independent and dependent variables: that is, they have effects on the variables of classic demography (population size, distribution, composition, and change), and these classic demographic variables, in turn, affect the culture, and so on. Social demography also expands the list of population composition variables to include many cultural, economic, political, and social constructs – examples include ethnicity, family structure, occupation, race, governing regime type, religion, social class, and value orientations.

To illustrate social demographic analysis, let's continue the discussion of the concept of the *sex ratio* brought up in the Introduction. The sex ratio, the number of men per 100 women, is deemed balanced when it is 100 – or very close to it. A balanced ratio means that half the population is male and half is female. As the ratio becomes imbalanced, tending to 90, or even lower, or tending to 110, or even higher, it has effects that ripple throughout society. As observed in the Introduction, a society that develops a low ratio has an increased chance of experiencing a women's movement. The linchpin interpretation is that

> unlike the high sex ratio situation, women would find it difficult to achieve economic mobility through marriage [and thus] ... [t]hey might try to achieve economic and political independence for themselves and other women. We would expect various forms of feminism to be accelerated [and] ... the attempt on the part of women to establish themselves as independent persons in their own right. (Guttentag and Secord 1983: 20–1)

What about the opposite situation from that of the United States during the late 1960s, that is, what about a society, such as present-day India, where the sex ratio is high, especially when considering young adults – who are generally at a stage in life when they want to establish families and careers? In such a society, traditional gender roles for women are more likely to play out, and we would thus expect a higher proportion of women to marry, not to use modern means of birth control, to have children, to set aside their educational and career aspirations, and thus be willing (or be coerced) to marry at a relatively young age (even in their teens). Indeed, Part 1 of Table 1.2 confirms these expectations regarding India versus the United Kingdom and the United States, while Part 2 of this table confirms them around the world when we examine those countries with very high versus very low sex ratios. (Note that differential sex ratios reveal their effects only at the very high and very low ends of the continuum.)

Table 1.2: The association of the sex ratio with total fertility rate, percentage of females married at ages 15–19, and percentage of women using modern birth control (BC) methods

Part 1: *India versus the United Kingdom and the United States*

	India	UK	US
Sex ratio	108.0	99.0	97.0
Total fertility rate	2.5	2.0	1.9
% females married at ages 15–19	27.6	0.4	2.8
% married women using modern BC[a]	47.0	84.0	79.0

Part 2: *10 highest sex ratios nations versus 10 lowest sex ratio nations*

	(a) 10 highest nations	(b) 10 lowest nations	(c) Ratio of (a) to (b) (%)
Average sex ratio	153.9	87.4	176.1
Total fertility rate	2.3	1.9	121.1
% females married at ages 15–19	9.2	5.9	155.9
% married women using modern BC[a]	33.5	45.1	74.3

Note: [a] Percentage of women of reproductive age (15–49) who are married or in a union and are using, or whose sexual partners are using, a contemporary and effective method of contraception, including the pill, IUDs (intrauterine devices/coils), condoms, or sterilization.

Data sources: Population Reference Bureau (2012, 2014); United Nations (2012a); *World Factbook* (2013)

Of course, as emphasized in the Introduction, to approach a full understanding of any individual or group phenomenon requires a complex explanatory model containing many variables from many perspectives, including the psychological, the cultural, the economic, the political, and the social. Thus, for example, China also has an imbalanced sex ratio (106 overall; and even higher, 111, for those entering the age range when career education and marriage are becoming increasingly important – in their late teens and early 20s), but because of a combination of rapid economic development and a political program of *wan* (later marriage), *xi* (longer delays before having the next child), *shao* (fewer children) – culminating in its One-Child Policy of the past several decades – its total fertility rate of 1.6 is equal to that of the average Western European nation, where sex ratios tend be balanced and slightly below 100 (see data from Population Reference Bureau 2012).

In short, when sex ratios become imbalanced, especially for younger adults, profound social and cultural consequences often unfold in predictable patterns – especially consequences involving gender roles and how they interact with the culture, economy, and polity. This powerful demographic variable will be examined further in Chapter 4.

The Importance of the Demographic Perspective in Understanding the World We Live In

Auguste Comte (1798–1857), a founder of modern social science, famously observed that "demography is destiny." By this he meant that human attitudes and behaviors, at the level of both the individual and the group, cannot be fully understood without taking into account the core variables of demography – including population size, distribution, composition, and change. As empirically demonstrated in the preceding section, the sex ratio is correlated with fundamental variables affecting many of us: for example, at what age our parents married (if they married at all); how many siblings we had; what roles our parents played in childrearing versus working in the paid labor force; and the opportunities our mothers had to take one path in life versus another, such as becoming homemakers versus throwing themselves full-force into careers. Indeed, population variables have critical effects on, and are in turn critically affected by, all five of the major social institutions upon which all human societies are based: the economy, education, the family, the polity, and religion. The contours of these institutions, in turn, have powerful effects on individual health, prosperity, world views, and the choices each of us is afforded and ultimately makes.

The following are some more brief examples of how population factors shape the world we live in – all of which are developed more fully in later chapters.

Health and Mortality

Improvements in individual and public health lie at the heart of the population explosion that carried the world from a billion individuals in the early 1800s, which took 200,000 years to achieve, to more than 7 billion today (taking just 200 years to achieve). These improvements have had the demographic impact of reducing the frequency of deaths. As argued earlier in this chapter, a society with a high death rate must encourage and realize a high birth rate or else it risks withering away to the point of extinction.

At the societal level of analysis, economic development and associated advances in technology have been at the core in improving rates of good health and declining rates of mortality. Economic prosperity is, in part, a function of a healthy population, and, in turn, prosperity supports the growth of technologies that further good health. These technologies include those related to the *Green Revolution* (dramatic improvements in agriculture involving better-quality irrigation, fertilizers, pesticides, and seeds), enhanced immunization, and better public sanitation – all of which have served to encourage improved public and private health and a decrease in mortality (which goes hand-in-hand with an increase in longevity). For example, in the 20 nations of Northern and Western Europe, all generally quite prosperous, *life expectancy* averages are in the early 80s, while in the 14 generally economically depressed nations of Middle and Southern Africa, life expectancy is in the early 50s (Population Reference Bureau 2012).

At the family and individual levels of analysis (the *micro level*), economic prosperity is also critical. For example, in the contemporary United States, the death rate for males with less than a high school education is more than three times the rate of their counterparts with at least some college (821 vs 249 per 100,000; see National Center for Health Statistics 2008). The prosperity–health/mortality relationships at the micro level of analysis hold across nations of both the developed and developing worlds.

The links between prosperity and health/mortality are accounted for by a wide variety of factors, many of which involve little personal choice (e.g., the level of violence in the neighborhood; access to quality healthcare), but many of which do (including smoking, alcohol consumption, diet, stress control, and exercise). The factors involving personal choice also account for many of the differences in health status and mortality within particular social class and race/ethnic groups (see, e.g., Murray et al. 2006).

Increasing longevity is putting financial pressure on families, communities, and nations across the world: Who will pay for the retirement of those in their 70s, 80s, and 90s? Who will pay for their healthcare costs, especially the astronomical costs associated with the final months of life? The problem is growing in both the developed and less developed worlds, but is especially pressing in those nations experiencing population declines because of fertility rates having fallen below the replacement level of 2.1. One clear answer lies in demography: the encouragement of immigration. Immigrants tend to be younger and motivated by economic incentives and thus are more likely to work and to pay taxes.

Fertility

As noted previously, at its most basic level of explanation, the rate of fertility for a society reflects its infant and overall mortality rates. Societies with high death rates that do not have concomitantly high birth rates eventually cease to exist. Thus, the subduing of death is at the heart of declining fertility rates that have been occurring in the developed world for more than a century and in the less developed world for the past several decades. In the past half-century, less developed nations have been able to dramatically reduce their death rates without the foundation of economic prosperity that was traditionally required; they have done this by importing the technologies of death prevention, including immunization, mosquito control, clean water projects, and enhanced farming productivity (e.g., disease-resistant grains requiring less water).

Declining fertility rates have dramatic impacts on gender roles, with women being freed from the demands of pregnancy, nursing, and large families. The causation works both ways: Increasing prosperity increases individual health and lowers infant mortality and thereby releases women from the universal cultural demand in human history to "be fruitful and multiply"; at the same, when women begin working less at home and more in the paid labor force, their aspirations for education, for individual freedom, for self-development, all increase and their motivation to have many children fades.

This change in motivation can spill over into the wider culture, and social demographers have thus found that changes in family size are sensitive not only to changes in prosperity but also to shifts in the wider culture. The impact of culture becomes increasingly powerful with the rise of mass education and the mass media, both of which foster secular attitudes and individualism. These trends are reflected in the decision process of younger adults in weighing how having a child (or another child) will affect self-fulfillment and the pursuit of a higher standard of living (van de Kaa 2004; van de Walle and Knodel 1980; Watkins 1991); of course, the final decision is often to postpone having a child, as well as to keep the total number of children small (usually just two).

The relationships among increased education, greater economic prosperity, and smaller families hold at both the societal and individual levels of analysis. Why do those nations, those communities, those neighborhoods, those families, and those individuals least able to afford children end up having the most? This is a fascinating question for social demographers, the answering of which gives a keen appreciation of the sociological approach to the study of population (see Chapter 4).

Migration

The population size of any specified geographic area smaller than the entire world must take into account the demographic process of migration. Many different forms of migration will be defined in Chapter 5, but all involve the crossing of a significant political or geographic border.

For example, *immigration* involves moving *to* one country from another; and, relatedly, reversing the perspective, *emigration* is the moving *from* one country to another. In either case, the basic demographic process of migration can have dramatic effects on the fortunes of the populations involved: that is, of both the country of destination and the country of departure.

One example that has been receiving increasing public and government attention and concern in recent years is the *population implosion* being experienced in Japan and in many European nations. An implosion is set up when the total fertility rate falls under the replacement rate of 2.1, and is considered critically serious when the rate goes below 1.6. Traditionally, each generation that reaches maturity in the labor force (formal education is over; work careers are well established) is expected to take over the care of the surviving members of the generations that came before it: that is to say, working adults are expected to contribute to the welfare of their aging parents, grandparents, and great-grandparents. When fertility rates are fairly high (the average women having at least two or three children) and when longevity rates are fairly constrained (few individuals living past their early 70s), as has been the case of most of human history, the traditional expectation was more or less readily realized. However, in at least 36 nations today, most of them economically developed, the fertility rates have dropped below 1.6, while longevity has been extended to the point where many individuals can expect to live well into their 80s (see Population Reference Bureau 2009, 2015). There simply are not enough working adults to support the heavy needs of the older population.

Japan is the archetypical example of this phenomenon: The replacement fertility rate for economically developed countries is considered 2.1 (a child to replace each parent, plus a little extra to account for childhood deaths and for women who do not bear any children). Japan was well above this figure in the 1950s, but by 1960, fertility began to drop, and by the early 1970s, its total fertility rate fell to the replacement rate of 2.1; by the 1990s, it was down to 1.6, and by 2011, to 1.4 – and it continues to creep downward (data taken from Population Reference Bureau 2015; United Nations 2012b). The impacts on individual Japanese have been widespread and dramatic:

> [E]veryone is involved, in one way or another, or knows someone who is: Someone who has seen an elementary school turned into a community center for the elderly; is overstretched trying to do justice to a care-dependent parent and a job; someone who is troubled by mounting medical costs and a stagnant retirement allowance. ... Politicians who call for pension reform and fail to pay their premiums do not escape media attention any more than elderly people who have no one to care for them and who, therefore, commit suicide. (Coulmas 2007: 2)

What would help resolve Japan's implosion (indeed, any nation's implosion) would be a healthy amount of immigration, as immigrants' most common motivation for coming to a new nation is to find work; and because they tend to be younger, in their 20s and 30s, their work and the taxes they pay can help to support an aging population.

Population Pressures on the Environment and on Peaceful Coexistence

The stunning rate of world population growth over the past 200 years has wreaked, is wreaking, and will continue to wreak havoc on the environment and on the desires of much of humanity to live with one another in peaceful coexistence.

Actually, the damaging influences of uncontrolled population growth on our environment and on the desire of many to live in social harmony have been with humanity since its beginnings. The difference between our past and near future is that the effects of overpopulation, including societal collapse, were felt locally or in a small region, whereas now they involve continents.

One example (of many) currently unfolding: In the western part of the United States, atmospheric chemists have identified China as the source of dust, ozone, carbon monoxide, and mercury now polluting the once pristine Cascade mountain range (such pollutants being carried across the Pacific Ocean on the jet stream). As better data continue to be generated, climatologists are building increasingly accurate models on how world regions are and will be environmentally damaged by the dramatic escalations of fossil fuel burning in China, India, and other rapidly developing Asian countries – not to mention by the already enormous *carbon footprint* of developed nations (Gillis 2014; IPCC 2015; Melillo et al. 2014; NASA 1996; Oskin 2013; Simons 2013; Unger 2006; carbon footprint is the label environmental scientists use to describe the burning of fossil fuels, creating carbon dioxide and other pollutants).

The recent decline in the rate of population growth has lulled some observers into thinking that the real problems regarding the size of the population involve its downsizing: the population implosions happening in selected nations, especially those of Europe, China, and Japan (see, e.g., Pearce 2010). As noted earlier, these implosions have real impacts on the people of the nations involved, but the world as a whole is not experiencing any such implosion: even though the replacement rate of 2.1 children per woman is not being met in most developed nations today (this figure is closer to 1.6), with a base population of 7.3 billion, and with women in less developed nations averaging 2.6 children per woman and in least developed nations 4.3 children per woman, the size of the human population is growing by 237,000 people *per day* (393,000 births versus 156,000 deaths each day; calculations derived from the Population Reference Bureau 2015).

The slowing *rate* of population growth will, *perhaps*, ultimately reduce pressures on the environment, on economies, and on governments dealing with the manifold and myriad effects of high growth, but for the immediate future, the world has to deal with the environmental, employment, health, and political problems associated with the absolute and enormous size of the world's population – over 7.3 billion now, and 8 billion by 2023. "Perhaps" is used in the preceding sentence because the current generation of adults coming of age across much of the world is increasingly seeking a Western lifestyle (cars, mobile phones, computers, luxury goods, public amenities, etc.), a lifestyle that entails a heavy carbon footprint.

Broad Theoretical Frameworks Informing Social Demography

Demographic Transition Theory. Demographers explain the world population explosion with one or more variants of *demographic transition theory.* Throughout the overwhelming bulk of human history (if we trace the origin of our species back to 200,000 BCE, then for 99% of *homo sapiens'* existence), populations were kept relatively small and in check because of high death rates. Around 1800 CE, humanity reached its first billion, as food supplies had increased via the development of agriculture during the preceding several thousand years and as death rates began to drop as humans began keeping their sewage separated from their drinking water supplies. These developments continued for the next 130 years, as did the processes of industrialization and urbanization, when humanity reached its second billion around 1930. In the next 30 years, these processes spilled over borders more rapidly, with less developed nations importing and acquiring in a few decades the death-controlling technologies (public sanitation, vaccinations, agricultural improvements) that had taken more developed nations centuries to create, and humanity reached its third billion by 1960. Since then, it has taken just a little more than a decade to add another billion (by 1974, there was 4 billion; by 1987, 5 billion; by 1999, 6 billion; and by 2011, 7 billion).

As death rates dropped dramatically, there was a *cultural lag* in norms and values regarding family size, and the number of children being born was far above replacement rates in both the developing and developed worlds. Thus, in between the high death/high birth rates of traditional (preindustrial) societies and the low death/low birth rates of modern societies lies the *demographic transition.* The transition unfolds unevenly and differently for each nation – depending on its particular culture, political system, and history of war and migration. Given this messiness in the human experience, the theory is crude and provides more of a perspective for understanding population growth than offering precise predictions. It cannot say, for example, that at a given level of economic development (e.g., as measured by per capita gross domestic product [GDP]) the death rate will fall to a particular level, then be followed by the birth rate also dropping to a particular level. However, its strength lies in its correct expectation that the transition will occur in every society experiencing modernization. (See Chapters 2 and 4 for fuller discussions of demographic transition theory, including a recent variant of the theory used to account for the extremely low fertility of many nations in recent decades – a variant that places greater explanatory emphasis on the increasing importance of postmodern values promoting individual self-development and less emphasis on material circumstances [this variant having become known as the *second demographic transition*].)

Malthusianism/Neo-Malthusianism.   In his classic treatise *An Essay on the Principles of Human Population*, Thomas Robert Malthus (1798) observed that humanity is continually motivated by material interests to increase its population size: More people create more markets for mercantile and business interests; for an agricultural family, more children means more farmhands and potentially more prosperity; for the capitalist owners of factories and farms, more laborers drive down the cost of labor. The motivation is magnified by our robust drive to reproduce (our high level of sexuality; our libidos) – and the ultimate outcome is that population size has strong tendencies to outstrip food resources, the consequences of which can be disastrous: famine, pestilence, war, and high mortality. Malthus deemed these consequences *positive checks* for keeping population size and resources in balance. However, he also offered that humans have the capacity for *preventative checks* (though he believed our strong sexual nature obviates us from taking these pathways until the positive checks loom large). Such checks include "immoral" ones, such as infanticide, prostitution, and birth control, and "moral" ones – mainly abstinence and delayed marriage. Although his ideas of morality, of humans' incapacity to lower birth rates except in the face of disaster, and of the limited capacity of an acre of land to yield food have all essentially been discarded – in part, because birth control has gained widespread acceptance, in part because he did not foresee the impact of technology to increase the output of farmland, and in part because he did not clearly foresee the near universal phenomenon of the inverse relationship between prosperity and family size (the prosperous use their extra resources not to increase their number of children, but rather to increase self-development and self-fulfillment and in these pursuits see more children as a barrier) – his name and the core idea that *population and resources must be in balance* are his enduring legacy.

Malthus's thinking underpins the sociologically imaginative arguments of contemporary *neo-Malthusians*, including Lester R. Brown (e.g., 2009), Jared Diamond (e.g., 2005), Paul R. and Anne H. Ehrlich (e.g., 2005), and Marvin Harris (e.g., 1991). These scholars find population growth and the human tendency for overconsumption central to understanding:

- the development of technology (e.g., technologies motivated to more efficiently feed, clothe, house, and transport a growing population);
- political change (e.g., population growth often outstrips economic growth, leading to unemployment, discontent, and eventual regime

change; or to the motivation of regimes to make war to increase resources);

- environmental degradation (e.g., deforestation and the pollution of land, air, and water);
- the destruction of local economies that are based on natural resource extraction, from mining to logging to fishing; and, relatedly,
- poverty (and its correlates, e.g., disease, mortality, and violence).

Although the tone of the neo-Malthusians is pessimistic – and even a cursory look at any of the UN's *Human Development Reports* (published since 1990, e.g., see 2011a) provides plenty of data in support of their pessimism – these scholars offer creative and potentially achievable economic and political solutions to the multitude of problems linked to overpopulation.

The tenability of these solutions rests on whether they can substitute for the economic development that is spurred by population growth: A rise in population expands the market, which in turn encourages job growth and prosperity. (For the clearest exposition of the positive relationship between population growth and economic development, see Boserup 1981; Clark 1967; Mosher 2008; Simon 1981.) The solutions rest on two basic premises: (1) that population growth is overwhelming developing nations and that limiting growth will eventuate in a higher standard of living; and (2) that different countries require different solutions in managing their population growth.

The actual solutions are developed from various combinations of (a) *family planning* (reduced fertility, e.g., via expanding and strengthening the distribution of contraception methods; via increasing the education of women; via government policies and programs; via the efforts of NGOs [nongovernmental organizations]; and via strengthening public health initiatives that can reduce mortality, especially infant mortality); (b) transforming sources of energy from carbon-based to more renewable types (e.g., from oil to sunlight); (c) increasing the *inter*national level of social justice by encouraging less exploitive economic relationships between developed and developing nations: that is, relationships based less on transferring the wealth generated by the natural and human resources of the latter to the former and more on keeping the proceeds of these resources under the control of local populations; and (d) increasing the *intra*-national level of social justice: that is, widening the distribution of the proceeds of local natural and human resources to include all segments of society – all social classes, all ethnic and religious groups, and paying special attention that women are not left behind – instead of simply making local (and often corrupt) elites richer.

Conflict Theory. Ironically, as it has been reformulated in recent decades, neo-Malthusianism is, in part, an outgrowth of the conflict theoretical perspective in the social sciences. Starting in 1877, various Malthusian Leagues were formed in Great Britain, the Netherlands, and other European countries and flourished until the late 1920s. Some League members identified themselves as *neo-Malthusian*. *Malthusians* expressed their belief in the fundamental dictum of Malthus, that population and resources must be in balance, while *neo* added a special twist and emphasis on Malthus's concept of preventative checks: that the key to preserving the population size/resources balance was the private and state encouragement of birth control, especially for the poor and working classes. The philosophy was at heart politically conservative and non-sociological, seeing the misery of the bottom half of society as rooted in its members having too many children – which, in turn, created misery not only for them, but for the greater social order as well (with over-population encouraging crime and insurrection). The poor and near-poor would ultimately not be helped by income redistribution policies (e.g., welfare, unemployment insurance, national health insurance), as these would only allow for – and even encourage the having of – more children. Instead, the ultimate solution was to be found in birth control and having fewer children.

In stark contrast, the conflict perspective in the contemporary social sciences sees the problems of the poor – and of the greater society in facing crime and insurrection – as being spawned by the unequal, and ultimately unfair, distribution of resources in society. This perspective is rooted in the nineteenth-century writings of Karl Marx and Friedrich Engels. For example, in the 27th chapter of his classic *Capital, Volume 1*, Marx (1867: 877–95) persuasively documents how large landowners of England and Scotland, the heart of the upper class from the fifteenth through the eighteenth centuries, used the power of the state (its laws, its armies) to maintain their position.

As the textile industry developed and landowners saw more profit in using their land for sheep grazing rather than for tilling, they used their power and influence to expropriate the peasants from their historic holdings and convert these holdings into sheep pastures. The weaker class, the peasants, were forced into states of privation and compelled to migrate to cities, where they toiled for low wages in the textile mills converting wool and cotton into cloth. In short, the rich stayed rich or got richer, and the poor got poorer – more miserably so. The same processes are evident [throughout] contemporary society. (Carter 2010: 391)

The conflict perspective is used to explain the workings of the social system *within* nations, emphasizing how advantaged individuals and groups use their educational, financial, and social networking advantages to maintain the upper hand in the realms of culture, economics, and politics. And the theory is used to explain relationships *among* nations, with the governments of economically developed nations supporting their capitalist firms in penetrating the economies of less developed nations – buying off the elites of these countries and exploiting their land, raw materials, and labor force. For example, large food corporations maximize profits when small landholdings are consolidated into larger ones; when manual labor is replaced by machine labor; and when diverse, staple crops that historically fed the local population are replaced by cash crops. The combined effect of these processes is to drive small farmers and their families out of business and into poverty; they then end up migrating to urban areas, where they are either forced into low-wage industrial jobs or migrate to another country in search of work. (The particular macro version of the conflict perspective used here has become known as *world systems theory*, an outgrowth of *dependency theory*; see Wallerstein 1980. In addition, for a discussion of this approach to social demography as related to the problem of international migration, see Castles et al. 2014: 31–3; and Massey et al. 1998: 34–41.)

Convinced by the explanatory power and generally strong empirical support of the conflict perspective for understanding the workings of the political and social order, neo-Malthusians reinvented themselves in the last third of the twentieth century with an emphasis on environmentalism and social justice – which scholar/activists like Paul R. and Anne H. Ehrlich see as connected. The middle and upper classes have developed lifestyles that overly strain the environment and ultimately put too much pressure on society to maintain political and social order. Thus, the formula for humanity's well-being and ultimate survival combines population control and reducing consumption by the top quarter of society – with greater equality in the distribution and use of the world's remaining and finite resources (key among these being clean air, clean water, clean land, and the ever-dwindling supply of fossil fuels). This formula is enhanced to the degree to which technological innovations make non-polluting, renewable energy sources (e.g., solar and wind power) more economically feasible, and to which these innovations produce more environmentally friendly efficiencies in food production, transportation, communication, architectural design, and manufacturing.

Contemporary demographic explanations of population growth, as well as of fertility, mortality, and migration, make modest and eclectic use of theory. They combine *micro* (individual-level), *medial* (group-level), and *macro* (country- and regional-level) theoretical perspectives. They emphasize the subtle influences of family and friends on individual decisions regarding childbearing (fertility), health behaviors (reflected in longevity/mortality), and geographic mobility (migration). They also emphasize (a) the harsher, less forgiving influences of macro-level economic and political changes (from industrialization and the growth of capital and credit markets to war, regime transformation, and a nation's level of influence and power in the global economy); and (b) cultural and economic globalization (to wit, the postmodern cultural emphasis on individual development/potential, decreasing the presumed and actual importance of race, ethnicity, gender, and age; and the globalization of economic exchanges that, by definition, increasingly and readily transcend national and political borders). And, finally, they acknowledge that human beings are part of nature and that, to thrive, humanity must abide by the natural laws that govern the health of the physical environment that nurtures us.

In sum, contemporary social demography, with varying emphases depending upon the problem at hand, is guided by three broad theoretical frameworks: (1) demographic transition theory, and a recent variant that has become known as the second demographic transition; (2) reformulated neo-Malthusianism, as it has become informed by the grand perspectives of conflict theory and environmental human ecology; and (3) postmodern globalization theory, a perspective that emphasizes (a) the rising importance of the global economy, which has accelerated the flows of people and products among countries – thus making them increasingly interdependent and increasingly in need of transnational governance; and (b) the worldwide rising importance of a value system emphasizing individual autonomy and fulfillment of individual potential, which has stemmed from – and contributed to – a relaxation of the tight political, religious, and social control of the individual so omnipresent in traditional societies. Within these broad frameworks, a large number of demographic theories have arisen to explain population growth, mortality, fertility, and migration. However, modern social demographers do not restrict themselves to a single theory when developing an explanatory model that involves one or more of these demographic processes as either dependent or independent variables. Rather, as is the approach taken in the present volume, they incorporate diverse and often unlabeled perspectives to develop causal models to explain the phenomenon at hand. Thus, for example, in Chapter 3, the complex explanation of mortality rates and longevity invokes macro factors involving economic development; the *epidemiologic transition* (the historical shift from the majority of deaths in a country coming from infectious disease to the majority coming from degenerative diseases); the improvement of living standards; the growth of public and private hygiene; the development of germ theory and resultant improvements in public health programs; the Green Revolution; and nationalized health-care. The complex explanation also similarly invokes a host of micro-level factors, with associated theoretical interpretations, that include modifiable lifestyle factors (e.g., smoking, drinking, and obesity); poverty, gender, race/ethnicity; and the impacts of genetics and epigenetics. Similarly complex and well-interpreted explanatory models are developed for fertility in Chapter 4 and for mortality in Chapter 5, always with an eye to how such variables are not only dependent variables but also act as independent variables in the realms of the economy, culture, polity, and society.

Nuanced discussion of key subcategories of the major theoretical frameworks – including neoclassical economics/rational choice theory, functionalism, historical structuralism, transnational, social network, and world systems theories, and approaches based on segmented labor markets, household decision-making, human agency/livelihood, and cumulative causation – can be found in Anderson (2015), Castles et al. (2014: Chap. 2), and Massey et al. (1998: Chap. 2). Anderson discusses theoretical frameworks and their subcategories as they apply to population growth, mortality, fertility, and migration, while Castles et al. and Massey et al. focus on migration.

Demographics, the Market Economy, and Social Planning

Demographics is the term used to describe a wide variety of practical uses of population data.

Accurate demographic information is at the heart of local, state, provincial, and national government planning and budgeting processes. How many people need *social safety nets* or other services, and how will these needs change in the short- and medium-range futures? For example, in the United States, the federal government needs to know how many people will live into old age (their late 60s and beyond) and require Social Security. Similarly, how many will need Medicare (medical assistance for those 65 and older)? How many people, young and old, will need Medicaid (medical assistance for the poor)? How many schools are needed to meet the needs of those at the elementary level, the middle school level, the high school level, the community college level, and the university level? How many immigrants can the United States accept without overwhelming the criminal justice, educational, healthcare, and welfare systems? How many immigrants does the occupational structure need to maintain its vitality at various levels (e.g., how many farm workers, how many unskilled workers, how many engineers, how many skilled professionals)? How many immigrants of working age are needed to maintain an adequate tax base for the services citizens have come to expect?

Beyond the operation of government, those seeking to hold political office combine survey data on the attitudes of different social groups (e.g., based on age, gender, or ethnicity) toward particular issues with demographic data on how prevalent these groups are in their election districts to develop campaign platforms and to craft political advertisements.

Demographics is central in the marketing of products and services. Consumer markets are highly segmented by age, gender, education, ethnicity, religion, social class, and life-cycle stage (among many other social background characteristics). Business owners and managers know that their products are differentially bought and used by people from these different social groupings, and they develop, refine, and advertise their products accordingly. Identifying where individuals in these groups cluster geographically is a big business in and of itself. *Geodemographics* companies like Nielsen Claritas develop neighborhood-level demographic databases that are in high demand by businesses for site selection, human resource management, and advertising.

Sources of Population Data

Population data abound in the contemporary era, and the Internet has democratized social science research, in general, and demographic research, in particular. Before the late 1990s, a researcher had to be at a major university or a major government organization to do serious demographic research. City, county, state, regional, and cross-national data were stored on magnetic tapes, or existed in hard copy, in generally difficult-to-access archives. Major research universities had the staff and professional connections to ensure that they were the first to receive, for example, US Census and UN data sets. In contrast, since the late 1990s, the average researcher, the average college student – indeed, just about anyone with motivation and access to the Internet – can readily access massive amounts of free population data – data, however, that can readily overwhelm a researcher not guided by specific goals or hypotheses.

For social demography, the same sources that offer data on the variables of classic demography – on population size, distribution, composition, and change – generally offer a wealth of other kinds of social science data related to culture, economics, politics, and social issues. These sources – the Central Intelligence Agency (CIA), the Centers for Disease Control and Prevention (CDC), the General Social Survey (GSS), the UN, the US Census Bureau, and a large number and variety of other inter- and intra-national governmental and nongovernmental organizations – often provide data in easily downloadable formats, and within a day or two, if not a morning, a researcher who has basic knowledge of Microsoft Excel can start a research project that would have taken months to launch in the pre-Internet era.

At the end of the chapter, under *Suggested Readings and Online Sources*, several major suppliers of high-quality social demographic data are listed (with enough detail that their associated homepages can quickly be located with any of the common Internet search engines, e.g., Google). At a lower level of collection, the following sources provide the raw numeric information that organizations like the UN and the US Census Bureau use to build their generally comprehensive and elegant data sets.

National Censuses

For social planning and election purposes, all national governments conduct some kind of population *census*, most commonly every 5 to 10 years. A census is meant to count every individual. Moreover, it gathers data on selected characteristics of individuals and families, including, for example, age, gender, immigration status, income, marital status, and national background. The data are published at the level both of the individual (e.g., annual income) and of the household (e.g., median household income).

In the United States, the decennial census is dictated in Article 1 of the US Constitution and had the original intent of apportioning representatives to Congress and of allocating taxes. The census still serves these purposes, but over the years it was lengthened to assist the government in social planning (e.g., the funding of schools, roads, employment programs, housing programs, and healthcare are all distributed on the basis of census figures) and it eventually incorporated a very long set of questions given to a sample of those counted. (Starting in 2010, this *long form* was replaced by the *American Community Survey* [the first one being in 2013].) The current *short form* can be completed for everyone in the household by a single individual and takes just a couple of minutes. The form includes questions on the number of people living in the household as of April 1 of the census year (e.g., 2010); the type of housing (house, apartment, or mobile home); the sex, age, ethnicity, and race of each household resident; and whether a resident lives or stays somewhere else too (e.g., a college dorm, a seasonal residence, or, if a child, with another parent) (see US Census Bureau 2010a).

Census questionnaires tend to be similar across countries, with differing questions reflecting differing national government needs (e.g., some ask questions about immigration status, religion, and marital status). However, many nations are now using multipurpose electronic databases on their citizens and immigrants to replace the old-fashioned (but still common) knocking-on-doors approach. These databases are relatively cheap to use (compared to hiring census-takers) and even sometimes more accurate than the traditional approach (e.g., census-takers sometimes find no one at home, even with multiple visits, and they may often miss very poor or highly transient individuals).

A final, critical note on the national and cross-national census-based data sets that the UN, Population Reference Bureau, CIA (*World Factbook*), and other organizations construct and disseminate for the benefit of policymakers, social planners, and researchers: Despite the best efforts of the researchers constructing these data sets, errors can and do creep into them from multiple sources, including *errors in coverage* and *errors in content*. Errors in coverage occur when the key units to be counted and measured (e.g., individuals or households) are missed or, less commonly, are double-counted. For example, in the United States, undercounts of the numbers of African Americans, Hispanics, renters, and homeless individuals are well acknowledged and understood, though difficult to rectify fully (US Census Bureau 2012a). Errors in content occur when the characteristics of an individual, a household, or other unit of analysis are incorrectly noted. The error may be at the level of collection: for example, a respondent to a census-taker gives mistaken information; this is especially likely when the individual is reporting on another individual in a household (typically, just one individual completes information for every individual in the household). Or the error in content may arise when correctly gathered information is incorrectly coded or entered into an electronic database (e.g., a data-entry worker inputs "91" for an individual's age instead of "19"). More generally, there is a strong positive correlation between the quality of the data gathered by a national government and the nation's level of economic development. Despite how critical the data are for social planning, they are expensive to collect, and that expense is often ranked lower on the priority list of needs for poorer countries. For example, the 2010 US Census was estimated to cost $13 billion. And the costs, plus internal turmoil, prevented some poor and conflict-suffering nations from taking any counts of their populations during the first decade of 2000 – meaning that current researchers are using data on these countries collected during the 1990s (they include Iraq, Lebanon, Myanmar, Somalia, Uzbekistan, and Western Sahara; see *The Economist* 2011).

Vital Statistics Registers

While a census provides a snapshot of a population at one point in time, the registration of *vital events*, including, at minimum, births and deaths, is ongoing, and government organizations publish these on a regular basis (e.g., monthly, quarterly, or yearly). The registration documents generally contain an abundance of information on the characteristics of the individuals involved. This information provides the raw data from which social demographers develop their explanatory models of fertility, mortality, health, marital status, and other key constructs.

As with national censuses, there is clear positive relationship between level of economic development and the quality and quantity of vital statistics records – more prosperous countries can afford the heavy costs of data collection, organization, analysis, and dissemination. Indeed, the UN observes that tens of millions of births and deaths go officially unrecorded in developing countries – and thus the birth and death figures they publish on many of these countries rely heavily on estimations calculated from *sample survey* data (for a brief discussions of this issue, see United Nations 2013b: 100–8; for a classic, detailed, and technical discussion on indirect estimation methods that demographers use, see United Nations 1983).

The United States provides a good example of high-quality and detailed vital statistics registration and reporting. The National Center for Health Statistics (NCHS) tabulates and publishes birth, death, fetal death (including abortion), marriage, and divorce data that it gathers on a monthly basis from 57 registration areas: the 50 individual states, plus the District of Columbia, New York City, American Samoa, Guam, the Northern Mariana Islands, Puerto Rico, and the Virgin Islands. Although each of these 57 political units is responsible for keeping track of its individual jurisdiction's data, they have all agreed to use forms similar to the NCHS's "standard certificates" (see Tolson et al. 1991). These certificates provide a great level of detailed information on social background characteristics of the individuals being registered (e.g., age, ethnicity, education, race, parents' education) – these characteristics providing the aforementioned data that social demographers use to develop their explanatory models (certificates can be viewed at National Center for Health Statistics 2003a, 2003b).

Sample Surveys

Sample surveys have become a primary source of demographic data for social science researchers, government organizations, and both profit and nonprofit agencies. National populations (and subpopulations) are simply too large for the interviewing and tracking of every individual, of every household. The cost and logistics are enormous. Sample surveys are less expensive, more tractable, and often more accurate than attempted interviews of the full population. (As noted earlier, census-takers sometimes miss the counting of the very poor or of highly transient individuals.)

All developed – and many developing – nations conduct a wide variety of demographic surveys; some as often as monthly or quarterly, with others on an annual or less frequent, though regular, basis. Here are a few significant examples from Brazil, China, India, the United Kingdom, and the United States.

National Household Survey (Brazil).   Since the late 1950s, the Brazilian Institute of Geography and Statistics (Instituto Brasileiro de Geografia e Estatística) has annually conducted its PNAD (A Pesquisa Nacional por Amostra de Domicílios [*The National Household Survey*]) to measure selected social and economic characteristics of the population. Questions asked on a regular basis involve the level of education, the labor force participation, the income, and the housing situations of a very large sample of individuals (e.g., in 2011, the PNAD surveyed some 360,000 individuals in approximately 146,000 households). Supplemental questions on a variety of topics are asked that differ each year, depending on the social planning needs of the government – with examples including migration, fertility, marriage, health, food security, and access to the Internet (Brazilian Institute of Geography and Statistics 2013a, 2013b).

Health and Nutrition Survey (China).   Since 1989, the National Institute of Nutrition and Food Safety at the Chinese Center for Disease Control has worked cooperatively with the University of North Carolina to survey the Chinese mainland population on a wide variety of health issues, especially as they relate to many of the core variables of social demography – including age, gender, education, marital status, and lifestyle (e.g., exercise, smoking, diet, stress control). The China Health and Nutrition Survey (CHNS) is conducted every two to four years, with recent surveys involving some 4,400 households and 26,000 individuals. The Chinese national government is especially concerned about the societal effects of the sweeping and rapid economic changes that the country has experienced since the late 1970s. The incomes of many Chinese individuals and families have grown dramatically, but this growth has created new and deep disparities in the socioeconomic status of the population. How these disparities can and do affect differences in individual- and community-level health is a key concern of the government, and it uses CHNS data to help shape social and economic policy. Similarly, the "aging of the population and increased life expectancy have contributed to an increased demand for long-term care systems. Meanwhile, in rural areas economic progress continues to be in direct conflict with family planning goals. China's response to these changing problems is expected to include ongoing policy adjustments," relying, in part, on CHNS research findings (see China Health and Nutrition Survey 2013).

Sample Registration System (India). As typically required by national governments, India mandates that all births and deaths be officially registered. Although experiencing huge gains in economic development in the past several decades, many urban neighborhoods, smaller towns, and rural districts of the nation are poor and thus have difficulty meeting this mandate. To fill in these reporting gaps, the Office of the Registrar General & Census Commissioner (2013a) regularly samples births and deaths via its Sample Registration System (SRS). The SRS "consists of continuous enumeration of births and deaths in a sample of villages/urban blocks by a resident part-time enumerator" (Office of the Registrar General & Census Commissioner 2013b); these enumerations are verified every six months via surveys conducted by "full-time supervisors."

Annual Population Survey (United Kingdom). To update the demographic changes that the UK undergoes between its decennial censuses, the Office for National Statistics (2013) collects key demographic, labor force, and health data on the British population via its Annual Population Survey. Sample sizes are huge, with recent surveys involving some 360,000 individuals, age 16 and older, living in 155,000 residential households.

American Community Survey (United States). As noted earlier, the US Census Bureau's American Community Survey (ACS) replaced the long form of the decennial census as of 2010. The ACS samples 3.5 million households each year, and provides annual reports on the wide variety of social and economic characteristics that once were part of the long form, as well as on short form that the Census Bureau now uses exclusively for its decennial census. These reports are so fine-grained that they are valid at the level of the community. Because the reports are based on samples taken during the previous five years, they provide a large enough number of respondents to be accurate even for very small communities.[1]

Current Population Survey (United States).   Every month, the US Census Bureau conducts a national survey of civilian labor force participation of those 15 or older in a sample of approximately 60,000 households (Bureau of Labor Statistics 2014c). The sample size is large enough to draw conclusions on the employment situation in all 50 states, plus the 12 largest metropolitan areas (e.g., New York and Los Angeles). Anyone following US national news realizes that the stock market rises and falls according to the monthly release of CPS unemployment figures.

The March CPS is especially useful to social scientists and policymakers as it includes an *Annual Social and Economic Supplement.* The supplement includes detailed questions on family characteristics, household composition, marital status, educational attainment, health insurance, the foreign-born population, income, work experience, receipt of non-cash government benefits, poverty program participation, and geographic mobility (see US Census Bureau 2013b).

Immigration Records, Parish Archives, Manifests, Wills, and Other Sources.   Social demographers whose interests rest in the distant past find their search for good data increasingly difficult as they go back further in time. Common documents they use to construct their databases include immigration records (e.g., in the United States, from the Immigration and Naturalization Service), parish records (e.g., in the 1500s, England began requiring priests to give the government weekly reports of their baptisms, marriages, and burials), shipping manifests (e.g., of the number of passengers transported on a ship from an English port to an American port), last wills (providing a record of, for example, family size), and a variety of sources that the average researcher does not run across: for example, archeological dig sites (e.g., the number of structures in a village), text on gravestones in historical cemeteries, bookkeeping records (e.g., of the number of slaves bought and sold at an established slave auction), and diaries of contemporary observers (e.g., estimates of a local native population as recorded by a visiting missionary).

Main Points and Key Terms

1   Demography is the formal study of human populations. Classic demography studies the size, distribution, composition, and change of a population in a given geographic area. Social demography extends these concepts into the realms of the culture, the economy, the polity, the society, and the constraints on and opportunities for the choices individuals make.

2   The UN classifies the socioeconomic development of the world's regions and countries as more developed, less developed, and least developed.

3   A population pyramid graphically represents the size, age distribution, and sex distribution of a specific population.

4   The sex ratio is the number of men per 100 women and is deemed balanced when it is 100, meaning half the population is male and half is female. As the ratio rises above 100 (more men than women), women are encouraged to take on traditional gender roles; and when it falls significantly below 100, women are more likely to be freed from these roles and gain greater access to education, the paid labor force, and political power.

5   Improvements in individual and public health lie at the heart of the population explosion that carried the world from a billion individuals in the early 1800s to more than 7 billion today. At the societal level, these improvements include rising prosperity and improvements in technology that have resulted in the Green Revolution, enhanced immunization, and better public sanitation. At the individual level, increases in the standard of living have produced better diets, increased access to healthcare, and greater levels of education.

6   The population explosion of the past 200 years has created huge strains on the environment and forced national governments to cooperate in the use of natural resources. Neo-Malthusian scholars and activists observe that population size and the resources to support it must be in balance, as overpopulation creates starvation, disease, war, and premature death. These scholar/activists recognize the value of conflict theory in alerting us to the difficulty of creating an equitable distribution of resources.

7   Developed countries reduced death rates and increased longevity over the long course of the nineteenth century and the first half of the twentieth century. The forces producing low death rates, low birth rates, and increased longevity are collectively integrated into

demographic transition theory. The demographic transition in developing countries has been unfolding since the 1950s and is occurring at a much faster rate than it did for developed countries because the former have been able to import and quickly acquire the death-controlling technologies that it had taken the latter two centuries to create.

8   Developed countries and many developing countries have entered a period known as the second demographic transition – characterized by low rates of marriage and fertility and a postmodern value orientation that prizes the development of the individual over that of the group, including the traditional family.

9   Migration can balance surpluses of labor in one location and deficits in labor in another. International migration from developing to developed countries helps the developed ones counteract the effects of population implosion – the situation of fertility rates falling below the replacement rate of 2.1. This situation eventuates in a small younger generation trying to fund and take care of the needs of larger older generations.

10   Demographics describes the practical uses of population data for government and business planning, marketing, and the crafting of political campaigns. These data are abundant and readily accessible; they are derived from national censuses, vital statistics registers, sample surveys, immigration records, and relevant historical documents such as ship manifests, parish archives, and wills.

American Community Survey (30–1)
Annual Population Survey (30)
carbon footprint (17)
census (26–8)
classic demography (5)
conflict theory (21–3)
cultural lag (18)
Current Population Survey (31)
demographic transition theory (18–19)
demographics (24–5)
dependent variable (8)
emigration (15)
error in content (27)
error in coverage (27)
family planning (20)
fertility (14–15)
geodemographics (25)
Green Revolution (13)
immigration (15)
independent variable (9–10)
least developed country (8)
less developed region/country (8)
Malthusianism/Neo-Malthusianism (19–20)

Review Questions

1   What is the key difference between classic demography and social demography?
2   If the base of a population pyramid is very wide and the top is very narrow, what does this tell us about that society?
3   Why does the infant mortality rate have such a strong relationship with the fertility rate?
4   How are the gender role expectations of women affected by a very high sex ratio?
5   What is the relationship between economic prosperity and life expectancy? Does this relationship hold at both the micro and macro levels of analysis? What interpretations might account for the relationship?
6   As birth rates decline in a society, why does the encouragement of immigration become so important?
7   Why should Americans care about air pollution in China?
8   From the Chinese perspective, why would Chinese patriots feel little guilt about what Americans think about China's air pollution problem?
9   What are the three major theoretical frameworks that inform social demography? At its core, what is (a) Malthus's thesis regarding population size and resources; (b) demographic transition theory's explanation of the massive population growth of the past two centuries; and (c) conflict theory's explanation of why the status quo is so hard to change?
10 What are two advantages of sample surveys over total census counts of the population?

Suggested Readings and Online Sources

One of the most comprehensive and authoritative single sources on the science of demography is Jacob S. Siegel and David A. Swanson (eds), *The Methods and Materials of Demography* (2007). More accessible sources that emphasize social demography include Barbara A. Anderson, *World Population Dynamics: An Introduction to Demography* (2015); Dudley L. Poston and Leon F. Bouvier, *Population and Society: An Introduction to Demography* (2010); and John R. Weeks, *Population: An Introduction to Concepts and Issues* (2016). A dated – but still highly useful – source for definitions of demographic terms is Christopher Wilson (ed.), *Roland Pressat – The Dictionary of Demography* (1985).

For an online introduction to some of the basic terms of social demography, see Population Reference Bureau, "Glossary of Demographic Terms." A relatively new addition to the construction of population pyramids is the *animated pyramid*, which shows changes in the age/sex composition of a population over time; an example can be found at the US Census Bureau's *US and World Population Clock* website. Another excellent example can be found at the Australian Bureau of Statistics *Animated Population Pyramids* site, revealing how the nation is transforming from one of many youths, to many middle-aged and older individuals. Swedish social scientist Hans Rosling has developed a much more comprehensive set of animated graphics-presentation tools for the study of social demography at his *Gapminder* website; a lively demonstration of *Gapminder* can be found on the Ted.com website ("the best stats you've ever seen").

Many organizations provide comprehensive and relatively easy to use cross-national demographic data sets; four of the most popular are (1) Population Reference Bureau, *World Population Data Sheet* (updated annually); (2) United Nations, *Demographic Yearbook* (updated annually); (3) United Nations, *World Population Prospects* (updated periodically); and (4) Central Intelligence Agency, *World Factbook* (updated annually). Beyond these basic sources, the many other inter- and intra-national databases referenced in this chapter appear in the References section at the end of this book. More specialized data sources, for example on the total fertility rate, appear at the end of subsequent chapters.

The destructive effects of human activity on the environment, especially as related to climate change, receive massive and detailed scientific confirmation in recent reports by the US National Oceanographic and Atmospheric Association (NOAA) and the UN's Intergovernmental Panel on Climate Change (IPCC); see Jerry M. Melillo, Terese Richmond, and Gary W. Yohe (eds), *Climate Change Impacts in the United States: The Third National Climate Assessment* (2014), as well as the various *Climate Change 2014* reports at the IPCC.ch homepage.

The fundamental tenet of the neo-Malthusians regarding population growth – that population and resources must be in balance, or else Mother Nature will put them in balance via pestilence, starvation, and war – finds a wealth of supporting data and alternative, realizable prescriptions for how humanity can and should constrain its population growth and size in James H. Brown, Joseph R. Burger, William R. Burnside, et al., "Macroecology Meets Macroeconomics: Resource Scarcity and Global Sustainability," *Ecological Engineering* (2014); Lester R. Brown, *Plan B 4.0: Mobilizing to Save Civilization* (2009); Paul R. and Anne H. Ehrlich, *One with Nineveh: Politics, Consumption, and the Human Future* (2005); Jorgen Randers, *2052: A Global Forecast for the Next Forty Years* (2012); Peter F. Sale, *Our Dying Planet: An Ecologist's View of the Crisis We Face* (2011); and the Worldwatch Institute's annual updates on the *State of the World* (see, e.g., *State of the World 2013: Is Sustainability Still Possible?*, and *State of the World 2014: Governing for Sustainability*). For a more philosophical view on neo-Malthusianism, see Robert A. Schultz, *Technology versus Ecology: Human Superiority and the Ongoing Conflict with Nature* (2014): "Ultimately, our survival rests with our being able to use our knowledge to respect the ecosystem and to live within its limits" (p. 284).

For a very brief but useful examination of how demographic data can be used for marketing, see Gail Sessoms, "The Importance of Demographics to Marketing," *Houston Chronicle* (2015). The kingpin of marketing-consulting firms, Nielsen, produces a number of demographics-based *Nielsen SiteReports* reports each year (e.g., 2015), including for individual companies and for wider distribution.

A highly readable introduction to the use of demographic data in guiding social planning can be found in the US Agency for International Development monograph *Population Analysis for Planners* (2015) by Linda Lacey and Ilene Speizer, as well as in Diane Conyers's classic *Guidelines on Social Analysis for Rural Area Development Planning* (1993, especially Chap. 5).

2

World Population Growth and Distribution

Rapidly expanding populations can keep nations mired in a cycle of poverty and contribute to social and political unrest. And biodiversity is lost when plants and animals are crowded out to make room for more development. Population growth stretches natural resources to their limits. Deforestation, food and water shortages, and climate change are all intensified by the addition of over 80 million people a year to the world's population.

Population Connection (2015)

Most fundamentally, human history over the past forty years has not conformed to [dire] predictions. By the most basic measure, human populations have continued to grow and no population collapse or broad-scale famine – caused by population outstripping food supply – has occurred. To the contrary. With localized exceptions, life expectancy across the globe has risen, as have per capita incomes. Food production has kept pace with population growth. Energy remains abundant. ... The discrepancies in average health and welfare among nations have declined rather than increased. Countries around the world generally continue to improve their well-being rather than slip backward in greater poverty and suffering.

The sustained population growth of the past forty years and growing human prosperity suggest that humanity has remained much further from its natural limits than [once] predicted. ... We do not know for certain how many people Earth can support, and it is possible that humanity has already set the age for its future demise. But that date still seems far off.

Paul Sabin (2013)

The History of Population Growth

The stunning rate of human population growth in the past two centuries is captured in Figure 2.1. For most of humanity's 200,000 years on earth (our best scientific guess for the age of our species of hominid; see National Science Foundation 2005), we lived in small *hunter-gatherer bands*, numbering from a few dozen to perhaps 100 individuals. These bands hunted wild game, fished, and gathered wild seeds, nuts, berries, fruits, and vegetables (and related plants such as bulbs and tubers). It took 190,000 years for humanity to reach its first million,

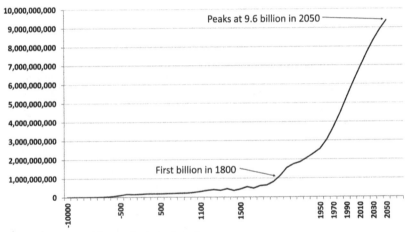

Figure 2.1:   World population growth
Notes: [a]Horizontal (year) axis is not drawn to scale.
[b]The plotted curve reveals that it took 200,000 years to reach 1 billion, but only 130 years to reach 2 billion (around 1930), and just 30 years to reach 3 billion (1960); since then, it has taken only a little more than a decade to add another billion (by 1974, there was 4 billion; by 1987, 5 billion; by 1999, 6 billion; and by 2011, 7 billion). Despite falling birth rates, the huge population base combined with falling death rates will keep the *billions* coming until we reach about 9.6 billion people in the year 2050 (for a discussion of the assumptions that underpin the 2050 estimate, see Haub 2013).
Sources: Raw data from United Nations (2013c) and US Census Bureau (2013c, 2013d)

at around 10,000 BCE, when the *Neolithic Agricultural Revolution* – the domestication of plants and animals – began in the Middle East along the Tigris and Euphrates Rivers in what is now modern-day Iraq. Over the next few thousand years, the domestication process sprang up in many areas of Europe, Asia, and Africa – and eventually in North and South America. The driving force was hunter-gatherer bands exceeding the *carrying capacity* of their local environments (carrying capacity is "the upper limit on production and population in a given environment under a given technology, without decreasing the resource base"; see Harris and Johnson 2007: 62). Major waterways allowed for major irrigation systems and the cultivation of major amounts of grains (barley, corn, rice, wheat); this abundance allowed for the growth of the human population to an estimated 27 million by 2,000 BCE, by which time major civilizations were developing in China (along the Yellow and Yangtze Rivers), the Indian peninsula (along the Ganges and Indus Rivers), the Middle East (along the Tigris and Euphrates Rivers), and Egypt (along the Nile, which eventually became a granary of the Roman Empire).

Because domestication can yield much greater amounts of plant and animal foods per unit of land, from this point forward, the human population increased more or less steadily – with intermittent setbacks from major famines, wars, and epidemics – until the start of the nineteenth century, when it reached its first billion. From then on, it experienced massive growth. This growth unfolded despite the ravages of the Great Chinese Famine (1958–62), two world wars (1914–1918, 1939–45), and dozens of violent internal conflicts (revolts and civil wars) that unfolded during the course of the twentieth century. The famine accounted for as many as 45 million deaths; the world wars an estimated 100 million more (from direct combat, genocide, and ancillary causes such as disease and famine); and at least another 85 million were victims of internal conflicts (see Leitenberg 2006).

The famed cultural anthropologist Marvin Harris (1979: 80) gives us the most fundamental reason why hunter-gatherer bands were kept relatively small throughout human history: Their "inability to control the rate of reproduction of the [plant and animal life of an area], especially of prey species, necessitates a low regional density of human population as well as small, mobile, camp-like settlements."

When a hunter-gatherer band's geographic area began to run low on food, the band often split into smaller groups and moved on; and when this failed to bring population size and food resources into balance, there was a resort to abortion, infanticide, geronticide (the killing of the very old), and moving into a neighboring band's territory – sometimes working cooperatively with the other band but often engaging it in deadly combat.

Although the degree to which our ancestral bands fought with each other is disputed among anthropologists, cross-cultural analyses reveal that food scarcity and other resource shortages comprise the strongest predictors of war between neighboring societies (see, e.g., Ember and Ember 1992). When none of these strategies worked, starvation would set in and individuals became more susceptible to disease and premature death. In short, mortality rates were high and limited technology for extracting food from the environment was the norm.

Based on anthropological studies of the few hundred remaining traditional societies that rely upon hunting, gathering, and limited agriculture, it would be a mistake, however, to think that life for these peoples was (and is) unceasingly brutishness, with 12 hours or more a day of toil to eke out a subsistence living. Indeed, estimates on the work-day of some of these bands reveal that it averaged as little as three hours a day – with much of the remaining time spent in game-playing and socializing with friends and family (see, e.g., Harris 1991: 13, 81; Lee 1968; though contrast with Kaplan 2000). And because possessions were few and wants were limited (contrast the possessions and wants of those living in the affluent societies of the contemporary era!), "hunters and gatherers [were] known for their relative 'prosperity,' leisure, and autonomy" (Harris and Johnson 2007: 66). Although anthropologists warn that we should not overly romanticize living life so close to nature (cold, heat, dirt, bugs, snakes, attacks from neighboring groups, etc.), life in many bands involved less work, more leisure, and greater equality than in the agricultural societies that replaced them. Indeed, contrast their lives with hundreds of millions of peasants eking out a living in the northern and western regions of both historical and modern-day China; the burdensome nature of their lives has surfaced "again and again in every dynasty, and will not go away ... the peasant is a second-class citizen from the day of his birth" (Chen and Wu 2006: 144, 176). Finally, even though few members of economically developed societies would want to give up the conveniences of modern life, their work days are significantly longer (about 8 hours a day in the contemporary United States) and their leisure-time activities (exercising, television, socializing with family and friends) significantly shorter in duration (3.5 to 4.5 hours a day) than their hunter-gatherer ancestors (see Bureau of Labor Statistics 2014a).

As displayed in Figure 2.2, until the last century, the rate of world population growth was steadily increasing throughout most of human history. As noted above, however, the growth rate has had a number of setbacks due to periodic wars, famines, and epidemics – including the mid-fourteenth-century pandemic plague that devastated the populations

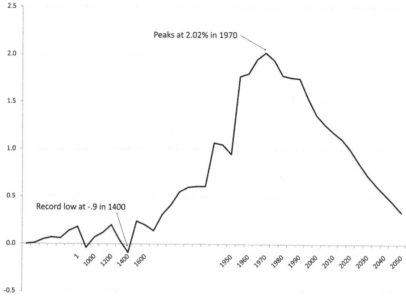

Figure 2.2:   Average annual rate of growth (%) of world population
Note: The horizontal (year) axis is not drawn to scale.
Source: Raw data from US Census Bureau (2013c, 2013d)

of Western Asia, the Middle East, and Europe. The various forms of the plague that become known as the *Black Death* have been traced to flea bites that transmitted the bacterium *yersinia pestis*. At the start of the pandemic, in 1347, the world population was estimated to be 445 million; within a few years, as many as 200 million individuals perished. One contemporary chronicler, Agnolio di Tura of Siena (Italy), apocalyptically observed in 1348 that "so many people have died that everyone believes it is the end of the world" (as quoted in Aberth 2007: 17), while the famed Italian scholar Francesco Petrarca (Petrarch), who lost his wife to the disease, wrote that "future generations would be incredulous, would be unable to imagine the empty houses, abandoned towns, the squalid countryside, the fields littered with dead, the dreadful silent solitude which seemed to hang over the whole world" (as quoted in Cartwright 1972: 37). In southern France, the number of dead was so massive that the Pope consecrated the river Rhône at Vignon – thus allowing corpses thrown into the river to receive a true Christian burial (Cartwright 1972: 37). The disease waxed and waned for nearly another three centuries; by 1500, the population had climbed back to 425 million, and in the middle of the seventeenth century, the world population was finally back to where it had been 300 years before.

The seventeenth century saw the easing of the plague, new food sources coming from the *New World* (especially corn and the potato), and continued improvement in agricultural technologies – including increasingly wider adoption of plows, crop rotation, and managed irrigation. Population rose steadily, and by 1700, the world population stood at 600 million.

The late 1700s and early 1800s saw the *Industrial Revolution* bring new technologies that would greatly enhance agricultural production – including iron plows, seed drills, and threshing machines. More food allowed for increasing population, which generated the need for even more food. Enough food was being generated to feed the populations in the urban areas that were springing up, out, and around the textile and other factories that arose by the thousands in Northern America (the United States and Canada) and Europe. Dramatic improvements in transportation, including steam-powered rail engines and ships, linked the rural regions where the food was produced to the urban regions consuming it. By the early 1800s, the world reached its first billion.

For the next 150 years, ever more efficient and ever more diversely applied technologies – to agriculture, manufacturing, mining, public health, medicine, transportation, and communication – resulted in the time in which the world population took to double growing ever shorter: from the thousands of years of the pre-agriculture era, to the hundreds of years after the adoption of agriculture, to the dozens of years in the last half of the twentieth century.

Demographers define this *doubling time* as the number of years it takes a population to double its size at the current rate of growth. Figure 2.3 flips the high and low points of Figure 2.2 and reveals how the falling growth rates of the past half-century – reflecting the falling birth rates that have occurred in both developed and developing nations during this time (see Chapter 1) – are significantly increasing the doubling time of the total world population.

Figures 2.4–2.7 show both the growth and the density of population over the past 2,000 years. The images reveal several facts about world growth: It has been most dramatic in the past century; it has only involved a very small part of the total land surface area, with the total population never taking up more than 17% of the surface area – as is the current figure – and before 1950, well under 10%; and it is concentrated on the coastlines, with half of the world living within 125 miles (200 kilometers) of the sea.

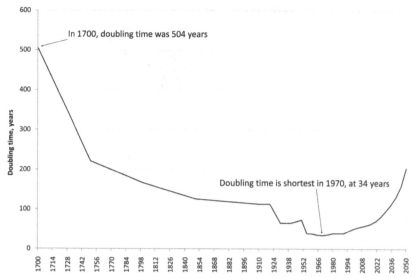

In 1700, doubling time was 504 years

Doubling time is shortest in 1970, at 34 years

Figure 2.3: Doubling time of world population since 1700
Note: Doubling time is calculated by dividing 69.3 (the natural log of 2, times 100) by the growth rate for the current year; thus, a population growing at 2% per year would take about 35 years to double (69.3 ÷ 2 = 34.6); in 2013, the growth rate was 1.095, and the doubling time was thus 64 years; by 2050, the US Census Bureau projects the annual growth rate to be 0.34, yielding a doubling time of 203 years. For quick calculations, 69.3 is rounded up to 70 and the doubling time calculation is labeled "the rule of 70".
Source: Raw data from US Census Bureau (2013c, 2013d)

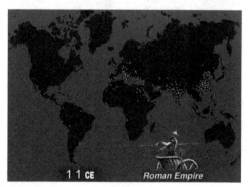

1 1 CE   Roman Empire

Figure 2.4: World population circa 11 CE
Notes: ᵃEach dot represents 1,000,000 people.
ᵇThe estimated 170,000,000 people alive in 11 CE were already heavily concentrated in the Indian peninsula and China, with the Mediterranean coast and the Nile River revealing the next heaviest concentrations. Mesoamerica (Mexico and Central America) and parts of South America had already reached population sizes in the millions – populations that from 1400 BCE onward were cobbled into major civilizations that would wax and wane according to pressures put on the environment and, after 1500, with contact with Europeans – who brought new diseases and greater warfare.
Sources: Image from Population Connection (2013); US Census Bureau (2013d)

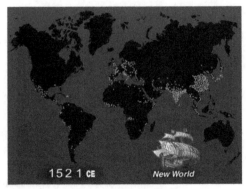

Figure 2.5: *World population circa 1521* CE

Notes: [a] Each dot represents 1,000,000 people.

[b] By 1521, world population stood at 430 million, with Europe being well on its way to recovery from the Black Death, and with India and China continuing their numerical dominance. In Mesoamerica, the Aztecs – much like the large civilizations that were built around the rivers of China (Yellow and Yangtze), India (Ganges and Indus), the Middle East (Tigris and Euphrates), and Egypt (Nile) – had used an intricate irrigation system built off the Cuauhtitlan River, as well as other major water sources, to develop a population of as many as 19 million people between the late thirteenth and the early sixteenth centuries.

Sources: Image from Population Connection (2013); US Census Bureau (2013d)

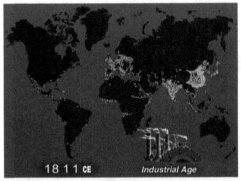

Figure 2.6: *World population circa 1811* CE

Notes: [a] Each dot represents 1,000,000 people; however, when areas become super-populated, as they are for China and India in this graphic, the dots merge and spread outward like a stain; thus, some dots appear in places that are not really densely inhabited: e.g., the bulk of China's population is more toward the coastline than the interior.

[b] In the early 1800s, the world population reached its first billion. Asia had continued to out-procreate the rest of the world, with nearly two-thirds of the world's people living there: 670 million in all of Asia, with China (350 million) and the Indian peninsula (205 million) maintaining their prominence. Africa stood at about 108 million; Europe at about 225 million; Northern America at 11 million; Central and South America at 27 million.

Sources: Image from Population Connection (2013); US Census Bureau (2013d); Wrigley (1969: 205)

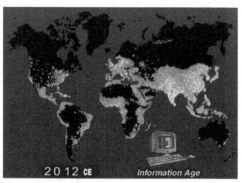

Figure 2.7: World population circa 2012 CE
Notes: [a]Each dot represents 1,000,000 people; however, when areas become super-populated, as they are for Asia and Europe in this graphic, the dots merge and spread outward like a stain; thus, some dots appear in places that are not really densely inhabited: e.g., for all continents, people are packed much closer to the coastlines than toward the interior.
[b]Between the early 1800s and the early 2000s, the world population exploded from 1 billion to 7 billion people.
Sources: Image from Population Connection (2013); US Census Bureau (2013d)

The Demographic Transition

Demographers explain the population explosion of the past two centuries with one or more variants of *demographic transition theory*. Throughout the overwhelming bulk of human history, populations were kept relatively small because of high death rates; and if a hunter-gatherer band or a nascent agricultural society were to overcome its high death rate, it needed to have a high birth rate. In the past half-century, death rates have fallen dramatically across the world, first in the industrialized, economically developed regions of the world (e.g., Northern America and Western Europe), where they had been dropping steadily since the onset of industrialization in the late 1700s, and then in the developing regions of Asia, Africa, and Latin America. In between the high death/high birth rates of traditional (preindustrial) societies and the low death/low birth rates of modern societies lies the *demographic transition*. Professional demographers argue about both the nuances and the overall validity of transition theory (e.g., Coale and Watkins 1986; Poston and Bouvier 2010: 273; Wilson 1985: 53). They note that there is no neat model whereby a given level of a nation's economic development will cause mortality to drop; a given drop in mortality will trigger rapid population growth; and an eventual culture adaptation occurs in which birth rates fall into line with death rates, resulting in little or no *natural growth* (growth that occurs when fertility outpaces mortality, as opposed to growth from immigration). Thus, the transition unfolds differently for each nation – depending on its particular culture, economy, political system, and experiences with war and migration – but as a general portrayal of population change, the theory is still useful. Indeed, its critics acknowledge that its strength lies in its correct prediction that the transition will occur in every society experiencing modernization. As social demographer Dudley Kirk (1996: 386) observes:

> No two countries have followed identical paths to transition, because there are so many possible combinations of nuptiality, fertility, mortality, and migration at each stage of the transition. However, this diversity is not irreconcilable with the universality of the transition. ... [D]ifferences [among countries] are not so great. They may accelerate or delay the transition, but the transition itself is inescapable.

Modernizing societies experiencing declining rates of mortality begin their eventual decline in fertility when (a) couples view fertility control as advantageous; (b) this control is morally acceptable in the wider society; and (c) effective birth control means (the pill, IUDs, condoms, etc.) are readily available (Kirk 1996: 365; Wilson 1985: 54).

The phases of the demographic transition are evident today, with several dozen nations at the beginning of the second (early transitional) stage (most from the UN's list of least developed countries), many developing nations toward the end of the third (late transitional) stage, and a few dozen developed nations – plus China – in the fourth stage. As originally formulated (Davis 1945; Notestein 1945; Thompson 1929), the theory did not predict the fifth stage that three dozen nations (Japan and most of those in Europe) have now entered: *population implosion*, whereby birth rates have fallen significantly below death rates. As noted in Chapter 1, an implosion is considered critical when the total fertility rate (expected number of births for women of childbearing age) falls below 1.6, which is already well below the replacement rate of 2.1 – and it is exacerbated if a country is experiencing little immigration or substantial emigration. The fifth stage has become so distinctive as to acquire the label *second demographic transition*. As first presented in the Introduction, and as will be examined further in an empirical analysis of the modern family in Chapter 4, this postmodern cultural transition is a product of delayed marriage; delayed childbearing; the growing preference for having one or two children, and even no children, in lieu of the historical preference of having many children; and the mounting acceptance of new family forms, including cohabitation without marriage, same-sex unions/marriages, non-marital childbearing, and blended families (individuals and children from prior unions/marriages forming new families through remarriage or cohabitation).

Table 2.1 presents selected examples of the demographic transition as it has unfolded in the contemporary era, while Figure 2.8 displays the idealized curve for population change according to transition theory.

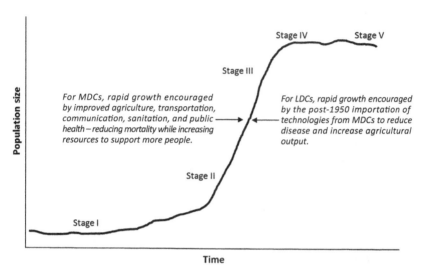

(For more developed countries [MDCs], Stage II begins for many by the late 1700s, and many have entered Stage IV by 1950)

(For less developed countries [LDCs], Stage II begins for many by 1950, and most will have entered Stage IV by 2050)

Figure 2.8:   Population change and the stages of demographic transition

Notes: [a] Transition theory accounts for population change according to the balance between deaths and births – and does not take into account migration to or from a nation.

[b] The transition curve plays out differently for each nation, depending on its culture, economy, and internal and external politics. For more developed countries (MDCs), substantial socioeconomic development was generally (but not always) a precursor to mortality decline, followed several decades later by fertility decline; within an MDC, however, cultural factors such as religion and ethnicity operated apart from economic development to encourage or discourage fertility control in various regions of the country. For less developed countries (LDCs), socioeconomic development has often been sidestepped in effecting mortality decline by way of positive interventions in disease control from the UN, selected MDCs, and NGOs (e.g., the Bill & Melinda Gates Foundation, CARE, OXFAM, and Save the Children). And similar to MDCs, the decline in fertility that has occurred in response to the decline in mortality in LDCs varies according to cultural, economic, and political factors.

[c] The pace of the transition has quickened over time, with Northern Europe taking 75–100 years for mortality to drop significantly; followed by Eastern Europe – which did so in 20–5 years; followed by LDCs – which have been doing so in less than two decades (Kirk 1996: 369; United Nations 2012d: xi–xii, 6).

Table 2.1: The demographic transition and where selected nations currently place

Stage	Description	Example nation	Death rate[a]	Fertility rate[b]	Growth rate[c]	Development level[d]
I	Preindustrial era (most of human history)					
	High fertility + fluctuating but generally high mortality = very low population growth					
	Fertility and mortality are nearly balanced					
II	Early transitional	Angola	15	6.3	3.2	Least
	High fertility +	Burundi	13	6.2	3.2	Least
	falling mortality =	Chad	15	7.0	3.6	Least
	high population	Malawi	12	5.6	2.9	Least
	growth	Mozambique	15	5.9	3.0	Least
	Fertility and	Niger	12	7.6	3.8	Least
	mortality are	Nigeria	13	6.0	2.8	Least
	imbalanced	Zambia	11	5.9	3.3	Least
III	Late transitional	Argentina	8	2.4	1.1	Less
	Falling fertility +	Dominican Republic	6	2.6	1.6	Less
	falling mortality =					
	modest	India	7	2.4	1.5	Less
	population	Indonesia	6	2.6	1.5	Less
	growth	Mexico	4	2.2	1.5	Less
	Fertility and	South Africa	11	2.4	1.0	Less
	mortality	Uzbekistan	5	2.3	1.6	Less
	returning to balance	Venezuela	5	2.4	1.7	Less
IV	Low fertility + low	Australia	6	1.9	0.7	More
	mortality = very	Belgium	9	1.8	0.2	More
	little population	Canada	7	1.6	0.4	More
	growth	China	7	1.5	0.5	More
	Fertility and	Denmark	9	1.7	0.1	More
	mortality are	France	9	2.0	0.4	More
	nearly balanced	Norway	8	1.8	0.4	More
		United States	8	1.9	0.5	More

Table 2.1   (cont.)

Stage	Description	Example nation	Death rate[a]	Fertility rate[b]	Growth rate[c]	Development level[d]
V	The second demographic transition	Croatia	12	1.5	−0.2	More
		Germany	11	1.4	−0.2	More
	Population implosion	Greece	10	1.4	0.0	More
	Very low fertility + low mortality =	Hungary	13	1.3	−0.4	More
		Italy	10	1.4	−0.1	More
	population decline	Japan	10	1.4	−0.2	More
	Fertility and mortality are	Poland	10	1.4	−0.2	More
	imbalanced	Portugal	10	1.3	−0.2	More

Notes: [a] Crude death rate (deaths per 1,000 population).
[b] Total fertility rate (expected number of children a woman will have).
[c] Percentage annual population increase from natural growth (from births exceeding deaths, ignoring immigration and emigration).
[d] UN designation of level of socioeconomic development.
Source: Raw data from Population Reference Bureau (2014)

The Contemporary Era and the Effects of Longevity on Population Size

The world population explosion of the past two centuries, and especially since 1950, has been fueled not only by declining mortality (which dropped until 1970 and has been slightly increasing since then) but also by increasing life expectancy. There is an *epidemiologic transition* accompanying the demographic transition of population growth: "Initial declines in the rates of death due to communicable diseases in the early stages of the transitions are followed by subsequent reductions in mortality attributable to non-communicable degenerative diseases in the advanced stages of the transitions" (United Nations 2012d: 1). As childhood deaths decline through immunization and clean-water projects that reduce diarrheal diseases, increasing numbers of children live into adulthood, and healthcare systems are able to concentrate more on the lifestyle- and environment-related diseases affecting adults, including cardiovascular disease and cancer – both of which are affected by behavioral factors including smoking, drinking, diet, and exercise, as well as by environmental factors such as air and water pollution. The upshot is that both less developed and more developed countries have experienced dramatic gains in longevity over the past six decades, with the former having greatly reduced the risk of childhood death and the latter the risk of middle-age and older-adult death. Because measures of life expectancy are especially sensitive to infant mortality (see Chapter 3), the life expectancy in less developed countries has actually been increasing at a faster rate than that for their more developed counter-parts (see Figure 2.9). The upshot for worldwide increases in longevity is the increasing contribution of older adults (65+) to the total popula-tion: They contributed 9% of the growth in world population between 1950 and 2010, and they are expected to contribute 36% of the growth that will occur between 2010 and 2050 (Pew Research Center 2014a).

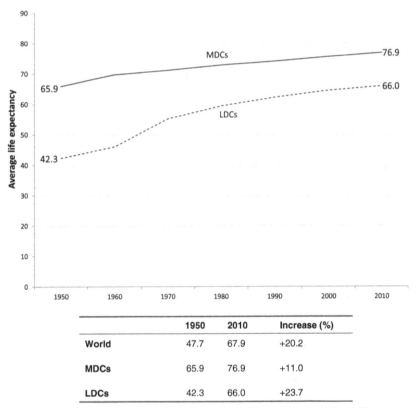

	1950	2010	Increase (%)
World	47.7	67.9	+20.2
MDCs	65.9	76.9	+11.0
LDCs	42.3	66.0	+23.7

Figure 2.9: Throughout the world, we are living longer, and the difference in longevity between more and less developed countries is decreasing over time
Source: Raw data from United Nations (2011b)

The increase underway in the proportion of older adults in national populations in more developed countries has been labeled the *longevity transition*. The large-scale economic, political, and social effects of this transition are examined in Chapter 4.

Contemporary Population Distribution by Major World Regions

Building upon Figure 2.7, Tables 2.2 and 2.3 break out the size, growth, and expected growth of the major regions of the world: Africa, Asia,

Table 2.2: *Population size (million) and growth (%) of major regions*

Region	1950	1980	2013	2050	Growth	Expected growth
					1950–2013	2013–50
Africa	229	478	1,111	2,393	385	115
Asia	1,396	2,634	4,299	5,164	208	20
Europe	549	695	742	709	35	–4
Latin America/Car.	168	364	617	782	267	27
Northern America	172	255	355	446	106	26
Oceania	13	23	38	57	192	50
Totals	2,527	4,449	7,162	9,551	183	33

Source: Raw data from United Nations (2013c: 2)

Table 2.3: *Percentage of world population by major region*

Region	1950	1980	2013	2050
Africa	9.1	10.8	15.5	25.1
Asia	55.3	59.2	60.0	54.1
Europe	21.7	15.6	10.4	7.4
Latin America/Caribbean	6.6	8.2	8.6	8.2
Northern America	6.8	5.7	5.0	4.7
Oceania	0.5	0.5	0.5	0.6
Totals	100	100	100	100

Source: Raw data from United Nations (2013c: 2)

Europe, Latin America/the Caribbean, Northern America (the United States and Canada), and Oceania (Australia and New Zealand, plus the island states of Melanesia, Micronesia, and Polynesia). The tables reveal that although population size has increased dramatically over the past 65 years, the rates of growth and absolute population sizes differ greatly among the major regions of the world – with Asia leading the way. Indeed, half of the individuals in the world today either can trace their roots to India and China, or now live in one of these two countries. Expectations are for (a) the continuation of high growth rates in Africa – as its HIV/AIDS epidemic of the late twentieth century is being increasingly brought under control and as it has witnessed increasingly strong economic development since 2010; (b) population decline in Europe; and (c) the continuation of moderate growth rates for the other four major regions of the world.

For any selected geographic area (from a village to a city to a country to a major world region), population size and growth represent a combination of the rates of mortality (deaths), fertility (births), and mobility (immigration and emigration) – each of which is explored in detail in the next three chapters. More generally, as per the discussion above, demographers explain the population changes in the world's major regions in the past two centuries with one or more variants of demographic transition theory.

Contemporary Population Distribution by Urbanity

Cities represent the largest and most densely populated human conglomerates, and 8 of the 10 largest cities are on the coast – which has been the trend throughout human history. Trade is heavily dependent upon ship transport, and port cities have been the beneficiaries – drawing in money, merchants, and factories of all kinds, and thus opportunities for employment and people seeking to take advantage of these opportunities (see Table 2.4).

The trend toward urbanization has been ongoing since the Neolithic Agricultural Revolution, but took off during the Industrial Revolution. Indeed, economic development and urbanization go hand in hand. For example, about 80% of the population of the UN's "more developed regions" of the world currently live in urban areas, while only about 50% of those in the "less developed regions" do so (United Nations 2014a). Along with improvements in transportation and communication, the twin technological forces of the mechanization of agriculture and the engineering of crops to be ever more bountiful will continue to

Table 2.4: Eight of the 10 largest cities are on the coast

City (urban area)	Population (2014)
1 Tokyo-Yokohama, Japan (coastal)	37,555,000
2 Jakarta (Jabotabek), Indonesia (coastal)	29,959,000
3 Delhi (DL-HR-UP), India	24,134,000
4 Seoul-Incheon, South Korea (coastal)	22,992,000
5 Manila, Philippines (coastal)	22,710,000
6 Shanghai (SHG-ZJ-JS), China (coastal)	22,650,000
7 Karachi, Pakistan (coastal)	21,585,000
8 New York City (NY-NJ-CT), United States (coastal)	20,661,000
9 Mexico City, Mexico	20,300,000
10 São Paulo, Brazil (coastal)	20,273,000

Note: Population estimates are for the urban area: that is, the city and surrounding suburbs.
Source: Demographia (2014)

push people from rural farmlands to urban areas, where the chances for employment are much higher. The pace of this push is increasing, and as of 2012, 5 million new residents are annually entering the cities of Africa, Asia, and Latin America, "absorbing some 95 percent of all global urban growth" (Williams 2012: 63).

Investments are drawn to the city because that is where factories and services cluster. Indeed, more than three-quarters of the world's GDP is generated in urban areas: "As cities attract businesses and jobs, they bring together both the human and the entrepreneurial resources to generate new ideas, innovations, and increasingly productive uses of technology" (United Nations 2012c: 15). Figure 2.10 shows the strong positive relationship between economic development and urbanization in the contemporary world. Thus, it is not surprising that the UN's statistical models of urban population growth predict that by 2050, more developed nations will see 86% of their inhabitants living in urban areas; however, as the mortality–fertility–wealth gaps between richer and poorer nations continues to fall (see Chapters 3 and 4), this percentage will rise significantly, to 64, for less developed nations. Overall, two-thirds of the world's population is expected to live in urban areas by 2050, with virtually all of world population growth occurring in these areas (United Nations 2012c: 1–2; for the huge movement of the world's population in urban areas, see Figure 2.11).

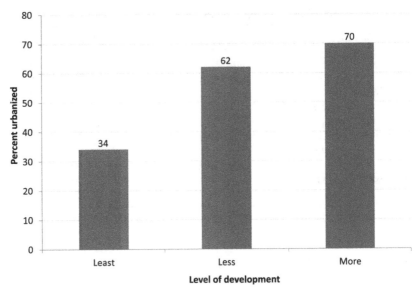

Figure 2.10:   Economic development and urbanization go hand-in-hand
Note: The correlation between the per capita gross national income (GNIPPP – see Figure 3.3, note b, p. 68 below) and percentage of the population living in urban areas is .67 ($p < .0001$).

For those unfamiliar with this statistic, which is provided in many subsequent figures in this book, The *correlation coefficient* measures the strength of the straight-line relationship between two variables: If the two variables are perfectly inversely related, the coefficient equals −1, and if the variables are perfectly positively related, the coefficient equals +1. In real-world analyses of demographic and related political and sociological data, the absolute values of correlation coefficients are always well below 1 (which is to say, no single dependent variable is very full explained by a single independent variable). (For an intuitive introduction to the correlation statistic, see Stockburger 2013: Chap. 15.)

Source: Averages calculated with raw data from Population Reference Bureau (2014); $N = 167$ countries

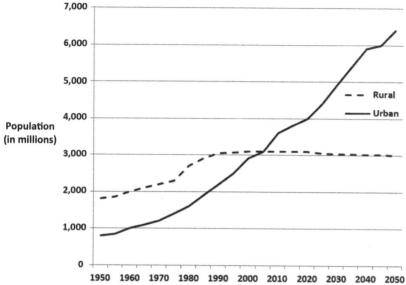

Figure 2.11:   Since 2005, the majority of the world's population has lived in urban areas

Notes: [a]The UN relies on each nation's census bureau's definition of what constitutes an "urban area" (e.g., in the United States, an *urban area* is defined as having at least 50,000 people, whereas an *urban cluster* is defined as an area with 2,500 to 50,000 people – "rural," meanwhile, encompasses all population, housing, and territory not included within an urban area; see US Census Bureau 2010b]).

[b]Although the populations of developed regions are one- and two-thirds more likely to live in urban areas (78% vs 47%), among the less developed regions, Latin America and the Caribbean have a very high level of urbanization (79%) – greater than that of Europe (73%). Africa and Asia, in contrast, remain heavily rural, with less than 50% of their populations living in urban areas.

Source: Raw data from United Nations (2014a: 7)

The Future: Population Implosions in an Increasing Number of Countries, But in the Context of Significant Worldwide Growth

Virtually all local, state, provincial, and national governments have a keen interest in the growth and social composition (e.g., age, socioeconomic status) of the populations they serve. Thus, it is not surprising that all of these levels of government expend considerable effort in gathering and analyzing projections of the changes their populations are expected to undergo. Aspects of population size and composition are examined in further detail in forthcoming chapters. The reduction of fertility far below mortality is creating population implosions (shrinkages) in those countries that experience little or no immigration or that, indeed, experience a negative net migration (more emigrants than immigrants). The impacts of these implosions were touched on in Chapter 1, and are further explored in Chapter 4. These implosions contribute to a rise in the average age of the population, which has both benefits and costs, and which is further analyzed in Chapter 4. The total population of the world is affected only by the balance between births and deaths, but the total populations of smaller geographic units of analysis – e.g., localities, counties, states, provinces, countries, regions – are affected not only by these but also by migration. The movement of people across political boundaries has effects on the areas they leave as well as on the areas into which they migrate. Such effects include the benefits and detriments to the economic, political, and social landscapes of their origin and destination areas. Some of the more important of these effects are reviewed in Chapter 5.

The demographic transition is unfolding in virtually all of the world's nations. They are steadily moving their ways through the major stages – and will reach a point where the world's population will be stable or in decline. In short, most nations are close to or are already in Stages IV or V (see Table 2.1). All of this said, the momentum of the birth rates of those 120 nations that were still above the replacement rate of 2.1 in 2014 (all of them on the UN's lists of "least" or "less developed" countries), along with the increases in longevity that will occur most strongly in less developed countries, will mean that planet Earth will see another two and a half billion people added to it by 2050. And, thus, as displayed in Figure 2.12, additions to world population are to come almost exclusively from the world's less prosperous nations.

The economies of many of these countries already struggle to provide adequate employment, healthcare, and even food to their populations – and the addition of so many more people, so quickly, can only increase the strains already felt by their resident populations and governments. For example, the UN tracks the proportion of children under the age of 5 who are malnourished and seriously underweight. The organization's most recent data reveal that these children reside mostly in the poorest nations of world – the very nations that are expected to be heavy contributors to the world's future population growth. To wit: 22.4% of children in least developed nations are categorized as "seriously underweight," that is, at least two standard deviations below normal; in contrast, just 2.4% of children in more developed nations are so categorized, with the percentage for less developed nations being 9.4 (United Nations 2014b).

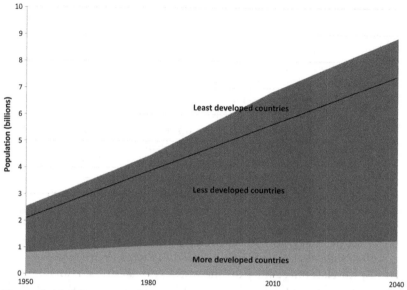

Figure 2.12: Future world growth will come almost exclusively from less developed countries

Note: Overall, developed countries will see little or no growth in the coming decades; their continued decline in fertility, which was at 1.6 in 2014, already well below the replacement rate of 2.1, will be compensated for by immigration from less developed countries; immigration will thus maintain the population of developed countries, as a whole, at or near current levels. Less developed countries will contribute most of the rise in world population. In 1950, they accounted for about 68% of the world's total population; by 1980, this had risen to 78%; by 2010, to 82%; and by 2040, it is expected to be 85%. Note that in 1950, least developed countries (the poorest subset of less developed countries) comprised about 12% of the total population of less developed countries; by 2010, this had risen to 15%, and it is expected to rise to 20% by 2040.

Source: Raw data from United Nations (2011b: 147–50)

The United Nations High-Level Panel on Global Sustainability questions whether the human family has yet to grasp the dimensions of the challenges stemming from population growth: "By 2030, the world will need at least 50 percent more food, 45 percent more energy, and 30 percent more water – all at a time when environmental boundaries are throwing up new limits to supply. This is true not least for climate change, which affects all aspects of human and planetary health" (United Nations 2012e: 11; also see the *Suggested Readings and Online Sources* at the end of Chapter 1).

Main Points and Key Terms

1   For almost all of their history, until the Neolithic Agricultural Revolution began around 10,000 BCE, humans lived in small hunter-gatherer bands numbering from a few dozen to perhaps as many as 100. They hunted wild game and foraged wild, edible plants.

2   The Neolithic Agricultural Revolution involved the domestication of plants and animals. It sprang up first around major rivers of the Middle East, then of Asia, Africa, the Americas, and Europe. Major waterways allowed for large-scale irrigation and thus the cultivation of surplus amounts of grains and vegetables – the end result being steady increases in the size of the human population and the growth of towns and cities, enabling large numbers of people to stay close to their food source. Cities became especially important after the onset of the Industrial Revolution, and since 2005, more than half of the world's population has lived in urban areas.

3   By the eleventh century CE, the world's population was an estimated 170 million; and by the early 1340s, it was an estimated 445 million. However, a catastrophic set-back unfolded in the late 1340s, the Black Death, a pandemic plague that killed as many as 200 million people in Europe, the Middle East, and Asia within a few years of its onset. The disease waxed and waned for 300 years, and world population did not return to its early 1340s level until the middle of the seventeenth century.

4   The Industrial Revolution that got underway in Europe in the late 1700s brought new technologies that greatly enhanced agricultural production, for example iron plows, seed drills, and threshing machines. Enough food was generated to feed the growing urban areas that sprang up by the thousands around the textile and other factories in Northern America and Europe. By the early 1800s, the world reached its first billion people. Despite lagging behind Europe and Northern America in industrializing, Asia accounted for two-thirds of this billion.

5   Industrialization motivated technological improvements not only in manufacturing and agriculture, but also in public health and medicine. In Europe and Northern America, the fall from the high death and birth rates of preindustrial societies to the low death and birth rates of modern societies in 1950 is attributed by demographic transition theory to these technological improvements and the increasing prosperity that they spawned.

6   While slow and eventually substantial socioeconomic development was generally the precursor to mortality/fertility declines in Western

and Northern Europe and in Northern America, the demographic transition occurred much quicker in the developing regions of the world (Africa, Asia, and Latin America). Socioeconomic development could generally be sidestepped in these regions because mortality decline was achieved by way of the post-1950 positive interventions in disease control from the UN, selected developed countries, and NGOs.

7   In both more developed and less developed countries, the decline in fertility that has occurred in response to the decline in mortality varies according to cultural, economic, and political factors.

8   Most developed countries, and an increasing number of developing countries, have entered a period known as the second demographic transition – a transition characterized by low rates of marriage and of fertility. This recent development has created population implosions in Japan and most of Europe. The youngest generation is now smaller than older generations and is thus experiencing difficulty in funding their retirement and healthcare costs, especially because of the significant increases in life expectancy throughout the world.

9   World population is expected to peak around 9.5 billion people in the middle of the twenty-first century. Africa is expected to have the highest growth rate (more than doubling in size between 2013 and 2050), while population decline will occur in Europe (–4%). In between the extremes of Africa and Europe are the moderate growth rates expected to unfold in Asia (+20%), Latin America (+27%), Northern America (+26%), and Oceania (+50%).

10   Most world population growth will occur in developing countries. The economies of many of these countries already struggle to provide adequate employment and healthcare for their populations – and the addition of so many more people, so quickly, can only increase the strains already felt by their resident populations and governments.

Black Death (40–2)
carrying capacity (39)
correlation coefficient (54)
doubling time (42–3)
epidemiologic transition
  (49–50)
hunter-gatherer band (39–40)
Industrial Revolution (42)

longevity transition (51)
natural growth (46, 49)
Neolithic Agricultural Revolution
  (39)
"rule of 70" (43)
second demographic transition
  (46–9)
urban area (55)

Review Questions

1   What kept population growth so low during humanity's long hunter-gatherer phase of history?
2   How does the concept of *carrying capacity* help us to understand the roots of the Neolithic Agricultural Revolution?
3   How did the Industrial Revolution promote population growth?
4   China has an annual growth rate of 0.5%; its population in 2014 was estimated at 1,355,692,576 according to the CIA's *World Factbook*. In what year can we expect China's population to be double its 2014 size?
5   What happens during the transitional stage(s) of a particular country's demographic transition?
6   What is the difference between a country's "growth rate" and its "natural growth rate"?
7   At a general level, what key differences are there between how the developed countries of Northern Europe experienced their demographic transitions and how less developed countries of Asia and Latin America have been undergoing their transitions?
8   How does increasing longevity affect population size?
9   Why are so many people drawn to urban areas?
10   Which countries do you think will have a tougher path to following in the coming few decades: those experiencing a population implosion, as currently are the countries of Eastern Europe; or those expected to experience significant population growth, such as the countries of west-central Africa? Why?

Suggested Readings and Online Sources

The UN has a wide variety of print and on-line sources covering the many cultural, economic, political, and social aspects of population growth and distribution. A few of the most cited of these sources include: *World Population Prospects: The 2012 Revision*; *World Urbanization Prospects: The 2014 Revision*; and the United Nations High-Level Panel on Global Sustainability, *Resilient People, Resilient Planet*. Excellent supplements to the *Resilient People, Resilient Plant* report include the Royal Society's comprehensive and nuanced analyses in *People and the Planet* (2012) and the work of the international think-tank Global Footprint Network (which not only provides country-level comparisons of the carbon output of nations and its destructive effects on the environment, but also allows individuals to calculate their personal carbon footprint). Analyses of the Global Footprint Network have led it to conclude that "if everyone lived the lifestyle of the average American, we would need 5 planets" (Global Footprint 2015). A fundamental conclusion of *People and the Planet* is that in no way can Mother Earth support even the world's current 7.3 billion people, let alone the 10 billion estimated to be living on the planet by the end of the twenty-first century, at the high levels of consumption enjoyed by the majority of the 1.3 billion individuals presently living in the developed world.

The UN publication on the growing importance of urban areas for the human experience is nicely complemented by two recent and important works on the city: Vishaan Chakrabarti, *A Country of Cities: A Manifesto for an Urban America* (2013), and Donald C. Williams, *Global Urban Growth: A Reference Handbook* (2012). The Chakrabarti book lays forth a strong empirical argument on how cities in the United States are the key to solving the pressing social problems of economic inequality and decreasing social mobility, as well as the destruction of our environment and ever-increasing healthcare costs. The Williams book also details the prospects cities offer us for greater prosperity, but in addition it presents stark data on the growth of massive slums in virtually all cities of the developing world. (The UN defines a slum as a settlement in an urban area where more than half of the inhabitants live in inadequate housing and lack basic services.) There are currently close to a billion people living in the urban slums of the cities of the less developed and more developed countries of the world, and this number is expected to reach 1.4 billion by 2020 (see Williams, p. 65).

The UN in its *Slum Profile in Human Settlements* (2014c) operationally defines a "slum" as "a contiguous settlement where the inhabitants are characterized as having inadequate housing and basic services. A slum is often not recognised and addressed by the public authorities as an integral or equal part of the city. ... [Slums] lack one or more of the following conditions: access to safe water; access to improved sanitation; secure tenure; durability of housing."

Regarding Mumbai's slums, a visiting British missionary, Matt Kottman, describes their conditions as "inhuman. A family will live in a tiny room with a hole in the wall for a window. There is no toilet, only public toilets down the road. Some of the slum rooms have a water pipe, but when the rainy season comes ... the sewage overflows and then contaminates the drinking water" (Kottman 2010).

Important print references for the impact of disease in reversing and retarding population growth over the course of human history include John Aberth, *The First Horseman: Disease in Human History* (2007); Frederick F. Cartwright, *Disease in History* (1972, 2000); and Irwin W.

Photo: **Matt Kottman**

Sherman, *Twelve Diseases That Changed Our World* (2007). All of these books devote significant attention to the Black Death, discussed in the present chapter. These books also observe that disease was much less important during the 190,000 years of our hunter-gatherer past and really did not have major effects until the Neolithic Agricultural Revolution (beginning around 10,000 BCE). The domestication of plants and animals allowed for the growth and permanency of human settlements. With settlements came sewage and garbage and polluted water supplies – all of which promote the introduction and spread of the bacteria and viruses that sickened, and often killed, much of the resident population.

Traditional societies in the contemporary world offer us a chance to compare the lives of peoples living a more or less pre-agricultural lifestyle versus living as agrarian laborers. See, for example, Jared Diamond's laudatory account of the former in his *The World Until Yesterday: What Can We Learn from Traditional Societies?* (2012) versus Chen Guidi and Wu Chuntao's depressing account of the latter in their *Will the Boat Sink the Water? The Life of China's Peasants* (2006).

For an online and accessible introduction to demographic transition theory and its applications to contemporary countries, see Population Reference Bureau, "Uganda: At the Beginning of the Demographic Transition" (2011a); "Guatemala: Beyond the Early Phase of the

Demographic Transition" (2011b); "India: On the Path to Replacement-Level Fertility?" (2011c); and "Germany: Beyond the Demographic Transition's End" (2011d). The concept of the *second demographic transition* was initially developed by Dirk J. van de Kaa in "Is the Second Demographic Transition a Useful Research Concept: Questions and Answers" (2004) to describe the dramatic changes in fertility and family forms that occurred in Northern and Western Europe in the last quarter of the twentieth century – changes associated with increasing levels of economic prosperity and of women's education and participation in the paid labor force, and the decreasing importance of religion in the rhythms of everyday life.

Many nonprofit organizations have relatively simple, straightforward, and neatly compiled data presentations on the history and future of population growth in the United States and the world. Good examples include the Pew Research Center's "Chapter 4. Population Change in the United States and the World from 1950 to 2050" (2014a); Population Connection's "World Population Video" (2013; text and video available at https://www.populationeducation.org/content/world-population-video; note that this video was the source of the images of population growth presented in Figures 2.4–2.7); and the Population Reference Bureau's "lesson plans" article entitled "Human Population: Future Growth" (2016).

Swedish social scientist Hans Rosling produces excellent graphical and video presentations of various population concepts, including that of population growth; see his clip "Population Growth Explained with IKEA Boxes" (2010a). Rosling's entertaining video shows that critical to curbing population growth (and the pressures on the economy and the polity to produce jobs and food, as well as on the environment) is to elevate the standard of living in the nations on the UN's list of "least developed"; by doing this, child survival rates will increase in these nations and thus the average number of children women have will fall.

3

Mortality

Nowadays, it is taken for granted that most parents can expect to live to see all of their children reach adulthood and to anticipate grand-parenthood. It was not always so. Only a few generations ago, infectious diseases were an ever-present danger that took the lives of people at all ages and in all social classes.... The retreat of death from the young and middle-ages is a social achievement that is all too rarely acknowledged.

Charles Hirschman (2005)

Measuring Mortality

The rate at which the very young die in a country tells us much about it. If many infants are dying, say as many as 120 or 130 in every 1,000 births, it tells us the country is poor and that it lacks adequate nutrition, healthcare, and security for its people. On the other hand, if as few as two or three infants perish for every 1,000 births, it tells us the country is well off and that it can feed its people and provide them with good healthcare and security from environmental and social threats. Figure 3.1 shows the relationship between a nation's level of socioeconomic development and its infant mortality rate. The relationship is clear, strong, and inverse: Prosperity buys life.

Infant mortality rates also vary according to inequality within countries – where inequality is high, infant mortality also tends to be high.

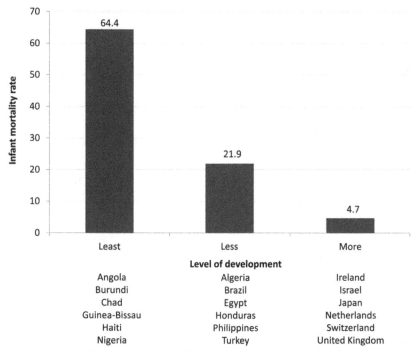

Figure 3.1: **Infant mortality**[a] **by level of development, with selected national examples**
Note: [a]Annual number of deaths of infants under the age of one per 1,000 live births.
Sources: Raw data from Population Reference Bureau (2014) and United Nations (2013c); data available for 140 countries

Poor individuals, families, and neighborhoods have fewer resources with which to encourage health and discourage premature death (see forthcoming discussion). But in countries with high levels of inequality, even the more prosperous tend to have high death rates because inequality reduces social cohesion – and reduced social cohesion raises the levels of stress, fear, and insecurity for the entire society (Institute for Policy Studies 2014; compare the similar findings and interpretations when US counties are the unit of analysis in Catlin et al. 2015: 6; and Sanger-Katz 2015). Illustrative of this relationship are comparisons between Japan and the United Kingdom in the last quarter of the twentieth century. In 1970, both nations had nearly identical life expectancies and income distributions (a life expectancy of 71.7 years in the United Kingdom vs

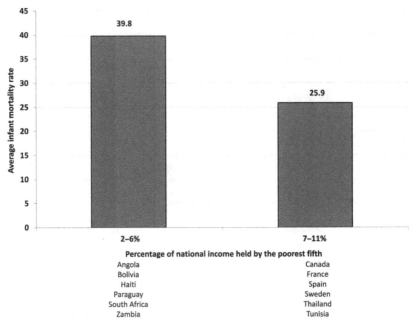

Figure 3.2: *Infant mortality by inequality,[a] with selected national examples*
Note: [a] Percentage share of national income that accrues to the poorest 20% of
the population (World Bank 2014a). The range goes from 2% in Bolivia, Haiti,
and Honduras, to 11% in Japan (average = 6.4; data available for 140 countries;
correlation = −.18, p <.05).
Sources: Raw data from Population Reference Bureau (2014) and World Bank
(2014a)

71.3 years in Japan). By 1990, however, the income difference between
the top and bottom segments of Japan had become the narrowest in the
world, while in the United Kingdom this difference had widened. The
consequence: Japan's life expectancy compared to other nations had
moved to the top spot, while the United Kingdom's international ranking
declined (a life expectancy of 75.0 in the United Kingdom vs 78.5 in
Japan). Changes in nutrition and healthcare did not account for the
increased difference in life expectancies of the two nations (Marmot and
Smith 1989; Williams and Collins 1995: 378–9). More generally, Figure
3.2 shows the inverse and statistically significant relationship between
intra-country equality and infant mortality.

Infant mortality is one of the many ways by which demographers
measure the mortality levels of a population. The following are the

operational definitions of some of the more common measurements, including infant mortality.

Crude Death Rate

$$\text{Crude death rate} = \frac{\text{Deaths in year}_i}{\text{Population year}_i} \times 1,000$$

where i is a particular year, and Population is the total population at midyear.

For example, for the United States in 2010, the

$$\text{Crude death rate} = \frac{2,468,435}{308,745,538} \times 1,000 = 7.995 \approx 8.0$$

The crude death rate allows us to compare the number of deaths across different geographic units (such as countries). However, because it does not take into account the age structure of the population, it can be misleading. On the face of it, we would assume that a nation with a high crude death rate was poor and lacking basic resources for its population. Yet the situation might be quite the opposite: The country might be prosperous and provide good amounts of healthcare, nutrition, and security to its population, and because of this, it has allowed for a high percentage of the population to live into old age (60+); and, not surprisingly, age is a strong predictor of death (as one grows older past the age of 60, the probability of dying from acute illnesses [like pneumonia] and degenerative diseases [like heart failure or cancer] increases significantly with each passing year). Thus, for example, in 2014, highly developed Germany had a crude death rate of 11, while much less developed Tanzania's was 9. What accounts for this difference is *not* the differences in development level, but the fact that 21% of Germany's population is 65 and older, while the equivalent percentage in Tanzania is 3. In short, crude death calculations can be deceptive and must be used cautiously. As a final note, it is important to recognize that the moderately strong inverse relationship between level of prosperity and the crude death rate at the cross-national level of analysis is accounted for mostly by the differences between the lowest and middle levels of prosperity (e.g., many Sub-Saharan African nations are very poor and also have high crude death rates); but for nations in the middle and upper levels of prosperity, the death rates do not show a consistent pattern (see Figure 3.3).

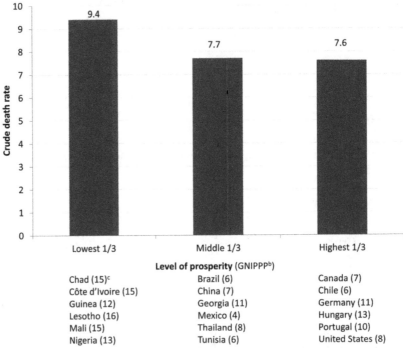

Figure 3.3: The inverse relationship between prosperity and the crude death rate^a is largely accounted for by differences between the lowest and middle levels of prosperity – not between the middle and highest levels

Notes: [a] Number of deaths per 1,000 population in 2013.

[b] *GNIPPP per capita* is gross national income in purchasing power parity (PPP) divided by mid-year population. International dollars indicate the amount of goods and services one could buy in the United States with a given amount of money. (Thus, for example, $20 in US currency would generally buy more food in the typical less developed country than it would in the typical more developed country; in short, PPP makes for better comparisons among countries for a given amount of money regarding what it can actually buy.)

[c] Crude death rate in parentheses.

[d] Correlation = −.63 ($p < .0001$); $N = 179$ countries; again, however, this correlation is largely a function of the strong relationship between the lowest and middle levels of prosperity, but it flattens out for the middle and highest levels.

Source: Raw data from Population Reference Bureau (2014)

Age-Specific Death Rate

Age-specific death rate

$$= \frac{\text{Deaths in year}_i \text{ of individuals of age}_j}{\text{Population in year}_i \text{ of individuals of age}_j} \times 1,000$$

where i is a particular year, and Population is the total population at midyear of individuals of age j (e.g., of age 40).

Age-specific death rates are often calculated for five-year intervals. Thus, for example, for the United States in 2010, for ages 40–4, the

$$\text{Age-specific death rate} = \frac{42,021}{20,895,574} \times 1,000 = 2.011 \approx 2.0$$

For all populations, whether living in least, less, or more developed countries, the risk of dying is highest in the first years of life, is lowest in later childhood and young adulthood, increases in middle age (after 40), and increases significantly in old age (after 60). For each society, depending on its level of socioeconomic development and political responsiveness, the starting point on the axis for the probability of dying varies – being highest for least developed countries and lowest for more developed countries – but the shape of the curve is the same: It forms a lazy J. Thus, for example, the curves for Liberia (a UN-designated "least" developed country) and the highly developed United States are near identical; the only difference is that Liberia's curve starts and ends much higher on the Y-axis, reflecting its higher death rates at all ages (see Figure 3.4).

Age-specific death rates are commonly used in demographic analyses to calculate (a) the infant mortality rate; (b) the mortality rate that is weighted by the age distribution (thus allowing comparison with, say, a high percentage of the population in their teenage years and a country with, say, a high percentage of the population over 65); and (c) life expectancy, as presented in a *life table* (see below).

Infant Mortality Rate

The age-specific death rate for infants is operationally defined as:

Infant mortality Rate

$$= \frac{\text{Deaths in year}_i \text{ of infants less than 1 year of age}}{\text{Total number of live births in year}_i} \times 1,000$$

where i is a particular year.

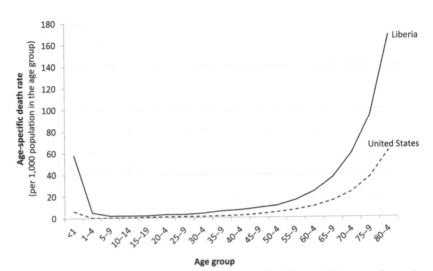

Figure 3.4: The relationship between the probability of dying and age is similar across countries – revealing a lazy J curve
Sources: Raw data for the United States from Centers for Disease Control and Prevention (2014a) for 2010; and for Liberia, from World Health Organization (2014b) for 2008

Child defecating publicly in India
In 2014, the UN has launched a campaign "to break the silence on open defecation"; as of 2014, an estimated 2.5 billion people worldwide lacked toilets and proper sanitation, with 1 billion of them practicing "open defecation" (United Nations 2014f).
Photo: Christine Werner, Sustainable Sanitation Alliance (public domain)

Children living next to a shared toilet facility – and open sewage – in Mathare slum, Nairobi, Kenya

Human waste polluting soil and water is increasingly seen as a cause of postneonatal deaths and of children with stunted growth in many developing countries (an estimated 162 million children in 2014; see Harris 2014; cf. World Health Organization 2014a). "Lack of improved sanitation largely contributes to the fact that a child dies every 2 and a half minutes from preventable diarrheal diseases. It also impacts vulnerable populations such as persons with disabilities and women, who are more exposed to sexual violence. Lack of private toilets in schools is a major reason why girls do not continue their education once they enter puberty" (United Nations 2014f).

Photo: Laura Kraft, Sustainable Sanitation Alliance (public domain)

Thus, for example, for the United States in 2010, the

$$\text{Infant mortality rate} = \frac{24,586}{3,999,386} \times 1,000 = 6.147 \approx 6.15$$

The infant mortality rate is one of the most cited statistics in all of demography, as it provides an overall indication of how well a population is being sustained by its economic, political, and healthcare systems. For analyses of more developed nations, and selected less developed nations with good vital statistics reporting, the infant mortality rate is sometimes reported as two components: the *neonatal mortality rate* (deaths of infants aged 0–27 days per 1,000 live births) and the *postneonatal mortality rate* (deaths of infants aged 28 days–11 months per 1,000 live births). For 2010, for example, the neonatal mortality rate was 4.05 in the United States, while the postneonatal rate was 2.10 (Murphy et al. 2013: 12; note that the sum of these two components equals the total infant mortality rate of 6.15). Neonatal deaths are reflective of inadequate nutrition and medical care for pregnant women, while postneonatal deaths stem from a lack of systematic immunization, good food, clean water, and sanitary environments. For example, in 2013, the postneonatal death rate for India was 23, which was and is very high compared to the rate in the typical developed nation (usually well below 3). The high Indian rate, as well as similarly high rates in many developing countries, is attributed, in large part, to the abundance of human waste polluting the soil and water – a function of the high concentrations of people with no indoor plumbing and who thus defecate outside (see Harris 2014; cf. World Health Organization 2014a). Figure 3.5 shows the strong, inverse relationship between infant mortality and access to toilets.

Life Expectancy and the Life Table

Age-specific death rates can be used to calculate the life expectancy of individuals belonging to the population or a subpopulation of a defined geographic area such as a nation state. The calculations assume that the age-specific death rates for a selected year will hold constant (which in actuality is rarely the case – as future death rates are often smaller than the current death rates being used for the life-expectancy calculations). The defined population may be the entire population, but because death rates vary significantly by sex (why females tend to outlive males is examined later in this chapter), more often the defined population is the subpopulation of either males or females. Furthermore, because death rates also vary significantly by race and ethnicity (why members of selected minority groups tend to live shorter lives is also examined later in this chapter), quite often the defined subpopulation is a racial or an ethnic category. For example, in the United States, age-specific rates are often calculated for black males, black females, white males, and white females – and sometimes for the subpopulations of Hispanic males and Hispanic females.

Life expectancy is estimated via a *life table*. A life table displays the calculations of each subpopulation's age-specific death rates and then applies them to a hypothetical population of 100,000 individuals born in the same time frame (e.g., a particular year).[1] The last column of a life table

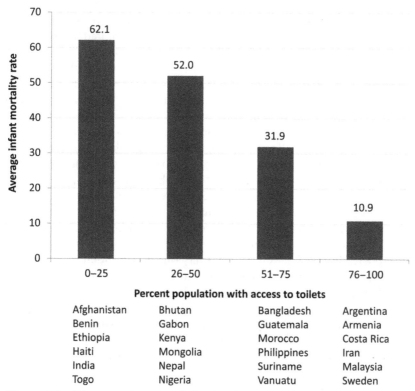

	Afghanistan	Bhutan	Bangladesh	Argentina
	Benin	Gabon	Guatemala	Armenia
	Ethiopia	Kenya	Morocco	Costa Rica
	Haiti	Mongolia	Philippines	Iran
	India	Nepal	Suriname	Malaysia
	Togo	Nigeria	Vanuatu	Sweden

Figure 3.5: The strong inverse relationship between infant mortality rate[a] and access to toilets,[b] with selected national examples

Notes: [a] Number of infants less than 12 months per 1,000 live births in 2013.

[b] *Access to toilets* is the percentage of the rural population with access to an improved sanitation facility, which the UN operationally defines as one that hygienically separates sewage from human contact.

[c] Although worldwide a higher percentage of the urban population has access to toilets, 79% versus 65% in rural areas, the correlation between these two variables is extremely high (.90); thus the relationship displayed here is identical when the horizontal axis is the percentage of the urban population with access to toilets.

[d] The correlation between infant mortality and the percentage of the rural population with access to toilets is −.80 ($p < .0001$), which is nearly identical to the correlation of the percentage of the urban population with access to toilets (−.79); $N = 183$ countries.

Sources: Raw data from Population Reference Bureau (2014) and World Health Organization (2014c)

for a particular population is years of life remaining (*life expectancy*). Table 3.1 cobbles together 18 of these columns to show the life expectancies of major age, sex, and race/ethnic groups in the United States.

Note that as an individual survives another year of life – that is, as he or she grows older – life expectancy increases. This is how the empirical calculations work out, but theoretically, it also makes sense: If individuals survive the traumas of childhood illnesses, then they have demonstrated a significant degree of sturdiness. Likewise, if they survive the risky behaviors of adolescence and young adulthood, they have confirmed that sturdiness at a higher level. Finally, if they do not succumb to heart disease or cancer or related diseases in their middle years of life, then there is further confirmation of their hardiness and of their bright prospects for long life. Thus, for example, based on Table 3.1, a white male born in 2008 can expect to live to the age of 76.1; but if he survives to the age of 30, he can expect to live to 77.6 (30 current years + 47.6 years of expected remaining life); and if he survives until the age of 60, he can expect to live to 81.2 (60 + 21.2). Of course, every one dies eventually, and, in this example, no white males are expected to survive past the age of 102.

Life expectancy at birth is one of the most popularly used statistics in the study of mortality across time and across geographic areas (e.g., cities, counties, states, regions, countries). Its main advantage is that it does not depend on the age distribution of the population – and thus it is a much improved measurement over the crude death rate.

Cause-Specific Death Rate

$$\text{Cause-specific death rate} = \frac{\text{Deaths in year}_i \text{ from cause}_j}{\text{Population year}_i} \times 100,000$$

where i is a particular year, and Population is the total population. (Note that the rate is now per 100,000 instead of per 1,000; this is because the numbers of deaths from a specific cause are small relative to the total population and thus using the multiplier of 100,000 eliminates difficult-to-read decimal fractions.)

Thus, for example, for the United States in 2010, the death rate for

$$\text{Cardiovascular disease} = \frac{597,689}{308,745,538} \times 100,000$$
$$= 193.586 \approx 193.6$$

Cause-specific death rates can be adjusted by age (controlling for the relative size of the younger vs older segments of the population), and

Table 3.1: Life expectancy by age, sex, race, and Hispanic origin in the United States, 2008

Age	All races and origins			White			Black			Hispanic			Non-Hispanic white			Non-Hispanic black		
	Total	Male	Female	Total	Male	Female	Total	Male	Female	Total	Male	Female	Total	Male	Female	Total	Male	Female
0	78.1	75.6	80.6	78.5	76.1	80.9	74.0	70.6	77.2	81.0	78.4	83.3	78.4	75.9	80.7	73.7	70.2	76.9
1	77.6	75.1	80.1	77.9	75.5	80.3	74.0	70.6	77.1	80.4	77.9	82.8	77.8	75.4	80.2	73.6	70.2	76.8
5	73.7	71.2	76.1	74.0	71.6	76.4	70.1	66.7	73.2	76.5	74.0	78.8	73.9	71.5	76.2	69.8	66.3	72.9
10	68.8	66.3	71.2	69.1	66.6	71.4	65.2	61.8	68.2	71.5	69.0	73.9	68.9	66.5	71.3	64.8	61.4	68.0
15	63.8	61.3	66.2	64.1	61.7	66.5	60.2	56.8	63.3	66.6	64.0	68.9	64.0	61.6	66.3	59.9	56.5	63.0
20	59.0	56.6	61.3	59.3	56.9	61.6	55.5	52.2	58.4	61.8	59.3	64.0	59.1	56.8	61.4	55.1	51.8	58.2
25	54.3	52.0	56.5	54.5	52.3	56.7	50.8	47.7	53.6	57.0	54.6	59.1	54.4	52.1	56.5	50.5	47.3	53.3
30	49.5	47.3	51.6	49.8	47.6	51.8	46.2	43.1	48.8	52.2	49.9	54.2	49.6	47.5	51.7	45.9	42.8	48.6
35	44.8	42.6	46.8	45.0	42.9	47.0	41.6	38.6	44.1	47.4	45.2	49.3	44.9	42.8	46.9	41.3	38.3	43.8
40	40.1	38.0	42.0	40.3	38.3	42.2	37.0	34.2	39.4	42.7	40.5	44.5	40.2	38.2	42.1	36.7	33.9	39.2
45	35.5	33.5	37.3	35.7	33.7	37.5	32.6	29.8	34.9	38.0	35.9	39.7	35.6	33.6	37.4	32.3	29.5	34.7
50	31.0	29.1	32.8	31.2	29.3	32.9	28.4	25.7	30.6	33.4	31.4	35.1	31.1	29.3	32.9	28.1	25.4	30.4
55	26.8	25.0	28.4	26.9	25.2	28.5	24.5	21.9	26.5	29.0	27.1	30.5	26.8	25.1	28.4	24.3	21.7	26.3
60	22.7	21.0	24.1	22.8	21.2	24.1	20.8	18.5	22.6	24.8	23.0	26.1	22.7	21.1	24.1	20.7	18.4	22.4
65	18.8	17.3	20.0	18.8	17.4	20.0	17.4	15.4	18.9	20.7	19.1	21.8	18.8	17.3	20.0	17.3	15.3	18.8
70	15.2	13.9	16.2	15.2	13.9	16.2	14.3	12.6	15.4	16.9	15.5	17.8	15.1	13.9	16.1	14.2	12.5	15.4
75	11.8	10.7	12.6	11.8	10.7	12.6	11.3	9.9	12.3	13.4	12.2	14.0	11.8	10.7	12.6	11.3	9.8	12.2
80	8.9	8.0	9.5	8.9	8.0	9.4	8.8	7.6	9.4	10.2	9.2	10.6	8.8	8.0	9.4	8.8	7.6	9.4
85	6.4	5.7	6.8	6.4	5.7	6.7	6.6	5.8	7.0	7.4	6.6	7.7	6.4	5.7	6.7	6.6	5.8	7.0
90	4.5	4.0	4.7	4.4	3.9	4.6	5.0	4.4	5.2	5.2	4.7	5.3	4.4	3.9	4.6	4.9	4.3	5.2
95	3.1	2.8	3.2	3.0	2.8	3.1	3.7	3.3	3.8	3.7	3.3	3.7	3.0	2.8	3.1	3.7	3.3	3.8
100	2.2	2.0	2.2	2.2	2.0	2.2	2.8	2.5	2.8	2.6	2.4	2.6	2.2	2.0	2.2	2.8	2.5	2.8

Source: Arias (2012: 4). The construction of the life tables from which the life expectancies in this table were calculated involves complex mathematics that vary according to various starting assumptions (see, e.g., Bell and Miller 2005).

thus they constitute an important means by which we can compare the eradication or reduction of a specific cause of death of a single country over time or of multiple countries at a single point in time. In general, as the economic, political, and healthcare systems become developed, the major causes of death transform from communicable diseases (like measles) to degenerative diseases (like cancer).

Figure 3.6 displays the strong inverse relationship between economic development and the percentage of deaths from noncommunicable (or degenerative) diseases. What this means is that economically developed nations have overcome what the UN labels as *Group I* causes of death;

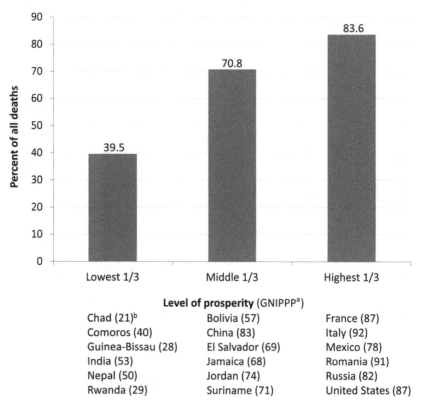

Figure 3.6:   The strong relationship between prosperity and the percentage of all deaths from degenerative diseases, with selected national examples
Notes: [a] *GNIPPP per capita* (see Figure 3.3, note b).
[b] Percentage of all deaths from degenerative diseases in parentheses.
[c] Correlation = .61 ($p < .0001$); N = 179 countries.
Sources: Raw data from Population Reference Bureau (2014) and World Health Organization (2011b)

these consist largely of communicable diseases transmitted from one person to another or from animals to humans – including respiratory infections, diarrheal and parasitic diseases, and sexually transmitted infections. Examples would include measles, tuberculosis, and HIV. Overcoming these diseases allows for much longer life. Everyone dies, but those living into old age are most likely to succumb to one of the well-known degenerative diseases; these fall under the UN's *Group II* causes of death and include cardiovascular disease, cancer, diabetes, and chronic respiratory disease. (A much smaller third category is reserved for traumatic deaths from accidents, murder, suicide, and group violence, which fall under the label *Group III*; see Table 3.2). The shift from the majority of deaths in a country coming from infectious disease to the majority coming from degenerative diseases is labeled the *epidemiologic transition* (see, e.g., Fetter 1997). As with the related and older concept of the *demographic transition*, social and medical scientists debate the nuances of epidemiologic transition theory, but its overall usefulness keeps it salient. The fundamental criticism is that the poorest individuals in least developed countries suffer heavily from both Group I and II causes of death: These individuals are least likely to be immunized and to have access to clean drinking water (encouraging Group I deaths). In addition, they are also likely to have a diet high in refined carbohydrates that is low on nutritional value and obesity-generating. And, finally, they are increasingly the targets of the tobacco, alcohol, and junk food industries (encouraging Group II deaths; see World Health Organization 2011a: 2; 2014d). However, it is

Table 3.2: *Leading causes of death in the world, 2012*

	N deaths	% of total
GROUP I[a] (*Communicable*)	12,822,000	23.0
Lower respiratory infections	3,052,000	5.5
HIV/AIDS	1,534,000	2.7
Diarrheal diseases	1,498,000	2.7
GROUP I (*Noncommunicable*)	37,892,000	67.8
Cardiovascular diseases	17,519,000	31.4
Malignant neoplasms (cancer)	8,206,000	14.7
Respiratory diseases	4,042,000	7.2
GROUP III (*Injury*)	5,144,000	9.2
Road injuries	1,255,000	2.2
Self-harm (suicide)	804,000	1.4
Falls	693,000	1.2
WORLD TOTAL	55,858,000	100.0

Note: [a] Only the top three causes of death are listed for each major Group.
Source: Raw data from World Health Organization (2014e)

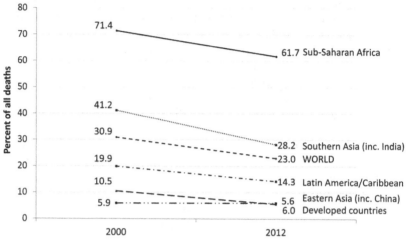

Figure 3.7: Changes in the percentage of all deaths from infectious diseases[a] *in the world, developed countries, and selected developing regions,*[b] *2000–12*
Notes: [a] Percentages refer to all Group I deaths.
[b] The operational definition of regions is that used by the UN's Millennium Development Goals program (United Nations 2014d).
Source: Raw data from World Health Organization (2014e)

clear from Figure 3.7 that regions of the world where the least developed countries predominate – largely in Sub-Saharan Africa and Southern Asia – are the most likely to have high rates of Group I deaths, while regions where developed nations are found (e.g., Europe and Northern America) are the least likely to have high rates of Group I deaths. Those countries in the middle, the UN's developing nations category, are in the midst of the epidemiologic transition: In 2010, about 50% of all deaths were accounted for by degenerative diseases; but by 2020, this figure is expected to reach 70 (World Health Organization 2014d).

Table 3.3 details the stages of the epidemiologic transition. Like its more general parent concept, the demographic transition (see Chapter 2), the transition was earlier and took longer for the prosperous nations of Europe and Northern America to undergo – as they slowly recognized and pursued the development of immunization, clean water, and other public health programs during the first half of the twentieth century. Developing nations were able to import these programs in the latter third of the twentieth century and the early part of the twenty-first century – and thus were quicker to begin the transition of a predominance of deaths from infectious diseases to one of degenerative diseases. Many developing nations made especially strong gains after 2000, when all 189 countries belonging to the UN, as well as 23 major international human welfare groups, signed the *Millennium Declaration,*

Table 3.3: *The epidemiologic transition and where selected nations currently place: as nations move from Group I[a] to Group II causes of death, their populations experience increases in life expectancy*

Stage	Description	Example nation	% of all deaths from Group II causes	Life expectancy
I	**Pre-transitional** Age of Pestilence and Famine (most of human history) *Group I deaths predominate* High mortality in both children and adults			20s–30s
II	**Early to mid-transitional** Age of Receding Pandemics (mid-nineteenth through mid-twentieth century for the developed countries of Europe and Northern America; mid-twentieth through early twenty-first[b] century for less developed countries) *Decreasing importance of Group I deaths* Declining mortality in children	Sierra Leone	18	40s–50s
		Guinea-Bissau	28	47
		Zambia	27	48
		Zimbabwe	21	48
		Nigeria	27	48
		South Africa	29	51
				54
III	**Late transitional** Age of Degenerative and Human-Made Diseases (1940s–60s for most developed countries; 1960s–early 2000s for all but the least developed of developing countries) *Predominance of Group II deaths* Most people survive to adulthood	Iran	72	70s
		Morocco	75	70
		Indonesia	64	72
		Brazil	74	72
		China	83	74
		Argentina	80	75
				76
IV	**Post-transitional** Age of Delayed Degenerative Diseases (1970s–present day for most developed countries; some less developed countries now entering this stage; but many least developed countries will not enter this stage for many decades) *Continued predominance of Group II deaths* Death delayed to even older ages	United Kingdom	88	80s
		Canada	89	80
		Netherlands	89	81
		Australia	90	81
		Sweden	90	82
		San Marino	85	82
				84

Notes: [a] Also included in this group are deaths related to pregnancy, labor, or delivery; as well as infant deaths from low birth weight and nutritional deficiencies. [b] Correlation between percentage of all deaths from Group II causes and life expectancy = .89 ($p < .0001$); data available for 189 countries.

Sources: Olshansky and Ault (1986), Population Reference Bureau (2014), and United Nations (2012d: 10).

which laid out eight major *Millennium Development Goals* (MDGs) that would show measureable success by 2015. There goals were to (1) eradicate extreme poverty and hunger; (2) achieve universal primary education; (3) promote gender equality and empower women; (4) reduce child mortality; (5) improve maternal health; (6) combat HIV/AIDS, malaria, and other diseases; (7) ensure environmental sustainability; and (8) develop a global partnership for development. The UN-coordinated pursuit of these goals pushed many developing nations rapidly along the epidemiologic transition. (There is more on the success of the MDGs in the last section of this chapter.)

Chile provides a good example of a developing nation that has gone through the epidemiologic transition. In 1960, it had a relatively high percentage of its deaths resulting from communicable diseases (almost 50%). However, this percentage fell with each passing decade: in 1970, to 35%; in 1980, to 23%; in 1990, to 12%; and by 2012, just 5%. At the same time, the life expectancy of its population grew each decade, from 40 years in 1960, to 78 years by 2010. Figure 3.8 provides a graphic display of how this dramatic transition has played out in this country.

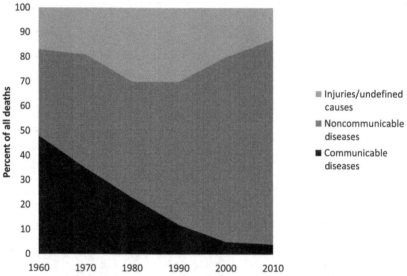

Figure 3.8:   Chile provides a good example of how the epidemiologic transition has unfolded in developing countries since 1960
Note: The three cause-specific categories of death represent the UN's operational definitions of Group I (communicable diseases), Group II (noncommunicable diseases), and Group III (injuries); see United Nations (2012d: 7–8).
Sources: Raw data taken from United Nations (2012d: 12) and World Health Organization (2014b)

Explaining Differences in Death (Who Lives a Long Life and Why): Macro and Micro Perspectives

Macro Factors Encouraging Lower Death Rates and Increased Life Expectancy

From a national level of analysis, improvements in the overall standard of living preceded major public health initiatives (e.g., vaccination) in moving death rates down and years of life expectancy up in Western Europe and in Northern America. McKeown's (1976) study of England and Wales empirically demonstrated that death rates began falling significantly in the latter half of the nineteenth century, well before the scientific understanding of *germ theory* and well before the consequent immunization programs that eventually got underway in the twentieth century. Major improvements in transportation in the nineteenth century – steam-powered rail engines and ocean vessels, as well as more and better-networked roads – began ensuring that both urban and rural populations had access to better-quality food year round. Better nutrition increased resistance to disease. Although Edward Jenner developed a relatively safe inoculation for the deadly smallpox virus in 1796, the use of which spread across Europe and the United States throughout the nineteenth century, most vaccines that would curb the outbreaks of epidemics were not developed until the twentieth century (see the Immunization Action Coalition's [2014] timeline for vaccine adoption).

As the nineteenth century progressed, cotton fabric became increasingly affordable, replacing much of the wool and flaxen clothing that had been predominant for centuries. Also, soap manufacturing grew in sophistication and scale after 1780, eventually both creating and responding to popular demand. Cotton fabric and commercial soap made for the easier laundering of clothes, and their adoption promoted regular washing – eventually becoming a cultural norm, not only for the middle and upper classes but also for the working class. One contemporary chronicler of the lifestyle of the English working class wrote in 1822 that "the woollen clothes, which [are] universally worn by them, last... for years and [are] seldom, if ever, washed" (Francis Place, as quoted in Razzell 1974: 15). However, by the mid-nineteenth century, cleanliness of both clothing and body had become socially desirable signs of stability and civility, as well as a perceived antidote to the dirt and chaos that industrialization had brought to urban areas (Eveleigh 2003; Razzell 1974). One consequence of the widespread regular washing of clothes was the reduction of body lice – the transmitter of typhus. And as frequent bathing became ensconced in the culture, the germs and parasites that harbored themselves on the human body were reduced and the inter-person spread of infections – including typhoid fever and dysentery – became less common.

The nineteenth-century improvements in living standards increased life expectancy by about 10 years: from the late 30s in 1800, to the late 40s by 1900. In the twentieth century, life expectancy continued to increase, but at a much faster rate. Key to this striking increase were the public health responses to germ theory, first advanced by Louis Pasteur in 1877. These responses included improvements in public sanitation and aggressive vaccination programs against diseases that had once devastated the general population, but especially children and young adults. These diseases, and the dates that vaccines were developed, included cholera (1896), diphtheria (1886), hepatitis A (1988), hepatitis B (1981), influenza (1942 – though not before the Spanish flu pandemic of 1918 killed 50 million+ people worldwide; less lethal but still deadly strains reappear every few decades), measles (1963), mumps (1967), pertussis (whooping cough, 1915), plague (pneumonic, 1897), pneumonia (bacterial, 1977), polio (1955), rubella (1971), tetanus (1949), tuberculosis (1927), typhoid (1896), and yellow fever (1935). The introduction of sulfa drugs (1935), penicillin (1943), and subsequent other antibiotics also contributed to declining death rates. (What today are considered minor infections could become life-threatening prior to the discovery and widespread use of antibiotics.) Figure 3.9 presents the United States as an example of how the dramatic change in life expectancy unfolded during the twentieth century in the developed regions of the world, when it rose by an average of 30 years (from the late 40s to the late 70s). The curve slopes markedly upward during the first half of the twentieth century and has continued upward at more modest levels ever since then.

The upward curve for life expectancy that started in the second half of the nineteenth century for developed nations began to unfold in the 1950s and 1960s in less developed regions of the world – as countries in these regions were assisted by the UN and many governmental and major nonprofit organizations in adopting technologies to increase food production and to deter disease through immunization, mosquito control, and clean-water campaigns. Thus, for example, in 1967, when smallpox was still common in many less developed countries, the UN's World Health Organization (WHO) launched the Global Smallpox Eradication Program, which promoted disease surveillance (to find out where new cases were breaking out) and vaccination programs in dozens of countries – ultimately having the astonishing effect of virtually eliminating the disease by 1980 (the first disease ever to be eradicated by human intervention!). Similar WHO programs were effective in reducing the

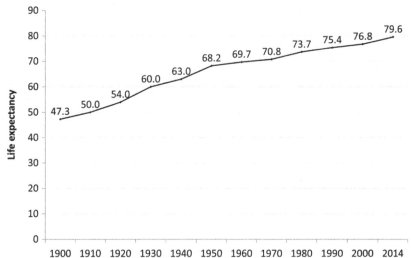

Figure 3.9: *The United States exemplifies the dramatic rise in longevity that contemporary developed nations experienced during the twentieth century*
Note: In the United States, life expectancy increased by two-thirds during the twentieth century, and has continued to increase since then.
Sources: Adapted from Arias (2004, 2012) and *World Factbook* (2014)

incidence (number of new cases) and *prevalence* (total number of cases) of cholera, HIV/AIDS, malaria, measles, polio, and tuberculosis. The WHO also advanced many initiatives to mitigate the devastation of chronic diseases (heart disease, cancer, diabetes), suicide, injuries, and other noncommunicable causes of death and ill health – all of which are still ongoing. It has partnered with the World Bank in leading the *International Health Partnership* – a group of nations and major nonprofit/nongovernmental (or "civil society") organizations committed to elevating the health level of the populations of developing nations to that of the populations of developed nations (see International Health Partnership 2014).

At the same time that the WHO and its allies began sponsoring major public health initiatives in developing regions during the 1950s and 1960s, the *Green Revolution* was unfolding in India, Mexico, Pakistan, the Philippines, Turkey, and other heavily populated developing countries. At its heart, the Revolution, which was sponsored by the World Bank, the Ford and Rockefeller Foundations, the UN, and various agencies of selected national governments, sought to take the high-tech farming that was created in developed countries in the first half of the twentieth century and bring it to the developing nations of Asia and

Latin America – and less so to Africa. Mexico, India (on the brink of mass starvation in the early 1960s), Pakistan, and the Philippines were early beneficiaries of the Revolution. This kind of farming uses high-yield maize, millet, rice, and wheat seeds; systematic and controlled irrigation; carefully planned farm-to-market roads; and massive amounts of synthetic fertilizers, herbicides, and pesticides. Within just a few years of the introduction of these high-tech approaches to agriculture, crop yields increased dramatically, quadrupling in some cases, and large grain importers such as India, Mexico, Pakistan, and the Philippines became self-sufficient – and even food exporters – by the mid-1960s (Gaud 1968). China and several other developing Asian nations followed suit and were largely self-sufficient by the early 1980s (Borlaug 2000). Figure 3.10 displays the dramatic effect of the Green Revolution on China and India during the last four decades of the twentieth century.

Figure 3.11 shows the dramatic effect on life expectancy that has been experienced in the developing nations of the world in the past several decades – largely as a product of imported public health initiatives and of the Green Revolution. The formula for calculating life expectancy, as noted above, reveals that it is particularly sensitive to early childhood deaths (small reductions in these yield large increases in life expectancy). And the dramatic reduction of these deaths in recent years has been one of humanity's greatest achievements. Indeed, between 1990 and 2012, the mortality rate of children under 5 declined from 90 to 48 deaths per 1,000 births (a 47% drop); in raw numbers, this means that 17,000 fewer children were dying each day in 2012 than in 1990 (World Health Organization 2014f: 13). Part and parcel of falling child death rates has been the huge reduction in worldwide hunger over the same time period: Although in 2013 an estimated 842 million were suffering from chronic hunger – regularly not getting enough food to conduct an active life – this is 17% fewer than were suffering in 1990 (United Nations 2014e).

While many developing nations were able to sidestep the economic development required by developed nations for their significant rises in life expectancy, this factor still plays a critical part in the explanation of differences in mortality and life expectancy among nations. The public health initiatives and Green Revolution that so dramatically improved health and increased life expectancy in Asia and Latin America were much less successful in the generally very poor nations of Sub-Saharan Africa. Although observers and scholars argue over the many reasons for the relative lack of success in this part of Africa, three key factors appear in most analyses. First, there is the widespread and seemingly incorrigible corruption of much of the political leadership – with money being diverted from healthcare initiatives into the pockets of the rich and into the building up of the military (see, e.g., Dugger 2007; Stevens 2004).

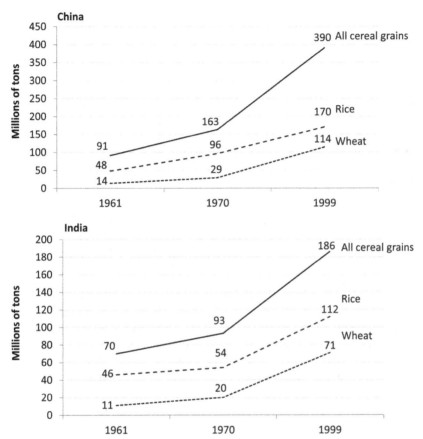

Figure 3.10: *The effects of the Green Revolution on grain production in China and India, 1961–99*
Sources: Raw data from United Nations (2000) and Borlaug (2000)

The second factor is fragile political stability of these nations due to the artificial drawing of their borders by European colonial powers in the late nineteenth century – in which peoples of markedly different languages, religions, and cultures were defined as nations not because of any natural affinities among these peoples, but because of the desires and political compromises of the six big colonial powers at the time (Belgium, France, Germany, Great Britain, Italy, and Portugal). (In 1870, these six controlled 10% of the African continent, but by 1914, they controlled 90% – with only Abyssinia [Ethiopia] and Liberia being independent. The map-drawing at the 1884 Berlin Conference prevented war among these six, as each of them was in an intense scramble for enrichment by colonizing as much of Africa as possible; see Pakenham 1992.) Note that the strong financial and credit markets needed to assist farmers in getting new seeds and new technologies require strong political stability. And the third factor is the relative lack of irrigation infrastructure and farm-to-market roadways in much of Africa when compared to Asia, where the Green Revolution has had its greatest successes (Alliance for a Green Revolution in Africa 2014; Dugger 2007). The upshot of the combined weight of these factors is that death rates have remained high and life expectancy low in much of Africa compared to the rest of the developing and developed nations of the world. Thus, for example, in the 20 prosperous and democratic nations that comprise Northern and Western Europe, life expectancies average in the early 80s, while in the 14 economically depressed nations of Middle and Southern Africa, life expectancies hover in the early 50s (Population Reference Bureau 2012). More generally, the UN estimates that a third of all deaths that have occurred since 2000 are rooted in poverty – and that would have been, and would still be, preventable with more nutritious food, cleaner water, and increased access to vaccines, antibiotics, antimalarial drugs, and related medicines (Stevens 2004; World Health Organization 2014f).

The World Bank and various arms of the UN predict that despite the numerous economic and political problems besetting Sub-Saharan Africa and many other least and less developed countries, the life expectancy gap depicted in Figure 3.11 will continue to close. The optimism is predicated on the recent successes of developing countries in bringing

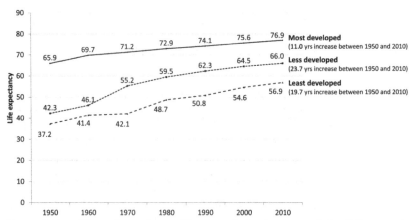

Figure 3.11: Throughout the world, we are living longer, and the differences in life expectancy among least, less, and more developed nations are decreasing
Source: Raw data from United Nations (2013d)

their food supplies, death rates, and fertility rates ever closer to their counterparts in developed countries. Especially important will be elevating the development of the world's least developed nations, particularly those of Sub-Saharan Africa, to a level where this UN designation (*least developed*) will no longer be needed. This quest is well underway with recent improvements in the implementation of Green Revolution technologies in African nations.

While agriculture sustains the economy of this region, providing a large share of the GDP, productivity in the sector has lagged considerably behind that of other continents, for reasons elucidated above, and well below the region's potential. "On average, about 65 percent of Africa's labor force is employed in agriculture, yet the sector accounts for about 32 percent of GDP, reflecting relatively low productivity." Thus, the majority of Sub-Saharan Africa's population has been mired in poverty "principally because of the inability to transform their basic economic activity – agriculture – to high productivity levels. Because of its contribution to the economy, the agriculture sector's poor performance is one of the major barriers to development on the African continent" (Alliance for a Green Revolution in Africa 2014: 14). One important effort to change this situation is the *Alliance for a Green Revolution in Africa* (AGRA) – founded in 2006, and funded primarily by the Rockefeller Foundation and the Bill & Melinda Gates Foundation. AGRA's research in 17 countries has revealed which areas need which solutions to increase agricultural production. In some cases, it is a lack of roads; in other cases, a lack of irrigation; in still other cases, a lack of credit to allow farmers to buy new high-yielding varieties of traditional cereals and starchy roots – mainly cassava, maize, millet, rice, sorghum, and wheat.

Recent successes of AGRA, and of related government- and NGO-sponsored approaches, include Ghana, Kenya, Mali, Tanzania, Uganda, and Zambia. For example, Ghana began transforming its agricultural system in the early 1990s. It started by helping its farmers – who constituted 50% of its work force at the time – to obtain disease-resistance strains of root vegetables and other crops. It also cut back the taxation of cash crops, especially of cocoa, resulting in raising the incomes of farm families. Finally, it invested in its physical and financial infrastructures (e.g., more and better roads; more and less costly credit) for getting crops planted and then transported from farms to market. The end results: Ghana's per capita food production rose 55% between 1990 and 2010, while the percentage of its population living in extreme poverty (less than $1.25 per day) during this period fell from 51.7 to 28.5%. The upper class in Ghana has profited greatly, but the major beneficiaries have been "small-scale producers of cocoa and farmers producing fruits and vegetables" (United Nations 2014e: 32).

A final note on the Green Revolution: Although it has been responsible for eliminating hunger and food insecurity for much of the total population of the developing world, as well as for increasing life expectancy, it is not without its downsides. A growing body of studies reveal that the Revolution has destroyed the livelihoods of millions of small farm families, as the cost of fertilizers, herbicides, pesticides, irrigation systems, and mechanized farm equipment ,was (and is) simply beyond their means. The bulk of the individuals affected have moved into (and continue to move into) the massive and growing slum areas of the nearest cities. The larger surviving farms use petroleum-based fertilizers that are ever more expensive, ever more polluting to the environment, and ultimately unsustainable (as opposed to natural fertilizers based on manure and decomposed plant matter). Finally, the diets of the local population are increasingly sustained by a single grain crop, with as much as 80–90% of calories coming from that grain. One result is nutritional deficiencies that are directly related to degenerative and infectious diseases (see Cordain 1999). As observed in Table 3.2, throughout the world, degenerative diseases are the leading causes of death, and as the least developed nations of the world become increasingly successful in combatting communicable diseases, their populations will have increased risks at younger ages of falling victim to degenerative disease – owing, in part, to the lack of balance in their diets; in part, to the heavy use of herbicides and insecticides that are major parts of the foundation of the Green Revolution; and, ironically, in part, to the rise of obesity. (This is the result, among other things, both of the extra fat produced by a high refined carbohydrate/low-protein diet, and of changing from the highly active lifestyle of rural living to the more passive lifestyle of urban living).[2]

The Green Revolution was based on high-tech approaches developed in the 1940s, 1950s, and 1960s. The solutions to the unintended negative consequences are also largely high-tech, but they are (and will be) using the high-tech approaches developed in the twenty-first century. For example, the large-scale farms already dominant in Northern America, and which are growing in numbers on all continents save for Antarctica, are beginning to use computerized tractors that have sensors to calculate the *minimum* amounts of fertilizers, herbicides, and insecticides that are needed – thus saving on petroleum-based products and reducing their harmful effects on the environment. Organic farming methods have been adopted for large-scale commercial use – such that cover crops, mulches, and compost can now replace large amounts of fossil-fuel based fertilizers. Organic farming also makes the soil and the plants grown in it more nutrient-rich, and as it requires less water, it produces run-offs that are less polluting to ground water and nearby rivers, lakes, and coastal waters. Water use is also being reduced by new high-tech, precise, sub-surface, drip-irrigation methods. Increasingly, grains that have been used to feed livestock for the meat industry are now directly consumed by humans with the return to traditional, grass-fed approaches. Finally, the huge amount of food waste that grew concomitantly with the Green Revolution – estimated at 25% of the world's food calories and 50% of total food weight – can be greatly reduced with new technologies for storing and transporting food, as well as cultural changes in how families, restaurants, and supermarkets handle and store it. Taken together, these steps "could more than double the world's food supplies and dramatically cut the environmental impact of agriculture on the world" over the coming few decades – when, as discussed in Chapter 2, world population is expected to grow by at least 2 billion people. (See Foley's [2014] illuminating discussion on how combining new technology with older organic farming methods can fix many of the negative effects of the Green Revolution.)

Macro Factors in Developed Nations: the Example of the United States. While the UN, the World Bank, major nonprofits such as the Ford, Rockefeller, and Bill & Melinda Gates Foundations, and many national governments have focused on the health and mortality problems of the developing world, the US National Research Council has tackled the problem of why a highly developed and prosperous nation like the United States lags behind its peer nations in so many health and mortality indicators – including infant mortality (see Figure 3.12), childhood death, drug-related mortality, degenerative disease (including heart disease and diabetes, but not cancer), and life expectancy. (See the Council's major findings in Woolf and Aron 2013.) Given that the United States spends more money on healthcare than any other nation, about $8,500 per person, more than twice that of the typical developed nation (see Figure 3.13), the expectation would be for it to rank at or very near the top for all of the common indicators used to measure the health of a national population. Indeed, earlier in this chapter, Figure 3.1 led to the conclusion that "prosperity buys life."

The Research Council compared the United States to its 16 closest peer nations (prosperous democracies): Australia, Austria, Canada, Denmark, Finland, France, Germany, Italy, Japan, Norway, Portugal, Spain, Sweden, Switzerland, the Netherlands, and the United Kingdom. Among the major findings revealed were as follows:

1   The US healthcare system is overly fragmented, with limited primary care (the first doctor a sick person should generally see; and the first doctor a healthy person should see to get a regular checkup) and a

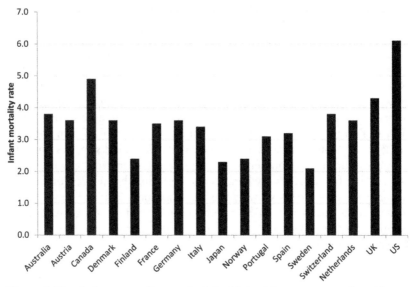

Figure 3.12: *Infant mortality rate*[a] *of the United States compared to 16 peer nations*

Note: [a] Deaths of infants 0–11 months per 1,000 live births (US rate = 6.1; the average of its peer nations = 3.4).
Source: Raw data from OECD (2013: 37)

large uninsured population. At the start of 2013, 14% of the US population – 44 million individuals – did not have health insurance or access to Medicaid, the government program offering healthcare to the poor. Legislation intended to reduce this percentage, the Patient Protection and Affordable Care Act, did indeed have an impact, and by the middle of 2014, these numbers had fallen to 10% and 31 million; so part of the uninsured problem is being addressed (see US Department of Health and Human Services 2014a, 2014b). Note, however, that the United States' 16 peer nations have national health insurance programs that cover their entire populations (OECD 2013: 139; note that in Germany, 89% of the population is covered by governmental health programs, while the remaining 11% is covered by private insurance).

2 Despite its rich and varied economy, the United States has levels of poverty and income inequality that exceed most of its peer nations. Children living in poverty are laying the foundations for chronic health problems in young and middle adulthood (normally the healthiest years of life), and the United States has a very high percentage of its children living in poverty compared to its peer nations.

Moreover, the United States has fewer safety-net programs than its peers to mitigate the ill health created by poverty.

3   The health-related lifestyle habits of US individuals deviate significantly from the habits of individuals in its peer nations. More particularly, in the United States, individuals are more likely to overeat (encouraging obesity – see Figure 3.13); to drive instead of walk to work or to do shopping (losing the health benefits of walking and thus also encouraging obesity); to drive while under the influence of drugs and alcohol; to abuse prescription and illegal drugs; to commit violence with firearms (inflicting much greater injury than other kinds of weapons); and to partake in unsafe sex practices in adolescence.

The National Research Council's major recommendation is that the United States can narrow the mortality and health gaps between its

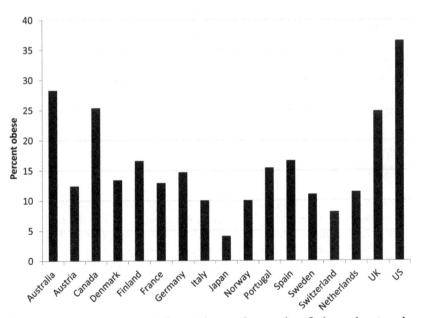

Figure 3.13: Percentage of the adult population classified as obese[a] – the United States compared to 16 peer nations
Note: [a] Obesity operationally defined as a *Body Mass Index* (BMI) of over 30 (obesity percentage in the United States = 36.5; average percentage in its 16 peer nations = 14.7).
Source: Raw data from OECD (2013: 59)

population and the populations of its peer nations by making a conscious and "strong societal commitment to the health and welfare of the *entire* population" (emphasis added). And that this should be reflected in "strengthening systems for health and social services, education and employment; promoting healthy life-styles; and designing healthier environments." The Council observes that this commitment in the United States' peer nations is "not solely the province of government: Effective policies in both the public and private sector can create incentives to encourage individuals and industries to adopt practices that protect and promote health and safety" (Woolf and Aron 2013: 6). Regarding cost, the Council concludes that not attending to the growing US health disadvantage will be more expensive in the long run – and will adversely affect "the economy and prosperity of the United States as other countries reap the benefits of healthier populations and more productive workforces" (Woolf and Aron 2013: 9).

The macro factors influencing death rates and life expectancy (e.g., immunization, clean water, balanced nutrition, and social stability) can be reconceptualized at the individual level of analysis – as presented in the next section. As already noted, the National Research Council's analysis of why the United States lags behind its peer nations in various key measures of mortality and health identified individual lifestyle behaviors as one critical part of the explanation. Indeed, 40% of all deaths in the United States are associated with just four bad health habits: tobacco use, unhealthy eating, physical inactivity, and overdrinking (see Mokdad et al. 2004, 2005).

Micro Factors Encouraging Lower Death Rates and Increased Life Expectancy

Micro factors promoting longevity are relevant to everyone, but a prosperous individual, whether living in a developing or a developed nation, tends to have more control over them. Some of these factors fall under the umbrella rubric of *lifestyle factors*. Others center on the negative consequences of being poor. Finally, genetic factors can predispose individuals to either ill or good health. However, the new science of *epigenetics* reveals that an individual's genes interact with lifestyle and inequality factors – with these factors having the ability to activate or inactivate many genes, including some associated with health and disease.

Modifiable Lifestyle Factors.   Among the most important behavioral factors contributing to *premature death* (i.e., of dying before the average age for those of the same sex born in a particular year) are smoking, overeating (obesity), poor nutrition, physical inactivity, and alcohol/drug abuse.

As of 2013, the WHO estimates that tobacco accounts for about 6 million premature deaths per year worldwide – including over 600,000 deaths from exposure to second-hand smoke (World Health Organization 2014g). (Recall from Table 3.2 that two-thirds of the world's 56 million annual deaths are from degenerative diseases, with heart disease and cancer being the leading two causes, both of which are closely linked to tobacco use.) Because tobacco companies have moved strongly into the markets of developing countries since the 1990s, the WHO predicts that this number will rise steadily, reaching at least 8 million by 2030 – with the majority of these deaths coming in developing countries. (Smoking has been on the decline in the developed world for decades – the key motivation for tobacco companies to grow their markets in the less developed world; note that alcohol companies are now following the lead of tobacco companies [see Lawrence 2011].) In the largest cross-national investigation of tobacco use as of 2015, involving the probability sampling of 3 billion individuals, the Global Adult Tobacco Survey (GATS) revealed that 49% of men and 11% of women in the 14 developing nations studied were tobacco users – and these percentages have been on the rise for decades. For example, 20% of the world's population lives in China, where the GATS estimates that 53% of the adult male population regularly smokes. Contrast this to the United Kingdom and the United States, where the equivalent percentages are 23 and 24 – and these have been on the decline since the 1970s (see Giovino et al. 2012).

The WHO estimates another 3.2 million annual deaths from lack of exercise; 2.3 million from overdrinking alcohol; and 1.7 million from grain-heavy diets that are low in fruit and vegetable consumption. All three of these variables are related to the worldwide growing rate of obesity, especially for the young. Low- and middle-income countries are, ironically, witnessing the fastest rise in overweight children (World Health Organization 2014g). These children, as well as many of their thinner counterparts, are reflective of what the UN's Food and Agriculture Organization (FAO) calls *hidden hunger*: a diet with sufficient calories, and at times well above sufficiency, but lacking in protein, healthy fats, and micronutrients. Undernourishment defined as sufficient calories has dropped dramatically in the developing world over the past several decades (from above 19% in the 1990 to 12% in 2013), while at the same time undernourishment defined as a nutritionally incomplete diet is on the rise. In 2013, the FAO estimated that 842 million people were calorically undernourished, while at the same time at least a quarter of the world's population (2 billion people) were suffering from hidden hunger, with 500 million of them obese (FAO 2014a, 2014b, 2014c).

In developing nations, obesity and undernutrition are reflective of the lack of affordable options in food choice: High-quality protein in the form of red meat, fish, poultry, eggs, and dairy is expensive, as is year-round access to fresh fruits and vegetables. What is affordable are highly refined grains: rice, wheat, maize, or others. Not only does the refining process remove most of the micronutrients from these foods, but it also lays the foundation for weight gain – as refined grains, as well as the sugar that is often added to them as multinational food corporations gain ever stronger footholds in developing nations (Lawrence 2011), create spikes in the hormone insulin, which is the body's key fat-storing mechanism.[3]

In developed nations, where the majority of the population can afford and have access to highly nutritious food, obesity has been linked to poor food choices – as related, in part, to an individual's social networks. In a major study of the spread of obesity in the United States, Christakis and Fowler (2007) found that an individual having a friend who has become obese within the preceding three years has a 57% greater chance of becoming obese in the coming three years than an individual with no such friends. Similarly, if one of his or her siblings becomes obese, the chance of the individual becoming obese is increased by 40%, while if the individual's spouse has become obese, his or her chance increases by 37%. The key interpretation of this groundbreaking finding – that obesity is "contagious" and is a phenomenon that is transmitted person-to-person over time – is that if an individual's most important friends and relatives become obese, then for that individual it becomes more socially and personally acceptable to tolerate, accept, or even embrace fatness.

The physiological mechanisms connecting tobacco use, alcohol/drug abuse, lack of exercise, obesity, and a poor diet to premature death from heart disease, cancer, chronic respiratory disease, diabetes, and dozens of serious but less prevalent diseases include elevated blood pressure, raised blood glucose, depressed immune function, and – in the case of tobacco – exposure to carcinogens. Because degenerative diseases unfold slowly over time, they can have much greater effects on the total *disease burden* of a country compared to the relatively quick deaths that often come from communicable diseases. Cross-national studies measure disease burden with the *disability-adjusted life year* (DALY) indicator – the number of years lost from poor health and premature death (see Homedes 1996; *Lancet* 2014; World Bank 2014b; World Health Organization 2014h, 2014i). Not surprisingly, the UN's list of least developed countries suffer the highest levels of disease burden (see Figure

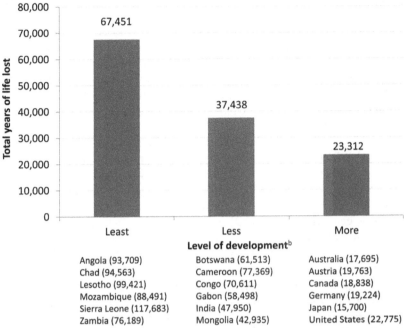

Figure 3.14: *The disease burden*[a] *is heaviest in countries least able to bear it*
Notes: [a] Average disease burden for each level of development in 2012; disease burden is measured by the DALY indicator, which is defined as the total amount of healthy life lost to all causes, measured in years, whether from premature mortality or from some degree of disability during a period of time (see Homedes 1996; World Bank 2014b). The DALY figures used here are age-adjusted (so that countries with relatively high or low populations of younger or of older individuals can be compared).
[b] UN level of socioeconomic development; example countries have their DALY indicator in parentheses.
Source: Raw data from World Health Organization (2014i)

3.14) – lacking the resources to prevent, as well as to treat, their burgeoning rates of chronic disease. In short,

> as diets and lifestyles in developing countries change, their patterns of disease are following those seen in industrialized countries in the north equally rapidly. But for poor countries there is a double whammy: they have started suffering from high rates of [degenerative diseases] before they have managed to deal with hunger and malnutrition. The double burden is devastating both their economic growth and their health budgets. (Lawrence 2011)

Inequality and Poverty. At the family and individual levels of analysis (the *micro* level), economic prosperity is a critical predictor of ill health and premature death. For example, in the United States, African Americans living in poor inner-city neighborhoods can expect to live to their early 60s, while their white and Asian counterparts in selected upscale neighborhoods have life expectancies that range as high as the early 90s (Murray et al. 2006; cf. Clarke et al. 2010). More generally, the age-adjusted death rate for males with less than a high school education is more than three times the rate of their counterparts with at least some college education (821 vs 249 per 100,000; see National Center for Health Statistics 2008). The socioeconomic status–health/mortality relationships at the micro level of analysis hold across nations of both the developed and less developed worlds (see, e.g., Kunst and Mackenbach 1994; United Nations 2013e: 12; Williams and Collins 1995: 351).

More generally, the WHO, and indeed the social science research community as a whole, concludes that the social determinants of health have strong effects on a person's health-related behaviors and can thus account for much of the disparity in health/life expectancy between poorer and more prosperous individuals. Social determinants are "the conditions in which people are born, grow, live, work and age. These circumstances are shaped by the distribution of money, power and resources at global, national and local levels" (World Health Organization 2014j; cf. US Department of Health and Human Services 2014c). Thus, explaining the differences in life expectancy and rates of disease between the less prosperous and the more prosperous involves examining differences between them in economic stability, neighborhood stability, access to healthcare services, and education.

The precise reasons for the inverse relationships between *socioeconomic status* (indicated by education, income, and occupational prestige) and ill health/premature death are complex, difficult to weight by level of importance, and generally not well understood. However, the relevant behavioral and social science research consistently reveals that among the most important reasons are the following:

1   *Affordability of healthcare*: In the United States, for example, one-third of those suffering a chronic illness spend more than $1,000 a year in out-of-pocket costs (Schoen at al. 2011; Woolf and Aron 2013: 112), and these costs prevent as many as 40% of Americans from seeking needed care, especially the poor (National Center for Health Statistics 2012: 272; Wendt et al. 2011; Woolf and Aron 2013: 112).

2   *Affordability of health-enhancing material assets*: Better food (fresher, higher in protein, less processed), better housing (with

nonleaded paint, quiet surroundings, adequately heated and cooled), better schooling (including the accoutrements that help in the educational process – such as having a computer at home, having access to the Internet, having tutors to help with learning difficulties), and better recreation (beyond television and drinking at home with friends or family) all have positive and well-documented effects on the health status of an individual (see, e.g., Adler and Newman 2002; Phelan et al. 2010). In short, poor individuals can afford fewer – or lower levels – of the material assets that contribute to good health.

3   *Having a job, and, better yet, having a job where the work environment is nontoxic*: Unemployment and job insecurity negatively affect health. For example, worries about plants closing and whether one will have a job in the near future are linked with elevated blood pressure (Schnall et al. 1992). Those with low levels of education suffer much higher rates of unemployment (e.g., in the United States, those without a high school diploma are about three times more likely to be unemployed than their counterparts with a college degree; see Bureau of Labor Statistics 2014b). Moreover, the working poor are more likely to have jobs that expose them to occupational injuries, as well as to harmful substances – including lead, asbestos, carbon monoxide, toxic chemicals, and industrial waste (Adler and Newman 2002).

4   *The level of support from friends and family*: Isolation, low engagement in social networks, and little trust in the people with whom an individual interacts on a regular basis are strong predictors of ill health (Adler and Newman 2002; Uchino 2004). The poor are less likely to be in school, to be employed, to attend church, to live in neighborhoods where trust levels are high, and to belong to organized recreational groups such as sports teams or dance clubs (see, e.g., Adler and Newman 2002; Wilcox et al. 2012).

5   *Behavioral choices*: As shown in Table 3.4, less educated individuals are more likely to be on the wrong end of those lifestyle behaviors noted in the preceding section that contribute to good health. Inspection of this table reveals that those of limited education, who generally have low incomes and higher unemployment rates and thus can least afford ill health, are much more likely than their better-educated counterparts to smoke and to be obese, while at the same time less likely to exercise and to get medical testing that can catch potentially fatal diseases in their early stages. The social class differences in these health-related behaviors account for much of the excess ill health and mortality of low-income/low-education individuals (see, e.g., the large-scale study by Jarvandi et al. 2012). Within a particular income or education grouping (e.g., the college/

Table 3.4: *Health-related behaviors/characteristics and general health by level of education (%)*

Health-related behaviors/characteristics	Level of education	
	No high school diploma	College or university degree
Smoking[a]	31	9
Obese[b]	39	26
Not exercising[c]	70	42
No colorectal test[d]	55	33
Trusting others[e]	14	55
Excellent health[f]	20	38

Notes: [a] Percentage of adults 25 and older who smoke cigarettes.
[b] Percentage of adults 25 and older with a Body Mass Index (BMI) of 30 or more. BMI is a measure adjusting body weight for height; it is weight in kilograms divided by height in meters squared. A healthy weight for adults is defined as a BMI of 18.5 to less than 25; overweight is 25 to less than 30; and obesity is 30 or greater.
[c] Percentage of adults 18 and over meeting neither aerobic nor muscle-strengthening physical activity recommendations of the US Department of Health & Human Services (http:// www.health.gov/PAGuidelines/; note that education for this variable is defined as no high school diploma vs some college or more).
[d] Percentage of adults 50 to 75 years old not having a colorectal test of any type within the recommend time-frame: a home fecal occult blood test (FOBT) in the past year; or a sigmoidoscopy in the past five years with FOBT in the past three years or a colonoscopy in the past 10 years. Note that the relationships of education to pap smears, mammograms, and other common medical disease-screening tests are similar to that for colorectal tests.
[e] Percentage of adults 18 and older asserting that "most people can be trusted."
[f] Percentage of adults 18 and older reporting their general health to be "Excellent" (as opposed to "Good," "Fair," or "Poor").
Sources: For (a)–(d), percentages excerpted from National Center for Health Statistics (2012: 64–6, 252); for (e)–(f), percentages calculated from the General Social Survey (2012)

university-educated or those without a high school diploma), differences among individuals in dying prematurely and of having poor health are strongly accounted for by differences in smoking, alcohol/drug abuse, obesity, exercise, medical check-ups, and the quality of social relationships (see, e.g., Murray et al. 2006).

Social forces strongly shape the choices available to an individual, as well as the probabilities of making particular choices, but his or her lifestyle decisions still matter, greatly so. The well-educated, prosperous individual who smokes cigarettes, overeats, and avoids exercise and the doctor's office is cutting years from his or her life compared to his or her well-educated and prosperous counterpart who chooses not to smoke, not to overeat, and not to avoid exercise and the doctor's office. The same thing can be said for poorly educated, less prosperous individuals: Those with a healthy lifestyle tend to outlive and to have better health than their counterparts with an unhealthy lifestyle.

Other Factors: Gender, Race/Ethnicity, and Genetics

Gender. In 2012, only two nations witnessed males outliving females (Botswana and Swaziland), and in only three nations were the life expectancies of males and females the same (Lesotho, Malawi, and Sierra Leone). In all five of these nations, life expectancy was, and is, very low (in the high 40s to low 50s). In general, the very few nations where females do not outlive males are nations having high female death rates from the traumas of childbirth in the presence of inadequate medical care. In 2010, an estimated 287,000 women died because of giving birth, and all but 1,700 of them were in developing countries. More than half of these deaths occurred in Sub-Saharan Africa (World Bank 2013: 10). However, save for a very small handful of the world's poorest nations, being female adds years to life expectancy. Worldwide, the average female can expect to live five to six years longer than the average male (73.3 vs 67.5 years; see Wang et al. 2012: 2075). The causal forces involve biology, psychology, and culture.

Biologically, women have several advantages in the game of life. They tend to be shorter and smaller, putting less stress on their hearts. Their high levels of estrogen prior to menopause relax blood vessels and reduce the chances of hypertension. These factors combine to produce overall lower rates of cardiovascular disease for women than for men (and recall, from Figure 3.2, that this is the number one cause of death worldwide).[4] Other biological mechanisms favoring females are the increased susceptibility of the XY chromosomal pattern to recessive disorders (e.g., hemophilia and muscular dystrophy), making males less healthy at birth, and the negative effects of testosterone on lymphocyte maturation, a major part of immune function, thus resulting in females having stronger immune responses to disease (Pongu 2013). In sum, the biological research "implies that when male and female children are treated equally, male children should suffer a higher incidence of infectious and noninfectious diseases and thus a lower survival rate. This is indeed the pattern observed worldwide, especially in regions where parents do not discriminate against children of a particular sex in the allocation of household resources" (Pongu 2013: 423).

Psychologically, females are more likely to express their emotions, including feelings of stress or weakness. This makes them more likely to open up to friends, more likely to seek medical attention, and less likely to internalize stress – which can be expressed as hypertension and poor-quality sleep (both predictive of heart disease and premature death; for gender differences in emotional expression and help-seeking, see Farrimond 2012 and Kret and De Gelder 2012). In addition, men are more likely than women to partake in risk-taking behaviors that involve bodily peril. The most important risky behavior in explaining male–female differences in life expectancy is cigarette smoking, which men are one and a half times more likely to do in a developed country like the United States, and four and a half times more likely in developing countries like China and India (Giovino et al. 2012; Oksuzyan et al. 2008: 92). Smoking differences between men and women explain 40–60% of the gap in their life expectancies (McCartney et al. 2011). Men's greater abuse of alcohol throughout the world also ranks high as a risky behavior that accounts for the gender difference in life expectancy. Men's greater likelihood to overdrink alcohol explains another 10–30% of the gender difference in longevity (McCartney et al. 2011; in the United States, men are three times more likely than women to suffer an alcohol-related death, and 1.6 times more likely to die from a drug overdose; see Murphy et al. 2013: 11). Other examples of men's willingness to put themselves at higher risk of injury, illness, and death include their greater involvement in violent crime, as well as many of their recreational choices (e.g., very few women play [American] football, box, wrestle, drag race, spear fish, or hang glide). In the United States, for example, 80% of violent crimes – aggravated assaults, rapes, robberies, and murders – are committed by men (FBI 2014), while men are twice as likely as women to die from traffic, recreational, and other types of accidents (Chang 2008: 5; Murphy et al. 2013: 5).

The greater-risk-taking psychology of men is related to cultural norms and values encouraging it. More generally, there is a survival advantage in cultural prescriptions that keep women of childbearing age (and girls, who will eventually be there) out of harm's way. A society with one man and 100 women could potentially produce 100 offspring in a year. A society with one woman and 100 men could produce just one baby. Thus, high-risk occupations – from being in the military, to working in dangerous environments like mines or steel factories – have generally been reserved for men. For example, in the United States, 92% of on-the-job deaths involve men (Bureau of Labor Statistics 2013).

Race/Ethnicity. Throughout the world, ethnic and racial minorities tend to have more health problems and have shorter life expectancies than the dominant group (Commission on the Social Determinants of Health 2008; Geiger 2003: 441–2). For example, inspection of Table 3.1 reveals that the life expectancy of the average non-Hispanic white person is 4.7 years longer than that of the average non-Hispanic black person. For all categories of chronic disease, US blacks have significantly higher rates than their white counterparts. The greater part of race/ethnic background–health relationships are the product of racial and ethnic minorities' greater likelihood of living in poverty (see, e.g., Clarke et al. 2010; Hayward et al. 2000; the same explanation for the race/ethnic disparities in health and mortality generally holds worldwide, see, e.g., Woolf and Aron 2013: 167). However, even when social class is controlled for, African Americans in the United States tend have more health problems and shorter lives. Why this is the case is not clearly understood, but one key interpretation is that they are much more likely to suffer constant background stress simply because they are black living in a white-dominated society. In the words of Williams et al. (2007: 56), "the stress of racism [is] virulent and pathogenic" (cf. Clarke et al. 2010: 1377; Williams and Collins 1995: 367). This stress has direct physiological effects on ill health that increase the likelihood of premature death, including raising inflammatory immune responses that lead to heart disease and some forms of cancer (Stix 2007); the stress also has indirect effects, as common coping responses to it include smoking and the overuse/abuse of alcohol and drugs. The racism blacks face is both *institutional* (primarily via residential segregation that results in their living in areas with substandard schools and public services) and *personal* (e.g., from suffering *racial profiling* by the police and store and airport security officers; to being the token black in some workplaces and thus feeling that one's behaviors are being seen not just as those of the individual but those of the entire race; to internalizing the dominant society's ideology that they are inferior; Williams and Sternthal 2010).

On the other hand, one exception to the relatively strong and consistent relationship between minority status and shortened life is Hispanic (Latino/a) Americans in the contemporary United States. Inspection of Table 3.1 reveals that Hispanics tend to outlive non-Hispanic whites (81.0 vs 78.4 years). This is unexpected given that Hispanics suffer from much of the same prejudice and discrimination inflicted on blacks, and given that the Hispanic poverty rate consistently averages twice that of non-Hispanic whites (11.6% for whites vs 23.0% for Hispanics; note that the average for Asian Americans is very similar to whites, 11.7%, while the percentages for African Americans and Native Americans are similar to that of Hispanics – 25.8 and 27.0, respectively; see Macartney et al. 2013: 3; poverty rates were averaged for the years 2006 through 2011). Health scientists have labeled this the "Hispanic Paradox." Although not fully understood, two current interpretations have intuitive appeal and modest empirical support:

1   Unlike the overwhelming majority of non-Hispanic whites and blacks, the large Hispanic population in the United States is much

more likely to be recently arrived, with half (49.8%) of all Hispanic adults being foreign-born (Krogstad and Lopez 2014; as of 2014, 17% of the total population was Hispanic; see US Census Bureau 2014a). In contrast, less than 4% of non-Hispanic whites and less than 9% of non-Hispanic blacks are foreign-born (Motel and Patten 2013: Table 6). In general, those who choose to migrate tend to be healthier persons than their counterparts who choose not to migrate. Indeed, Rubalcava et al (2008) found in a study of over 6,000 recent Mexican migrants to the United States that their health tended to be better than their counterparts who stayed in Mexico, even after controls for education and rural vs urban residence. Bostean's (2013) similar large-sample study of 35,000 individuals partially confirmed the Rubalcava et al. findings – in that recent Mexican migrants to the United States tended to have fewer physical limitations (a composite measure that included the ability to carry a bucket and to walk 5 kilometers) – but found that they were no healthier regarding chronic/degenerative diseases (diabetes, heart disease, hypertension, or cancer).

In sum, selective migration of those who are generally healthier may account for a small part of the Hispanic Paradox. Relatedly, selective migration may also explain a small part of why Asian Americans, two-thirds of whom are foreign-born, have life expectancies that also exceed non-Hispanic whites. More importantly, however, Asian Americans have the highest overall level of education of any race or ethnic group in the United States – with 49% of Asian American adults versus 33% of non-Hispanic white adults having a four-year college or university degree; the strong effects of education on health behaviors and mortality have been noted previously.

2   Latin American cultures, despite their great diversity, have several common traditions (Marin and Marin 1991), at least two of which can contribute to the health of the individual: a generally strong emphasis on the family, as well as a generally strong emphasis on religion. Compared to non-Hispanic whites and blacks, Hispanics are more likely to have strong family ties and large family networks (Gaines et al. 1997). In turn, family-focused individuals have been found to handle stress better and to have the motivation and resources to take better care of themselves, including seeking medical care and tests when sick (see the literature review of Gallo et al. 2009; Asian Americans also benefit from their generally strong familism).

Relatedly, Hispanics are significantly more likely than non-Hispanic whites to attend religious services on a regular basis (see Table 3.5). In turn, religious involvement is positively correlated with a sense of well-being, the ability to cope with ill health, and better

Table 3.5:   *Attendance of religious services by ethnic background (%)*

Frequency of attendance	Ethnic background	
	Non-Hispanic white	*Hispanic*
At least monthly	40.6	52.4
Less than monthly	30.3	28.3
Never	29.1	19.3
Total	100	100

Note: $\chi^2 = 15.5$, $p < .0001$, N = 1,571. (Chi square, χ^2 is a simple test of statistical signifi-cance; for a lucid explanation of this statistic, see Stockburger 2013: Chap. 22.)
Source: Raw data from General Social Survey (2012)

health behaviors (e.g., seeking counseling, quitting smoking, and getting medical check-ups). In part, the effect is mediated through social interaction: An individual attending religious services having a health problem is likely to receive messages of self-worth and of practical advice (e.g., "I care about you – please see my dermatologist about that mole I've seen getting larger on your neck"). And, in part, the effect is the individual's hearing the advice, and actualizing it, that life's heavy problems – regarding finances, health, interpersonal relationships – and the stresses they involve should not be borne alone, but "given over to God." A *meta-analysis* of 91 studies of the effect of involvement in organized religion on health and longevity revealed clear, positive, independent effects (i.e., the relationships hold even after controlling for smoking, drinking, exercising, and socioeconomic status; note that a meta-analysis study combines results across different studies to see if an overall pattern emerges). In short, religious involvement increases an individual's chances for good health and for a long life (Chida et al. 2009).

The cultural explanation of the Hispanic Paradox fits into the broader tradition of research showing the strong connections between social support and good physical and mental health. Indeed, after a careful review for more than 300 empirical studies, Uchino (2004: 181–2) arrived at this conclusion:

[Being habitually alone fosters a sense of isolation and despair that is only deepened when faced with life's challenges. In contrast, the strength of social bonds manifests in the joy, sense of acceptance, and resources we experience as part of our relationships. This not only promotes positive mental health, but can also influence how long one lives. Evidence...suggests the role of social support in predicting lower all-cause as well as disease-specific mortality. This conclusion is based on more than twenty years of research conducted in Asia, Europe, and North America with tens of thousands of research participants.

Genetics.   The collaborative international research program of the late twentieth and early twenty-first centuries that became known as the *Human Genome Project* produced a complete map of the human genome – which is the sum total of our 20,500 genes. Since the map was completed in 2003, medical scientists have used it to better understand inherited tendencies for individuals to suffer selected diseases. All of the major degenerative diseases – including heart disease, cancer, diabetes, and Alzheimer's – have genetic bases that can partially explain why some individuals get a particular disease while others do not, as well as the timing and course of the disease (Cure Alzheimer's Fund 2014; National Institutes of Health 2012, 2014). However, the growing science of epigenetics has revealed the influence of environmental factors – which can begin in the womb or at any time after birth – on gene expression (activating or deactivating a gene without modifying the DNA sequence of the gene; for technical explanations of the mechanisms involved, such as changes in DNA methylation, see, e.g., Balazs 2014; Tammen et al. 2013). The relevance of epigenetics to the demographic study of mortality comes, in part, via the new science of *nutrigenomics*. This science seeks to reveal the connections between dietary factors and the expression or suppression of genes that enhance or hurt the health of the individual. Animal studies have revealed a wide variety of dietary factors that turn on or off cancer and other disease-causing genes. Human studies have followed, some of which have confirmed the findings with animals. Among the dietary factors that suppress cancer, for example, are polyphenols found in tea, grapes, berries, and turmeric; isoflavones found in soy and fava beans; isothiocyanates found in cruciferous vegetables like broccoli, cabbage, and cauliflower; several chemical forms of selenium, as found in nuts, chicken, game meat, and beef; and folate found in green vegetables. On the other hand, heavy alcohol consumption is associated with harmful epigenetic impacts – including the development and progression of colon, head, and neck cancers (see, e.g., Hardy and Tollefsbol 2011).

The upshot for the individual is that a diet rich in a wide variety of plant products – fruits, vegetables, and nuts – is most likely to activate health-promoting genes. Indeed, as noted earlier, the WHO attributes nearly 2 million deaths a year worldwide to low fruit and vegetable consumption – and the individuals involved come overwhelmingly from developing nations where varied and complex traditional diets have been replaced by heavy reliance on a single grain (as much as 90% of calories), as well as from low-income individuals in developed nations like the United States (where calories obtained from refined, nutrient-deficient grain products are much cheaper than from meat, fruit, and vegetables).

Relatedly, other epigenetic research has begun to reveal the effects of a stressful childhood environment on the central nervous system and subsequent response to stress in later life. Genes related to depression are activated by childhood stress, as are those related to the activation of an individual's fight-or-flight response (Tammen et al. 2013; Weiss and Wagner 1998). Like the link between poverty and diet, there is a clear link between poverty and increased levels of childhood stress (Institute for Safe Families 2013: 15), so the poor are disproportionally affected. Childhood stressors include abuse; neglect; having insufficient food or clothing; witnessing domestic violence; living in a home where a parent abuses drugs or alcohol or is the victim of mental illness; or having a parent leave the home because of divorce, separation, or prison. Since 1997, the US government's Centers for Disease Control and Prevention has co-sponsored an ongoing major study of childhood stressors on adult health, and has concluded that they are connected to statistically significant, *dose–response*-increased chances of chronic disease, alcohol/drug abuse, mental illness, interpersonal violence, and premature death; indeed, the "worst health and social problems in our nation…arise as a consequence of adverse childhood experiences" (Centers for Disease Control 2014b). (Note that a dose–response finding means that an increasingly stronger level of a causal factor produces an increasingly strong effect.)

Future Trends: Will Millennium Development Goals Continue to Be Realized?

For the past century, the dominant trends for mortality have been falling death rates, rising life expectancies, the replacement of communicable diseases with degenerative ones as the primary cause of death, and the narrowing of the once very large gap in life expectancies between developing and developed nations. These trends reflect the rising standard of living throughout the world; the increased efficacy of medical science and public health strategies in fighting disease; the abundance of food generated by the technologies of the Green Revolution; the increasing sophistication of communication and transportation networks; and the manifold and conscious efforts of governmental, intergovernmental, and civic agencies to cooperate and to share resources and technologies to improve health and prevent premature death. Regarding this last set of efforts, the UN's Millennium Declaration of 2000 and its well-defined eight goals for increasing the welfare of all humanity have been critically important. All eight goals, individually and in combination, were directed at significantly reducing premature death, reducing the huge gaps between the richest and the poorest segments of the human community (the developing and developed worlds), and increasing the quality of life for all people by 2015. As of that year, the pursuit of these goals had realized much, but not full, success, and thus they have been revised and renewed for the world community to achieve by 2030 (United Nations 2013f, 2015a; World Bank 2014c). (The new goals deal with the same global issues but have been refined and extended to now number 17.) If the 2030 goals are met to the degree that the 2015 goals were, then the chances are good that the world will reach its predicted population of 9.6 billion by 2050. Below is a brief overview of the success of selected targets (measureable objectives) for each of the eight goals as of 2015 (for a more detailed review of all 21 targets, see United Nations 2014g, 2015b):

Goal 1: Eradicate extreme poverty and hunger
Target 1A: *Halve, between 1990 and 2015, the proportion of people whose income is less than $1 a day* [the operational definition of "extreme poverty"; note this was later adjusted to $1.25]. This target was met for the world community, though not in every country. In 1990, 47% of the people living in developing countries were doing so on less than $1.25. By 2015, this percentage had dropped to 14. In raw numbers, 1.9 billion people were living in extreme poverty in 1990, and this number fell to 0.84 billion by 2015. Two-thirds of those still living on less than $1.25 a day are found in five countries: India (33% of the world's extreme poor), China (13%), Nigeria (9%), Bangladesh (5%), and the Democratic Republic of Congo (5%). Most of the remaining extreme poor are found in Sub-Saharan Africa and Southern Asia. (Other than India and Bangladesh, this region includes Afghanistan, Iran, Pakistan, and Sri Lanka, plus several smaller nations.)

Target 1C: *Halve, between 1990 and 2015, the proportion of people who suffer from hunger*. This target has been nearly met. In 1990, 23.3% of the world's people were suffering from chronic hunger (not having enough food to regularly conduct an active and healthy life). By 2015, this percentage had fallen to 12.9, which is 90% of the 11.65 percentage figure that would have met the goal. In raw numbers, 795 million people (1 in 9 of the world's population) were estimated to be chronically hungry in 2015, with 780 million of them living in developed countries. Most of Asia (including China) and Latin America reached the Target 1C goal; slower progress in Sub-Saharan Africa kept it from being fully met, as did violent conflicts in Western Asia. (This region includes war-torn Iraq, Syria, and Yemen – and nearby countries into which refugees have spilled: Jordan, Lebanon, and Turkey; see discussion on the impacts of these conflicts on migration patterns in Chapter 5.)

Goal 2: Achieve universal primary education
Target 2A: *Ensure that, by 2015, children everywhere, boys and girls alike, will be able to complete a full course of primary schooling.* The goal of 97% of children completing primary school (usually defined as the basic education given to children until the ages of 11 or 12) has not been met, but substantial progress has been made. In 1990, 96% of primary-school-age children in the developed nations of the world were enrolled in school; this percentage was the same in 2015. However, in developing countries, this percentage rose from 80 to 91%. Sub-Saharan Africa made the greatest progress, going from 62 million (52%) of its children of primary school age being enrolled in school in 1990, to 153 million (80%) by 2015. However, it still lagged well behind all other regions of the world, and of its 33 million children not in school, 55% were girls. Although 22% of the world's primary-school-age children live in Sub-Saharan Africa, the region contributes 58% of the total number of primary-school-age children not enrolled in school. Key to Sub-Saharan Africa's problem in catching up with other regions has been the many armed conflicts it has experienced since 1990; indeed, 50% of its out-of-school children live in conflict-ridden areas. Similarly, because of its war-torn countries (including Iraq, Syria, and Yemen), Western Asia has been contributing an increasing proportion of the world's primary-school-age children not in school: for example, just 12% of the tens of thousands of Syrian children ages 6 to 14 living in Lebanese refugee camps were enrolled in school as of 2015 (United Nations 2015b: 26; see more on the Syrian conflict in Chapter 5).

Goal 3: Promote gender equality and empower women
Target 3A: *Eliminate gender disparity in primary and secondary education, preferably by 2005, and in all levels of education no later than 2015.* Substantial, but not full, progress had been made toward these targets by 2015. The key measurement of gender disparity in education is the percentage of girls enrolled divided by the percentage of boys enrolled (labeled the *gender parity index* [GPI]). Thus, for example, if 85% of girls are enrolled and 90% of boys are enrolled, then the GPI would be: $85 \div 95 = 0.89$; and if the percentage of girls were also 95, then the calculation would be: $95 \div 95 = 1.00$. The UN defined full success as a GPI between 0.97 and 1.03.

Worldwide, this target had been met for primary education, though some developing nations have fallen short. In 1990, the GPI in the developing world was 0.86, and by 2015 it had reached 0.98. Lagging behind were Sub-Saharan Africa and Western Asia (countries that most people think of as comprising the Middle East, e.g., Iraq, Saudi Arabia, and Syria), with GPIs of 0.92 and 0.93, respectively.

Regarding secondary education (that given to children from ages 12 to 16 or 17), the developing world has made huge progress and has almost met the goal, going from 0.77 in 1990 to 0.96 by 2015. Not surprisingly, Sub-Saharan Africa lags far behind with a GPI of 0.84 (even though it, too, has made substantial progress since 1990, when its GPI was 0.76)

The UN's definition of tertiary education equates to enrollment in colleges, universities, and post-secondary vocational schools. Here, too, the developing world has made great progress and has met the goal, going from a GPI of 0.69 to 0.99. However, the average GPI of 0.99 masks many gender inequalities, with males actually coming up short in several regions: In East Asia (the dominant nation being China, holding 85% of the region's population), Latin America, and Northern Africa, females significantly exceed males in tertiary enrollments (GPIs of 1.08, 1.28, and 1.12, respectively), while in Sub-Saharan Africa and South Asia (dominated by India, holding 72% of the region's population), females lag behind males, with GPIs of 0.64 and 0.81, respectively. The most stunning progress has been made in East Asia, where the GPI was 0.48 in 1990, but had reached 1.08 by 2012.

Goal 4: Reduce child mortality

Target 4A: *Reduce by two-thirds, between 1990 and 2015, the under-5 mortality rate.* Though not met, progress toward this target has been substantial and one of humanity's greatest achievements. The child mortality rate is defined as the number of children under the age of 5 dying per 1,000 births. In the developed world, this rate was 15 in 1990, and it had dropped to 6 by 2015 (complete success would have been 5). In the developing world, the rate was 100 in 1990, and thus fulfillment of the target goal would have been 33, and by 2015, the actual rate was 47 (and thus has been 70% achieved). The target has actually been met in North Africa, Latin America, and East Asia. Although Sub-Saharan Africa made huge progress, dropping from a rate of 179 to 86 between 1990 and 2015, it is still almost double the average rate of 47 for the rest of the developing world. The greatest progress has been made in East Asia, which saw a 79% drop in its child mortality rate between 1990 and 2015 (from 53 to 11).

Goal 5: Improve maternal health

Target 5A: *Reduce by three-quarters, between 1990 and 2015, the maternal mortality ratio.* The *maternal mortality ratio* is operationally defined as the number of women, ages 15–49, dying from pregnancy- or childbirth-related causes in a particular year per 100,000 live births. Maternal mortality is almost exclusively a problem of the developing world in the modern era, as 99.4% of maternal deaths occur in developing countries. (The UN's most recent data are for 2013, with 289,000 maternal deaths recorded in that year.) The extremes are exemplified by Sierra Leone, on the one hand, which had 1,100 maternal deaths per 100,000 live births in 2013, and by Belarus, on the other hand, with a rate of 1 maternal death per 100,000 live births. Sub-Saharan Africa accounts for nearly two-thirds of the world's maternal deaths and South Asia for another quarter of them. The leading countries are India, with 50,000 maternal deaths, and Nigeria, with 40,000. All of this noted, the world did make significant progress between 1990 and 2013, with a 45% drop in the maternal mortality rate, from 380 to 210, though this is far shy of the 2015 target rate of 95. At the same time, the trend is improving for skilled health personnel to attend births in developing countries: 59% of births had this kind of personnel in 1990, which had risen to 71% by 2015.

Goal 6: Combat HIV/AIDS, malaria, and other diseases

Target 6A: *Have halted by 2015 and begin to reverse the spread of HIV/AIDS.* Although great success was made during the first dozen years of the twenty-first century in halting the spread of HIV infection, the target goal of bringing the incidence of new cases worldwide to zero was not met. As of 2014, a record high 35.3 million people were living with HIV worldwide.

Globally, the incidence (number of new cases per 100 adults ages 15 to 49) fell by 40% between 2001 and 2012. In the developing world, the incidence dropped from 0.10 to 0.06; the developed world saw no progress, with a rate of 0.03 in both 2001 and 2012 (although it did see great progress in saving lives via *antiretroviral drugs*). Sub-Saharan Africa saw great progress, with its rate falling from 1.98 to 1.02 by 2012; however, this rate is still many times greater than any other region (e.g., East Asia had a rate of 0.01, Latin America's was 0.03, and North Africa's was 0.01). Key to all public health attempts to rein in disease is educating the public about risk-increasing and risk-decreasing behaviors. The UN's analysis of why this Millennium Target goal was not met revealed that young people in the 15–24 age group, especially in Sub-Saharan Africa, had little understanding of how HIV is spread, and had high rates of practicing unsafe sex. For example, the UN had wanted 95% of those in this age group to have basic knowledge about the disease and to use condoms for high-risk sex (sex with a non-regular sexual partner). However, in 2012, 43% of males in this age group, and 63% of females, who had had high-risk sex in the previous year had not used a condom. Despite these high percentages, the UN estimates that 6.6 million AIDS-related deaths, 82% of them in developing regions, were averted between 1995 and 2012 because of the dramatic rise in access to antiretroviral drugs in both the developing and developed worlds. In 2003, a few hundred thousand individuals in developing regions were receiving antiretroviral therapy; but by 2014, this number had soared to 13.6 million (with 12.1 million of these individuals living in developing countries; United Nations 2015b: 46).

Goal 7: Ensure environmental sustainability

Target 7C: *Halve, by 2015, the proportion of the population without sustainable access to safe drinking water and basic sanitation.* The first part of this target was met. In 1990, 24% of the world's population did not have safe drinking water. By 2015, this percentage had fallen to 9, and it is still trickling downward. In raw numbers, 2.6 billion individuals gained access to safe drinking water between 1990 and 2015 – with the 650 million lacking this access heavily concentrated in Sub-Saharan Africa and South Asia (the majority in India). On the other hand, the second part of Target 7C was not met, though progress was made. In 1990, 54% of the global population lacked adequate sanitation facilities: that is, did not have access to septic or sewer systems, but instead used open pits or simply the ground, which is especially problematic and disease-generating in urban areas. (A third of urban residents in developing regions were living in slums lacking adequate sanitation as of 2015.) By 2015, 32% of the global population still lacked adequate sanitation. As noted earlier in this chapter, open defecation, which pollutes ground water and encourages the rapid spread of diarrheal and other disease, was being practiced by a billion individuals, most of them in South Asia and Sub-Saharan Africa, with the highly populous India and Nigeria being singled out as countries where the problem is especially severe (United Nations 2014g: 45).

Goal 8: Develop a global partnership for development

Target 8A: *Develop further an open, rule-based, predictable, non-discriminatory trading and financial system.* When businesses in developing countries, especially in least developed countries, can export their products to developed countries without duties or tariffs being added to the price of the product, sales increase and the net effect is to improve the economy and raise the standard of living in these countries. The Development Assistance Committee of the Organization for Economic Cooperation and Development (OECD) has 29 member states (from Europe, plus Australia, New Zealand, Japan, South Korea, and the United States) that work together to fund development in poor nations.

Through the efforts of this committee, the proportion of imports admitted duty-free to developed nations from developing nations rose from approximately 50% to 79% between 1996 and 2014 (United Nations 2014g: 50; 2015b: 64; note that oil and weapons are excluded from the duty-free list of imports).

In sum, despite humanity's manifold follies – as exemplified by environmental destruction, internal wars, ethnic cleansings, racism, sexism, unrestrained ethnocentrism, and selfishness – the UN's projections of the world's population reaching 9.6 billion individuals by the middle of the twenty-first century, and 10.6 billion by the end of the century, are realizable. (For more on these estimates, see United Nations 2013c: xviii.) Based on the success of the 2000–15 Millennium Development Goals, the new goals for 2015–30 bode well for further successes in improving health and delaying death, though at slower rates. If this is actually how reality unfolds, then the UN predicts that the average life expectancy in some developed countries will exceed 90 years during the course of the century, with an average of 89, and that in most developing countries, it will exceed 80, with an average of 81 (United Nations 2013c: xx, 15). Whether these optimistic projections will be realized will be heavily dependent on the current battle between humanity and the planet (see the discussion of neo-Malthusianism in Chapter 1) and the continued and sustained decline in fertility rates (Chapter 4).

Main Points and Key Terms

1 Infant mortality is a key indicator of the level of socioeconomic development a country has achieved. A low rate of infant mortality, under 6 deaths per 1,000 births, indicates that the population of a country is well fed, drinks clean water, has a good sanitation system, enjoys access to good healthcare, boasts a low level of inequality, and lives in a state of security.

2 The age-specific death rate is a better indicator of a country's mortality problem than the crude death rate. A high crude death rate might well be indicating that a nation lacks basic resources for its population; however, on the other hand, it might just as likely be indicating that the nation is prosperous and providing good amounts of healthcare, nutrition, and security – and because of this, it has allowed a high percentage of its population to live into old age (and the old die at a much faster rate than the young).

3 Regardless of a nation's level of prosperity, the age-specific death rate forms a lazy J curve: The risk of dying is highest in the first

years of life, is lowest in later childhood and young adulthood, increases in middle age, and increases significantly in old age.

4   The lack of proper sewerage encourages open defecation and thus the polluting of soil and water. Stunted growth, high death rates from diarrheal diseases, and sexual violence are among the serious problems the UN has identified as outcomes from the 1 billion people currently practicing open defecation.

5   As a country becomes more economically developed, the proportion of its population dying from Group I causes (communicable/ infectious diseases) decreases and the proportion from Group II causes (degenerative diseases like cardiovascular disease and cancer) increases.

6   The epidemiologic transition mirrors the courses of its more general parent concept, the demographic transition. For most of human history, Group I deaths predominated. Western Europe and Northern America entered the transitional stage of lower rates of Group I causes of deaths, replaced by Group II causes of deaths, over a longer period of time during the 1800–1950 period, as they slowly recognized the importance and pursued the development of immunization, clean water, and other public health programs during the first half of the twentieth century. Developing nations were able to import these programs in the latter third of the twentieth century and the early part of the twenty-first century, and thus were quicker to begin the transition to Group II diseases as being the predominant causes of death.

7   The Green Revolution brought the developing nations of Asia and Latin America high-yield seeds, systematic irrigation, and massive amounts of synthetic fertilizers, herbicides, and pesticides. The Revolution quickly and dramatically increased crop yields and greatly reduced the problem of famine throughout the developing world.

8   Although responsible for eliminating hunger for much of the population of the developing world, the Green Revolution destroyed the livelihoods of millions of small farm families, as the cost of fertilizers, herbicides, pesticides, irrigation systems, and mechanized farm equipment was simply beyond their means. The bulk of the individuals affected have moved into the massive and growing slum areas of the nearest cities. The larger surviving farms use petroleum-based fertilizers that are ever more expensive, ever more polluting to the environment, and ultimately unsustainable (as opposed to natural fertilizers based on manure and decomposed plant matter).

9   Social class is a strong predictor of life expectancy because the more prosperous have better access to healthcare, work in cleaner

environments, and have reduced stress from having higher job security. Reduced stress decreases the chances of handling remaining stress in unhealthy ways, such as smoking, overdrinking, abusing drugs, and not exercising. Many of the differences in good health and low mortality that exist among various ethnic and racial groups within a society are due to the differences in the social class standings of these groups.

10   The reduction of infectious diseases, hunger, and poor sanitation that has resulted in large increases in health and prosperity world-wide has been due, to a large degree, to the conscious and deliberate efforts of the UN and its allies as they sought to realize eight Millennium Development Goals (MDGs) during the first 15 years of the twenty-first century. These goals were met fully or significantly so, and included measureable objectives involving the reduction of extreme poverty, hunger, child mortality, and infectious diseases; and the increasing of schooling opportunities, gender equality, maternal health, environmental sustainability, and trade regulations to encourage less developed countries to become part of the global economy.

Review Questions

1 What is the key advantage of using the age-adjusted mortality rate instead of the crude mortality rate when doing cross-national analyses?

2 What does its infant mortality rate tell us about a particular country?

3 Briefly describe the three major groupings the UN uses to classify the causes of death. Which group predominates? And why do you think this is so?

4 What is the epidemiologic transition? In which stage would you be most likely to find a Sub-Saharan African nation such as Zambia or Zimbabwe?

5 At a general level, what key differences are there between how the developed countries of Northern Europe experienced their epidemiologic transitions and how less developed countries of Asia and Africa have been undergoing their transitions?

6 Why did the Green Revolution have much quicker and more widespread success in Asia and Latin America than it did in Sub-Saharan Africa?

7 What are the key reasons for the United States lagging behind many of its peer nations in so many indicators of health and disease, including infant mortality and life expectancy?

8 Discuss the modifiable lifestyle factors affecting health and life expectancy. Why do those of limited means tend to fall short on modifying these factors in their lives compared to their more prosperous counterparts?

9 Why have some health scientists concluded that obesity is contagious?

10 Why do women tend to outlive men? In what kind of social setting do we find the opposite: that is, men tending to outlive women?

Suggested Readings and Online Sources

There is a wealth of health- and mortality-related data sets that are readily available online. For example, the WHO annually monitors and publishes the most complete statistics for international health and mortality: *World Health Statistics*. It complements these statistics with an excellent A–Z Index of fact-sheets on a wide variety of health-related topics (http://www.who.int/mediacentre/factsheets/en/). The World Bank also publishes massive amounts of country-specific health/mortality data in its *World Development Indicators*, which is updated annually and maintains the data in a time-series format. Child mortality, the reduction of which was one of the eight major Millennium Development Goals, is carefully tracked by the UN's Inter-agency Group for Child Mortality Estimation (http://www.childmortality.org/). Between 2001 and 2015, the UN published a comprehensive assessment of all eight goals; see its yearly *Millennium Development Goals Report*.

Most individual countries, and all developed countries, have national offices that keep track of health and death data. For example, in the United States, the Centers for Disease Control and Prevention (CDC) annually publishes data on the causes of death, and also has an easy-to-use online data-retrieval program for the causes of death due to accidents and violence (WISQARS – Web-based Injury Statistics Query and Reporting System). The CDC also monitors the leading causes of death on an annual basis (http://www.cdc.gov/injury/wisqars/leadingcauses.html) and has a user-friendly A–Z Index that directs the user to hundreds of individual health topics (http://www.cdc.gov/az/a.html). The Index is also an excellent resource for finding heath data on countries other than the United States, as 117 individual countries appear in it. Other major data sources giving detailed data on the United States and other countries include USAID's *Demographic and Health Surveys* (2015) and its *StatCompiler* (http://statcompiler.com/); the US Census Bureau's *Statistical Abstract* (2015b); the US Social Security Administration's *Life Tables for the United States Social Security Area 1900–2100*; and the CDC's annually updated *Health, United States*, as well as its *Healthy People* database and website (http://wonder.cdc.gov/DATA2010; http://www.healthypeople.gov/2020/default.aspx; this comprehensive data source tracks progress toward national heath targets that are akin to those linked to the UN's Millennium Development Goals).

The date of your own death is predictable; highly so if you know some of your basic personal and family health data (e.g., blood pressure; history of heart disease and cancer in your immediate family). Among the most accurate can be found at this University of Pennsylvania website developed by Dean P. Foster, Choong Tze Chua, and Lyle H. Ungar: http://gosset.wharton.upenn.edu/mortality/perl/CalcForm.html (see its explanation at http://gosset.wharton.upenn.edu/mortality/).

Hans Rosling's *Gapminder* videos series (2010b) covers many aspects of mortality, including cross-national comparisons of child mortality, various cancers, and HIV.

For a simple presentation on the construction of life tables, see the Population Reference Bureau's *Population Handbook* (Haupt et al. 2011).

Important print references on mortality and healthcare systems include David Hemenway's engrossing and well-written account of the public health approach to preventing disease, injury, and premature death: *While We Were Sleeping: Success Stories in Injury and Violence Prevention* (2009). For a comprehensive and detailed description of public health programs and healthcare systems of all 194 UN countries, see Sarah E. Boslaugh's *Health Systems around the World: A Comparative Guide* (2013). Note that John C. Caldwell's review of empirical studies revealing which poor countries far out-perform their expected high levels of mortality and lower levels of longevity reveals that the most important choice a political regime can make is to invest in its nation's healthcare and educational systems (see Caldwell's classic 1986 scholarly article "Routes to Low Mortality in Poor Countries").

Other important and highly readable print resources include Bert N. Uchino's review of the massive scholarly literature demonstrating the strong relationships of health and mortality with social support (*Social Support and Physical Health: Understanding Consequences of Relationships*, 2004). By social support, social scientists mean information from others that one is cared for, loved, esteemed, and part of a mutually supported network (Uchino 2004: 4).

C. Everett Koop et al. (eds), *Critical Issues in Global Health* (2002) is another important print resource. Although slightly dated, its in-depth essays on virtually all of humanity's most important health issues address their underlying causes, which have not changed.

Mortality and morbidity statistics consistently reveal differences among racial and ethnic groups within a society – with a large part of these differences accounted for by differences in socioeconomic status among the groups. In the United States, the CDC closely monitors minority health and publishes its findings and recommendations on its *Minority Health* website. Relatedly, the Institute of Medicine of the National Academies has published an extensive analysis of the mechanisms creating the disparities in healthcare and its outcomes (disease/mortality) among racial/ethnic groups in the United States: *Unequal Treatment: Confronting Racial and Ethnic Disparities in Health Care* (Smedley et al. 2003). For a comparable treatment at the international level, see the analyses produced by the WHO's Commission on the Social Determinants of Health (World Health Organization 2014j).

A landmark work on the relationship between socioeconomic status and health/mortality is Michael Marmot's *The Status Syndrome: How Social Standing Affects Our Health and Longevity* (2004), which shows how relatively small differences in education, income, and occupational prestige yield significant effects on health. The effects of social ties, social standing, and the degree to which individuals have access to a modern healthcare system are nicely brought together in Dan Buettner's *Blue Zones: Lessons for Living Longer from the People Who've Lived the*

Longest (2010). Buettner summarizes his book in a fascinating TED Talk entitled "How to Live to Be 100+" (2009). Regarding the strong link between having low income in a prosperous society and suffering from emotional stress, see the widely publicized report from the American Psychological Association, *Stress in America: Paying with Our Health* (2014); poorer individuals are more likely to feel a lack of control over their lives, leading to emotional stress – which, in turn, has direct negative effects on the immune system and indirect effects on health. Finally, that high inequality itself is a causative factor in reducing life expectancy and other indicators of good health is confirmed in the excellent and downloadable US county-based data set available at the University of Wisconsin's Population Health Institute (http://www.countyhealthrankings.org/). For the inequality analysis, see Bridget Catlin, Amanda Jovaag, and Julie Willems Van Dijk's *2015 County Health Rankings: Key Findings Report* (2015: 6), as well as the detailed cross-national empirical analyses of Richard Wilkinson and Kate Pickett in their book *The Spirit Level: Why Greater Equality Makes Societies Stronger* (2009).

Norman Borlaug has been deemed the Father of the Green Revolution. Leon Hesser has produced a fascinating biography of this agricultural scientist's life and manifold achievements (*The Man Who Fed the World: Nobel Peace Prize Laureate Norman Borlaug and His Battle to End World Hunger*, 2006). The downsides of the Green Revolution (e.g., environmental destruction, the loss of farms and subsequent forced migration of many small farmers, and the growing disease susceptibility of the populations initially benefitting from the Revolution) are explored in Richard Manning's 2014 article in *Mother Jones*, "Hidden Downsides of the Green Revolution: Biodiversity Loss and Diseases of Civilization." The growing dominance of refined grains, increasingly laced with sugar, in many developing nations is one of a number of causal factors underlying the rising global obesity rate, as explored in Jamie Pearce and Karen Witten (eds), *Geographies of Obesity: Environmental Understandings of the Obesity Epidemic* (2010).

Epigenetics is difficult to understand for those without some preparation in biochemistry. However, Pamela Peeke has prepared an informative TED Talk for the novice entitled "Epigenetic Transformation – You Are What Your Grandparents Ate" (2014).

Finally, the cross-national study of mortality and disease involves many analyses that paint Sub-Sahara Africa as a bleak and doomed region. However, this is far from the truth: As briefly noted in this chapter, there are many signs of economic and social progress beginning to strongly unfold for this region, details of which can be followed at the *African Economic Outlook* website.

4

Fertility

On the aggregate level…changes in procreative behavior are influential accompaniments of virtually every variation in the fortunes of society. A disturbance of the rate of production of new members portends for the population successive modifications in the numbers of consumers in each higher age group, the demands placed on the educational structure, the flow of young adults into the labor force, the housing requirements of newlyweds, and so on throughout the life span to the ages beyond retirement when the old seek to derive financial if not psychological security from their savings, their progeny, and their government.

Norman B. Ryder (1959)

Contemporary populations…far exceed any historical limits on subsistence. Can we continue? Even with renewable sources of energy and materials, there would be an eventual collision between continued population growth and a finite world. But the collision may be averted because population growth has been slowing in recent decades, not from rising mortality, but because of voluntary controls on fertility.

Charles Hirschman (2005)

Measuring Fertility

Fertility represents *actual* levels of childbearing and can be measured at the individual or group level of analysis. It is often contrasted with *fecundity*, the *theoretical* ability of a woman to bear children. Given two or more women, two or more families, or two or more social groups, the question of why fecund women vary in their levels of childbearing is one of the fundamental questions in the study of fertility.

Knowing the number of children women tend to have in a society tells us much about it. If the average woman is having one or two, it tells us that that she is under little cultural or social pressure to bear a lot of children. Most likely, this pressure is lacking because her society has a high level of economic development and thus has high levels of food, medical care, and social stability to ensure that almost all children make it to adulthood – and do so with the wherewithal and opportunities to lead productive lives. On the other hand, if the average woman is having four or more offspring, it tells us that she is under cultural and social pressure to produce many children, as the society suffers many childhood deaths. This high mortality rate means that if the society is to survive into the next generation, its women must bear many children. These ideas are supported by the evidence presented in Figure 3.1 in Chapter 3 (infant mortality is strongly predicted by socioeconomic development) and in Figure 1.2 in Chapter 1 (fertility is strongly predicted by infant mortality).

Crude Birth Rate

The most commonly used measurements of fertility are the *crude birth rate* and the *total fertility rate*. The operational definition of the former is identical to that of the crude death rate developed in Chapter 3, but now, of course, the numerator is the number of births:

$$\text{Crude birth rate} = \frac{\text{Births in year}_i}{\text{Population year}_i} \times 1,000$$

where i is a particular year, and Population is the total population at midyear.

For example, for the United States in 2010, the

$$\text{Crude birth rate} = \frac{4,007,000}{308,745,538} \times 1,000 = 12.978 \approx 13.0$$

General Fertility Rate

Although standardizing for population size (per 1,000 people) allows birth rates to be compared across social groupings, including countries, this measurement has a problem in that it does not take into account sex and age distributions. More specifically, a country with many females in the age range of 15–44 (the ages of high fecundity) will be more likely to have a higher crude birth rate than a comparison country with fewer women in this age range – despite any socioeconomic differences between the two countries. Thus, a more refined measurement of fertility is the

General fertility rate

$$= \frac{\text{Births in year}_i}{\text{Population in year}_i \text{ of females of ages 15–44}} \times 1,000$$

where i is a particular year, and females of ages 15–44 is the specific part of the population most likely to bear children.

[Thus, for example, for the United States in 2010, the

$$\text{General fertility rate} = \frac{4,007,000}{61,481,000} \times 1,000 = 65.175 \approx 65.2$$

Age-Specific Birth Rate

The general fertility rate is related to a less commonly seen indicator of fertility, the *age-specific birth rate*, but the calculation of age-specific rates is a necessary step for the calculation of the most popularly used fertility measurement, *the total fertility rate*:

Age-specific birth rate

$$= \frac{\text{Births in year}_i \text{ of females of age}_j}{\text{Population in year}_i \text{ of females of age}_j} \times 1,000$$

where i is a particular year, and Population is the total number of females of age j (e.g., of age 30).

After the age of 19, age-specific birth rates are often calculated for five-year intervals. Thus, for example, for the United States in 2010, for women in the age range of 30–4 the

$$\text{Age-specific birth rate} = \frac{962,170}{9,868,000} \times 1,000 = 97.504 \approx 97.5$$

For all populations, whether living in least, less, or more developed countries, the chance of a female having a child begins to rise in the late teen years, peaks in the late 20s and early 30s, then steadily decreases

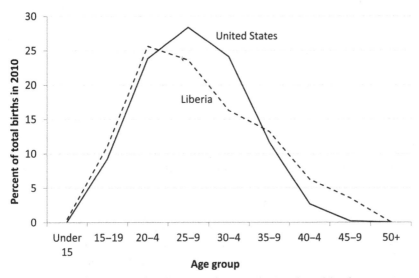

Figure 4.1:   The relationship between the percentage of total births in a given year and the ages of the females giving birth is similar across countries – revealing an inverted U curve

Note: The shape of the curves is almost identical, with the only notable difference being that Liberian women have their peak fertility in their early 20s (ages 20–4, representing 25.6% of the total births), while US women's peak is in their mid- to late 20s (ages 25–9, representing 28.4% of all births). This difference would be typical of the women in developed versus developing nations, as the women in the former generally have higher levels of education and delay childbirth until they are done with their schooling.

Sources: Raw data for the United States are from Martin et al. (2012); and for Liberia, from United Nations (2013g: Table 10)

until the early 50s, when it essentially bottoms out. In short, the shape of the curve is the same: it forms an inverted U. Thus, for example, the curves for Liberia (a UN-designated *least* developed country) and the highly developed United States are near identical; the only difference is that Liberia's curve is more to the left on the X-axis, reflecting that its females start having a significant number of children at younger ages than in the United States (see Figure 4.1).

Total Fertility Rate and Replacement Level of Fertility

Age-specific birth rates can be used to calculate the *total fertility rate* (TFR), which is the sum of the individual age-specific rates (usually for ages 15–44, and usually for five-year age groupings, e.g., 15–19, 20–4, etc.; the rates used are *per woman*, not per 1,000 women). This indicator has two key advantages that make it the first choice for the analysis of fertility: (1) it has the intuitively straight-forward interpretation of representing the number of children a female can expect to have during the course of her lifetime; and (2) because it adjusts for age differences that might exist among different populations, it allows for comparisons across time, social groups (e.g., blacks vs whites), and geographic areas (such as countries).

For developed countries, ignoring the impact of immigration and emigration, a population will stabilize – that is, neither grow nor decline in size – if it has TFR of 2.1 (2 children to replace the parents, plus the 0.1 to account for childhood deaths and infertility). The *replacement level of fertility* is operationally defined as a TFR of 2.1 in developed countries, and for very poor countries, where death rates can be very high, a TFR of greater than 2.1 (the actual TFR depending upon the country's death rate; see United Nations 2014h). One of the most dramatic and far-reaching changes in human history is an unpredicted shift in the *demographic transition*, with 83 countries – 45% of the world's population – below the 2.1 replacement level of fertility as of 2014 (including Canada, China, Japan, the United States, and all of Eastern, Northern, and Western Europe).[1] Recall that *demographic transition theory* describes humanity as having high death and high birth rates yielding very low growth for most of its history; then transitioning into rapid population growth as death rates fell and a cultural lag kept birth rates high for a period (nineteenth and twentieth centuries); and, finally, ending in low birth and low death rates yielding little or no growth (late twentieth/early twenty-first centuries). The theory did not predict that another stage would follow, with *very* low birth rates unable to keep up with low (but not *very* low) death rates. In this new stage that humanity is now entering, deemed the *second demographic transition*, the global population will decline. And, indeed, some social demographers disagree with the UN's prediction that humanity will reach 9.6 billion by 2050, and 10.6 billion by 2100 (United Nations 2013c: xviii), and, instead, have population models based on very low TFRs resulting in just 8.8 billion by 2050, with declines from that point onward (see, e.g., Norris 2013; Wise 2013).[2]

Explaining Differences in Fertility (Who Has Many Children and Why): Macro and Micro Perspectives

Selected Macro Factors Encouraging Fertility

Socioeconomic Development and the Control of Mortality. From a national level of analysis, the most important determinant of fertility is the death rate, especially of the very young: As argued earlier, if a society has high rates of infant and child mortality, its culture will encourage women to be "fruitful and multiply"; at stake is the very survival of the society. As described in earlier chapters, the *demographic transition* from high death and birth rates to low death and birth rates in the developed nations of the world was pushed along by economic development. As these nations gained increasing prosperity during the nineteenth and twentieth centuries, they advanced their public health, medical care, food production, transportation, and communication systems – all of which drove death rates down and life expectancy up. And, as also described in earlier chapters, the less developed nations of the world – in Asia, Africa, Latin America, and Oceania – were able to sidestep much of the economic development required of developed nations to lower their death rates via importing technologies for controlling death (from immunization and clean-water campaigns to the Green Revolution). However, even though less developed nations were able to sidestep much of the otherwise-required level of economic development, they were not able to sidestep all of the requirements, and thus socioeconomic development still strongly predicts fertility (Figure 4.2), because it is also predictive of infant and child mortality. We can sketch the model as follows: Level of Economic Development→Infant Mortality→Fertility. If this model is correct, then Economic Development and Fertility should be highly correlated, which they are (per Figure 4.2), and, further, if Economic Development transmits its major effect on Fertility via its effect on Infant Mortality, then the Economic Development/Fertility correlation should weaken greatly when Infant Mortality is held constant. (Think of a combination shot in pool. If the white ball hits the yellow ball, which then hits the green ball, then the movement of the green ball is caused by the yellow ball being struck by the white ball; the white ball is making the green ball go in via the movement it causes in the yellow ball. But if someone puts his or her thumb down on the yellow ball so it cannot move, then the white ball will lose its effect on making the green ball move. It's the same here, with Economic Development being the white ball, Infant Mortality being the yellow ball, and Fertility being the green ball.) Indeed, Figure 4.3 shows that when Infant Mortality is not held constant, then there is a strong inverse relationship between Economic Development (measured by GNIPPP) and the TFR; however, when Infant Mortality is held constant (by examining only those countries with a low level of Infant Mortality), the relationship weakens dramatically – just as would be predicted by the Level of Economic Development→Infant Mortality→Fertility causal chain.

Indicative of the cultural push toward high fertility in societies with high rates of infant death is the expressed desire of the individuals living

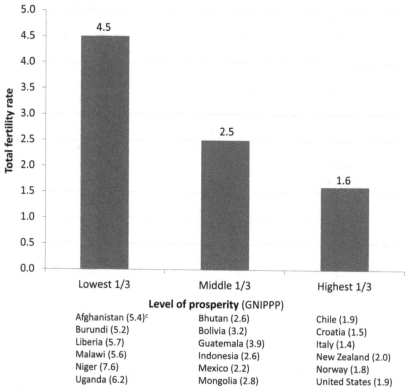

Figure 4.2: *The strong relationship between prosperity[a] and fertility,[b] with selected national examples*

Notes: [a] GNIPPP (see Figure 3.3, note b).
[b] TFR represents the expected number of children a woman will have during her lifetime.
[c] TFR in parentheses.
[d] Correlation = −.58 (p < .0001); N = 179 countries.
Source: Raw data from the Population Reference Bureau (2014)

in these societies to have many children. For example, in Liberia a 2007 nationally representative sample of over 13,000 adults revealed that the average "ideal number of children" reported by women was 5.0, while the average for men was 5.6. Moreover, two-thirds of the women reported getting married in their teenage years (14% by the age of 15, and another 44% by the age of 18; see Liberia Institute of Statistics and Geo-Information Services 2008: 4). An additional indication of the cultural forces encouraging high fertility is the degree to which sexually active women use birth control (either traditional methods like *coitus*

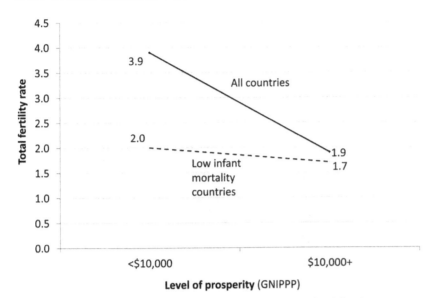

Figure 4.3: The strong relationship between prosperity[a] and fertility is trans-mitted via the effect of prosperity on infant mortality[b]

Notes: [a]The global median GNIPPP per capita in 2014 was approximately $10,000; thus countries in the bottom half of the distribution (the poorest 50%) are being compared to their counterparts in the top half of the distribution (richest 50%).

[b]Infant mortality = number of infant 0–11 months dying per 1,000 births. "Low infant mortality" countries are defined as those below the global median of 17.0 in 2014.

[c]The correlation between GNIPPP and TFR rate with no controls = −.58 ($p <.0001$; $N = 179$ countries); however, when controlling for the infant mortality rate, this correlation falls dramatically to −0.13 and becomes statistically insignificant ($p < .083$). Thus the partial correlation coefficient and the graphic lines depicted in this figure support this causal chain: Level of Economic Development→Infant Mortality→Fertility (i.e., that prosperity transmits its effects on lowering the fertility rate by way of reducing infant mortality).

Source: Raw data from the Population Reference Bureau (2014)

interruptus, or modern methods such as condoms, the pill, and IUDs). In Liberia, just 1 in 10 sexually active women reported using birth control in the 2007 survey.

Contrast the ideal number of children in highly developed, industrialized democracies such as Japan and the United States: in Japan, 96% of adults report that the ideal number of children is 2 or 3 (mean = 2.6), while in the United States, 84% of adults agree that 2 or 3 is the ideal number (with the mean being identical to that of the Japanese, i.e., 2.6;

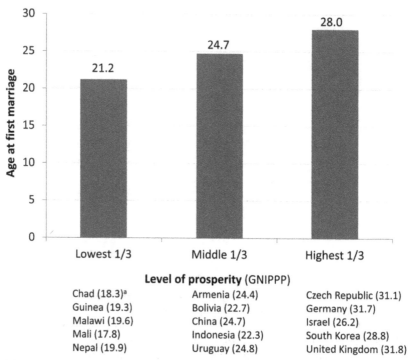

Level of prosperity (GNIPPP)

Chad (18.3)[a]	Armenia (24.4)	Czech Republic (31.1)
Guinea (19.3)	Bolivia (22.7)	Germany (31.7)
Malawi (19.6)	China (24.7)	Israel (26.2)
Mali (17.8)	Indonesia (22.3)	South Korea (28.8)
Nepal (19.9)	Uruguay (24.8)	United Kingdom (31.8)

Figure 4.4: The strong relationship between prosperity and age at first marriage for females, with selected national examples
Notes: [a] Average age at first marriage for females in parentheses.
[b] Correlation = .68 (p < .0001); N = 175 countries.
Source: Raw data from the Population Reference Bureau (2014) and World Bank (2014d)

see General Social Survey 2012 and Japanese General Social Survey 2005). Moreover, contrast the young age at which Liberian women marry with the average age of first marriage for women in Japan, 29.7 years old, and in the United States, 26.9 years old (US Census Bureau 2012b). Finally, in Japan, 55% of sexually active women practice birth control, while in the United States the percentage is 79 (Population Reference Bureau 2014). In short, these comparisons indicate that the pressure on women to fulfill traditional roles of marriage and motherhood are much stronger in poorer nations than in more prosperous ones. Indeed, Figure 4.4 shows the consistent cross-national pattern between prosperity and the age at which women first marry, while Figure 4.5 reveals the similarly close connection between prosperity and the use of birth control.

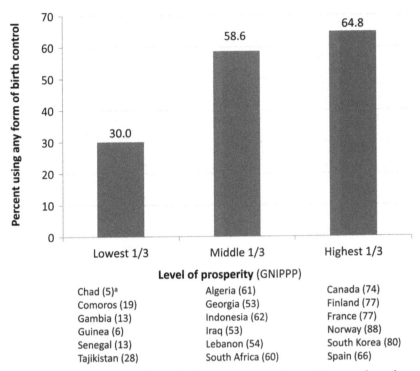

Figure 4.5: *The strong relationship between prosperity and the use of any form of birth control by sexually active women, with selected national examples*
Notes: [a] Percentage using any form of birth control in parentheses.
[b] Correlation = .48 ($p < .0001$); $N = 159$ countries.
Source: Raw data from the Population Reference Bureau (2014)

Government Programs and Policy. Population growth can stimulate an economy: Many babies, and the adults they grow into, encourage manufacturing for all of the products they need (from baby bottles to diapers to clothes); encourage agricultural development for their food; encourage construction industries for their housing, workplaces, and schools; and encourage services of every manner – from healthcare to childcare to educational and recreational work. However, if growth outstrips the ability of the economy to develop the infrastructure to handle so many new individuals – from transportation to communication to public healthcare systems, to the financial policies and institutions to facilitate the economic exchanges needed to support a growing populace – then growth can burden an economy and immiserate the population. Thus, fine-tuning the level of growth is a problem that all governments face and one that is not easily solved.

In the early 1970s, the Chinese regime concluded that its massive population of 800 million and its high TFR of around 6 children per woman – yielding a doubling time of 26 years – was soon going to lead to another disaster like the *Great Chinese Famine* of just a decade earlier (1958–62, which killed an estimated 45 million people). The result was the 1971 *wan* (later marriage), *xi* (longer delays before having the next child), *shao* (fewer children) program, which by 1979 had evolved into the *One-Child Policy*. (China's most powerful leader at the time, Deng Xiaoping, said "one child is best.") A host of carrot-and-stick government policies were created and widely enforced. Prominent among these was the awarding of a certificate to those married couples having just one child. The certificate entitled them to small cash stipends, improved childcare services, longer maternity leave, and preferential housing assignments. With acceptance of a certificate, the couple agreed to have no more children, and the woman was encouraged to get either sterilized or to have an IUD implanted. In rural areas, where the majority of the Chinese population still lives, local officials found greater resistance to the One-Child Policy and rural couples were generally allowed to have a second child, especially if the first-born was a girl. A large-scale public awareness operation accompanied the adoption of the One-Child Policy, and billboards, advertisements, flyers, and pamphlets bore slogans like "One Child is Best" and "Marry Late, Conceive Late." However, other, harsher slogans were also used: "If you don't get sterilized, your house will be demolished"; "Kill all your family if you don't follow the rule"; and "If you escape sterilization, we'll hunt you down; if you want to hang yourself, we'll give you the rope" (Marsh 2012; in recent years, the harsh slogans have been replaced with gentler messages). The harsh slogans were reflective of the penalties for violating the One-Child Policy: The most common was, and is, a stiff fine, often more than the combined annual salaries of the couple involved (a complex "social compensation" formula is used that often produces fines in the $3,000 to $10,000 range). Accounts of forced sterilizations and abortions have been documented by reputable outside sources (see, e.g., Public Radio International 2013), and the sins of the parents are inflicted on children born outside the framework and rules of the One-Child Policy: These children are denied access to schools, healthcare, and other services. (The children don't exist in the eyes of the government; see, e.g., US Department of State 2004.) The one-child framework, which undergoes periodic modifications, dictates one child for urban couples unless both the husband and wife are only children. Rural couples are allowed to have a second child if the first-born is a girl, in which case they can try for a boy. If the first child born has serious birth defects, a second child is allowed. Moreover, the small proportion (less than 10%) of the Chinese population that do not have a Han ethnic background (e.g., Muslim Uighurs and Tibetans) are generally free to have more than one child. Finally, there is significant local control over the one-child framework and, thus, there are significant differences among China's 420 prefectures in how strictly it is applied. (China's 34 provinces are divided into administrative prefectures – roughly equivalent to large counties in the United States.)[3]

Billboards extolling the One-Child Policy in China. Since the 1970s, the Chinese government has used billboards to exhort its people to conform to the goals of its One-Child Policy. Since 2000, the billboards have become less common in urban areas, as the populations there have generally been in compliance with One-Child policies.
The billboards are still a common sight, however, in many rural areas. The slogan on the billboard on the left translates as "I have got my Only-Child certificate," while the slogan for the right billboard exhorts "Vigorously implement the One-Child family policy!"
Photo: Alice de Jong

Because the implementation of the One-Child Policy was coterminous with a huge push toward industrialization and opening the country to international trade, the effects of the Policy are difficult to estimate exactly, as China's massive economic growth and rising prosperity post-1979 also drove down the fertility rate. Indeed, a comparison of mainland China with its off-shore neighbor Taiwan reveals that the birth rate in Taiwan, which has had no One-Child Policy, has fallen at the same rate as it has in mainland China, where the Policy has been in full force since 1979 (see Weeks 2016: 249; for an in-depth analysis, see Cai 2010). This said, the Policy has been credited with as many as 200 to 400 million fewer births between 1980 and 2010. (China's official estimate is 400,000,000, while some demographic analyses put the estimate as low as 200,000,000; see Olesen 2011: 138.) Another indication of its success is that even though the strict one-child limit has only applied to about a third of Chinese couples, in the coming few decades, almost two-thirds of Chinese couples (representing both urban and rural areas) are predicted to limit their families to just one child (Gu et al. 2007: 144).

The One-Child Policy is the extreme example in the global community of how a country can influence its fertility rate. India, the world's second most populous nation at 1.3 billion in 2016 (vs 1.4 billion in China), attempted a similarly aggressive campaign in the 1970s. The most controversial aspect was the required sterilization of a man with two or more children. Resentment of this policy was part of the backlash against the government of Prime Minister Indira Gandhi, who was forced from office in 1977. More generally, however, the regimes of most developing countries began family planning policies in the 1970s to curb their rapidly growing populations: In 1965, 21 countries had government-sponsored family planning programs; by 1975, this number rose to 95; and it stood at 160 as of 2015 (representing 81% of the 197 countries recognized by the UN; see United Nations 2013h: 17). These policies are varied and nuanced, but they largely center on public information campaigns and easy access to various means of inexpensive birth control *encouraging* (not *requiring*, per the One-Child Policy) couples to have fewer children. The policies' underlying ideology is that fewer children means a better life for everyone in the family and, indeed, for everyone in the greater community (the core idea behind neo-Malthusianism; however, a countervailing, Marxist-rooted resistance ideology arose in response in selected nations of Eastern Europe and Latin America). This ideology was also linked to the growing women's movement, which emphasized that women should have equal access to education – and when that access was realized, that they should be granted greater power over the number of children they bear. As with men, more education moves women to seek greater economic success at the price of having fewer children. The results have been substantially and steadily declining birth rates in developing nations until the present day (TFRs falling from the 5's and 6's to the 2's, and in the all-important case of China, below 2; with the percentage of women using modern contraceptive means rising from less than 10% to nearly 60%; note, however, that many of the countries in Sub-Saharan Africa still have relatively high TFRs and relatively low levels of birth control use). As in the case of China, it is difficult to assess the exact effect of government-encouraged family planning on declining birth rates, as socioeconomic development and urbanization were on the rise at the same time. In rural-agricultural areas, children are seen as an economic asset – as they begin contributing to family income by the ages of 6 or 7. In urban-industrial areas, children are seen as an economic liability, as they are in school until the age of 16 or beyond. After achieving many years of schooling, both men and women typically want income-producing jobs and children become seen as a barrier to the opportunity of making more money and of having, more generally, a higher standard of living. All of this said, the World Bank's comprehensive analyses of government-sponsored family planning programs support the conclusion that at least half of the decline of fertility in the developing world since 1970 has been due to such programs (Sinding 2007). Indeed, these programs stand "alongside the Green Revolution in agriculture as a demonstration of what collective political will and strong international cooperation can achieve" (Sinding 2007: 11). More circumspectly, social demographer John R. Weeks (2012: 505) concludes that "government policy is not a necessary precursor to change, but it can help to both solidify and accelerate changes that are under way."

Since 2000, many national governments have been less concerned with birth control/family planning and are more or less satisfied with their current TFRs. As of 2015, the UN estimates that 30% of national governments had policies to maintain fertility at current levels. Another 43%, virtually all in developing regions, continued with pre-2000 policies to lower fertility, while 27% had reversed their pre-2000 fertility control policies and were trying to raise their birth rates closer to the replacement level of 2.1. Almost all in this last category are developed countries with low TFRs (well below 2.1; see United Nations 2013h: 6). The key motivation is that their newer and smaller generations will not be able to support the retirement and healthcare costs of their older and larger generations. *Pro-natalist programs* encourage fertility by offering generous income tax deductions for children; offering cash stipends for new children; increasing maternity leave; allowing fathers or significant caregivers to also take leaves from work; increasing benefits while on leave; and, in a few cases, increasing restrictions on abortion and birth control. However, the government-sponsored attempts to raise fertility have to date been much less successful than their 1970s–1990s counterparts meant to reduce fertility.

Japan and Singapore offer good examples of how these kinds of programs have thus far met with little success. Since 1997, Japan has reported in periodic UN-sponsored surveys of national governments that it views its growth as "too low" and that its "concern levels" for the

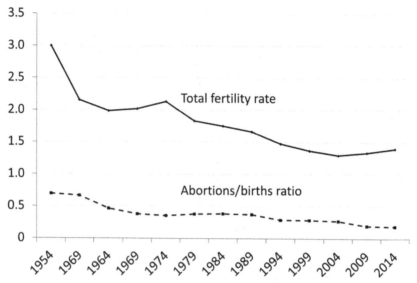

Figure 4.6: Decreasing abortion rates[a] in Japan have not been associated with increasing birth rates[b] – indeed, the data reveal just the opposite: Drops in abortion correlate with drops in fertility

Notes: [a] Abortions/births ratio = total number of abortions divided by the total number of births.

[b] TFR = expected number of children a woman will have during her lifetime.

[c] Correlation = .88 ($p < .0001$); $N = 13$.

Sources: Raw data from Johnston (2015), United Nations (2013i), and *World Factbook* (2014)

welfare of its working population and for its aged population are "great" (United Nations 2013h: 216). Well known for the use of abortion as a means of birth control, Japan increased restrictions on abortions after 1997 (United Nations 2014h: 69). However, the evidence presented in Figure 4.6 reveals that the history of abortion and fertility in Japan has unfolded as a *positive* correlation (the lower the abortion rate, the lower the birth rate!) – so the likelihood of the success of this approach is low.

Singapore's government has responded to its dramatically falling fertility rates with a variety of programs since the 1990s. The response was motivated by its TFR dropping from 6.3 in 1960, to 3.7 in 1970, to 1.8 in 1980, to 1.7 in 1990, and to 1.6 in 2000. The programs include increased availability of childcare, work leave for new mothers and the parents of young children, and cash awards for the birth of a child (the government matching, dollar-for-dollar up to $18,000, a family's child-dedicated savings account; see Yew 2012). The results? In 2005, the TFR fell to 1.4, in 2010 to 1.3, and in 2014 to 0.8!

Systematic research on public policies to reverse the declining birth rates in Europe confirm the Singapore example: In other words, "generous arrangements for parental leave, child benefits, and childcare may be considered desirable in their own right, but such policies *alone* are unlikely to succeed in raising the fertility level on a grand scale" (Hoem 2008: 256). More generally, social demographer Paul Demeny concludes that it is "foolish arrogance on the part of governments to assume that they can set some population size as the optimum and try to achieve it through appropriate policy measures." Rather, he sees declining fertility rates creating declines in population size, declines that will eventually stabilize and ultimately increase the well-being of humanity: "If the aggregate of individual fertility choices (the key variable in the growth equation) results in a *slow* demographic decline in modern affluent societies, such societies should be capable of making the necessary adjustments to a declining population size. Such adjustments could be consistent with maintaining and indeed raising the already high material standards of living..." (Demeny 2005: 8).

However, as of 2015, there were a few countries with extremely low fertility rates that were seeing success in reversing the trend. Most notable among these was France. The French government is credited with buttressing its family-focused approaches – like increasing tax deductions for children and offering maternity benefits – with a coordinated set of broader public policies. The latter have involved "a range of interlocking areas (economic policy, employment policy, housing policy, gender policy, core family policy, and more) that are implemented in a spirit that furthers childbearing in general, and do not just consist of making more money available to married families in selected situations" (Hoem 2008: 256). In short, France continually increased the breadth and depth of its post-World War II *welfare state* to the point where it represented a new paradigm, the *dirigiste* state (a term coined to describe the government's heavy financial investments in the economy, as well as the replacing of private- with state-owned industries, especially those involved with national defense). With a strong welfare state in place, France was able to enhance aspects of it over the past three decades that would favor increased fertility. These aspects included (a) increased state-funded maternity/paternity leave, childcare/preschools, and home nurses/nannies; (b) tax credits for employers with employees on family leave; and (c) support to city governments that provide benefits for children and families. The upshot: In 1990, France's TFR bottomed out at 1.72; as the comprehensive approach began to take effect, its TFR rose to 1.88 by 2000, then to 1.97 by 2010; and as of 2014, stood at 2.08 (data from United Nations 2013i; *World Factbook* 2015). The sum total of France's multifaceted family-friendly government programs and policies is to make it easier for women to balance their work and family lives. This is *the* key to the success of any set of national policies seeking to raise fertility.

The Nordic nations of Denmark, Finland, Iceland, Norway, and Sweden also put forth coordinated and comprehensive family-friendly approaches to increasing fertility that built on their strong welfare states and, like France, saw success, but only for a decade or so: After decades of declining fertility rates, they had rising rates in the 1990s and early 2000s. However, they have all seen reversals since 2005. For example, Sweden's TFR bottomed out in 1985 at 1.64. After aggressive family-friendly policies to reverse declining fertility – emphasizing generous support for parental leave, increased services for children, and gender equality – the rate rose to 2.01 in 1995; however, by 2014, its TFR was back down to 1.88. One problem with the French-style comprehensive approach is that it is expensive, "and today the question is not if similar policies can work, but if they can be funded" (Kramer 2013, as quoted in Achenbach and Jackson 2014; see Gauthier [2005] for an analysis of the problem in Europe's 55 nations).

Selected Micro Factors Encouraging Fertility

Socioeconomic Status and Age of Marriage.   The macro-level importance of socioeconomic development on fertility rates is replicated at the micro level of analysis: At both family and individual levels of analysis, as education, income, and job prestige increase, fertility decreases. Phrased differently, those most able to afford children are the least likely to have them, while those least likely to afford children are the most likely to have them. For example, Figure 4.7 shows the clear inverse relationship between the education level of US adults and the number of children they have. This basic pattern is found worldwide – and indeed for decades the UN and the World Bank have advocated for the "better schooling for girls as a means of achieving lower…fertility" (Cleland 2014: 187).

There are multiple and interrelated reasons for the education–N children relationship, but the simplest and most straightforward of these is the dramatic differences among the individuals of different socioeconomic standing regarding the age at which they start having children. For example, in the United States, 58% of women with no high school degree have their first child under the age of 20; in contrast, this percentage drops to 35 for women with a high school degree, to 24 for women with a junior college education (1–3 years of college), and to just 4 for university-educated women. On the other hand, 36% of women with a

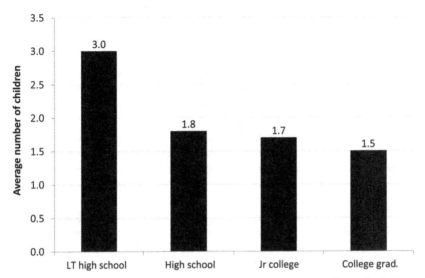

Figure 4.7: As education level increases, the average number of children decreases
Source: Raw data from General Social Survey (2012); N = 1,971 US adults

university degree have their first child between the ages of 30 and 34, while just 4% of their counterparts with no high school degree do so (Martinez et al. 2012: 19). Again, this pattern holds worldwide: The younger a woman starts to have children, the more extended her opportunities for having children, and thus the more children she is likely to have (United Nations 2013j: 24–5).

The interpretation of the inverse relationship between education and fertility also includes the *opportunity cost* an educated woman bears if she has more children: In short, she is less able to take advantage of the higher-paying jobs that an education opens up to her. Men are brought into the decision-making process in that the spouse (partner) of an educated woman realizes that the family's income will drop when the woman gives up work, or works less, after having a child; and thus the spouse of an educated woman is more likely to encourage her to delay having children and to have fewer children.[4] Relatedly, as a woman's economic contributions to the family increase, so does her decision-making power and control over her body, which often results in her pursuing paid work over childbearing. Thus, it is not surprising to find that education (and socioeconomic status in general) is positively related to the use of modern forms of birth control.

Some studies suggest that poorer women are more likely to subscribe to traditional gender roles (wife and mother) and thus are more likely to value children (see, e.g., Edin and Kefalas 2005; Kane 1995). However, many poor women realize the benefits of fewer children and smaller families, but they are more likely than their better educated and more prosperous counterparts to have unwanted pregnancies because they are less likely to use birth control. Indeed, in the largest empirical study to date, of nearly 4,000 US women, Musick et al. (2009: 543) found that the inverse relationship between socioeconomic status and fertility "comes largely from unintended childbearing, and it is not explained by child-bearing desires or opportunity costs." Finally, it is important to note that the causal arrow runs both ways: Educated women are likely to delay childbirth and have fewer children; but women who have children at a young age (less than 20) are less likely to complete their schooling.

As in the case of mortality, racial, ethnic, and religious differences in fertility are due, in significant part, to socioeconomic differences among them. Thus, although in the United States, blacks have, on average, more children than whites, this difference largely disappears when educational differences between whites and blacks are taken into account. For example, the 2012 General Social Survey reveals that the average white adult has 1.8 children and the average black adult has 2.3. However, as shown in Figure 4.7, education is strongly predictive of fertility, with the less educated having more children. And, in the United States, compared to their white counterparts, blacks are less likely to be high school- or college-educated and more likely to be high school dropouts. Thus, when holding education constant, and examining just high school graduates, the 0.5 child difference between blacks and whites reduces to 0.2. Similar reductions in this difference occur when looking just at junior college graduates or just at college graduates. The one exception is for high school dropouts, where the black–white difference is actually accentuated to 0.8 (3.5 children for blacks vs 2.7 for whites). Musick et al. (2009) demonstrate that this difference is largely due to the less frequent use of birth control on the part of less educated black women compared to their white counterparts – resulting in more unintended births.

The choices open to an individual are pushed in certain directions by the cultural norms and values of the greater society in which he or she lives. This core tenet of sociology is dramatically illustrated when considering the situation for many girls and young women in much of the developing world regarding their choices on when to marry, when to bear children, how much schooling to get, and whether to use birth control. Indeed, according to UN estimates, a third of girls in developing nations (excluding China) are forced into child marriages before the age of 18, and one in nine before the age of 15. In the 48 UN-designated "least developed" countries, the rate of female child marriage is even higher: One in two girls is married before the age of 18 (United Nations 2012f: 6). The highest levels of child marriage (before the age of 18) are in Sub-Saharan Africa, with Niger (75%) and Chad (72%) leading the way. With its huge population of 1.3 billion, India contributes the largest number of child brides each year, witnessing 47% of its girls married before their 18th birthday. In the Western hemisphere, countries with high rates of child brides include Brazil (36%), the Dominican Republic (40%), Guatemala (30%), Haiti (30%), and Honduras (39%).

The United Nations (2012f: 10) does not mince its words in characterizing child marriage as having "devastating – even life-threatening – consequences":

The term "child marriage" is used to describe a legal or customary union between two people, of whom one or both spouses is below the age of 18. While boys can be subjected to child marriage, the practice affects girls in greater numbers and with graver consequences. Child marriage is often referred to as "early" and/or "forced" marriage since children, given their age, are not able to give free, prior, and informed consent to their marriage partners or to the timing of their marriage....

[F]or millions of girls, marriage is anything but safe and anything but consistent with their best interests....Once married, girls are likely to feel, and in many cases are, powerless to refuse sex. They are likely to find it difficult to insist on condom use by their husbands, who commonly are older and more sexually experienced, making the girls especially vulnerable to HIV and other sexually transmitted infections....

Married girls are often under pressure to become pregnant immediately or soon after marriage, although they are still children themselves and know little about sex or reproduction. A pregnancy too early in life before a girl's body is fully mature is a major risk to both mother and baby. Complications of pregnancy and childbirth are the main causes of death among adolescent girls ages 15–19 years old in developing countries....Nearly 16 million teenage girls aged 15–19 years old in developing countries give birth every year. In nine out of ten cases, the mother is already married. Preventing child marriage would significantly help to reduce early pregnancy, and the associated maternal death or disability. At the same time, girls would face a reduced risk of HIV infection.

Beyond the immediate implications, child marriage denies girls the opportunity to fully develop their potential as healthy, productive and empowered citizens. Child marriage robs girls of their girlhood, entrenching them and their future families in poverty, limiting their life choices, and generating high development costs for communities.

The preceding paragraph is indicative of several core postmodern values impinging upon fertility that spread across most of the developed world during the course of the twentieth century and that are becoming increasingly adopted in developing nations – that is, adopted when females are given the choice in doing so. These values are part of the *second demographic transition* described earlier in the Introduction and Chapter 2 and include: (1) the importance of individual autonomy; (2) a relaxation of the tight political, religious, and social control of the individual so omnipresent in traditional societies; and (3) an increased expectation that a person should lead a life that can maximize his or her individual potential and recognition. The rise of postmodern values oriented toward "the self is accompanied by a relative decline in the importance attached to family formation and childbearing" (Philipov et al.).[5]

That child marriage is buttressed by strong social forces is evidenced by the UN's *Millennium Development Goals Report* of 2014, which revealed little progress in the previous two decades in reducing the number of births to adolescent girls aged 15–19 in Sub-Saharan Africa (117 births per 1,000 girls), Latin America (76 births per 1,000 girls), and the Caribbean (also 76 births per 1,000 girls; see United Nations 2014g: 31). As introduced in Chapter 1, one of these forces is the distorted *sex ratio* in many developing nations, where young adult males far outnumber their female counterparts; as shown in Table 1.2, an expected outcome of this situation is pressure on child and adolescent girls to marry and to live out traditional gender roles. Distorted sex ratios are intermeshed with other strong social forces that the UN (2012f: 14) emphasizes in accounting for the high incidence of child marriages persisting in much of the developing world. These forces include the following:

1   *Men exercising greater economic, political, social and interpersonal power than women*, reflecting gender norms that place a higher value on males than females. "When girls from birth lack the same perceived value as boys, families and communities may discount the benefits of educating and investing in their daughters' development."

2   *Child marriage being viewed as a safeguard against premarital sex*, "and the duty to protect the girl from sexual harassment and violence is transferred from father to husband."

3   *Poverty* – with many parents believing "that marriage will secure their daughters' futures and that it is in their best interests. Alternatively, girls may be viewed as an economic burden, as a commodity, or a means for settling familial debts or disputes, or securing social, economic, or political alliances. Customary requirements

such as dowries or bride prices may also enter into families' considerations, especially in communities where families can give a lower dowry for younger brides."

4   *Humanitarian crises*: Girls' vulnerability to child marriage "increases during humanitarian crises when family and social structures are disrupted. In times of conflict and natural disaster, parents may marry off their young daughters as a last resort, either to bring the family some income in time of economic hardship, or to offer the girl some sort of protection, particularly in contexts where sexual violence is common. These girls are called 'famine brides,' for example, in food-insecure Kenya. Young girls were married to 'tsunami widowers' in Sri Lanka, Indonesia, and India as a way to obtain state subsidies for marrying and starting a family. During the conflicts in Liberia, Uganda, and Sudan, girls were abducted and given as 'bush wives' to warlords, or even given by their families in exchange for protection."

The UN's analysis is exemplified and given life by the plight of Aguet N. of South Sudan. According to her testimony to the advocacy group Human Rights Watch (2013: 6), she was forced to marry a 75-year-old man when she just 15:

This man went to my uncles and paid a dowry of 80 cows. I resisted the marriage. They threatened me. They said, "If you want your siblings to be taken care of, you will marry this man." I said he is too old for me. They said, "You will marry this old man whether you like it or not because he has given us something to eat." They beat me so badly. They also beat my mother because she was against the marriage.

Intimate Social Circles.   Although socioeconomic status is a powerful predictor of fertility, within any level of education, income, or occupational prestige there are large differences among individuals and couples in their childbearing. Their decisions on the timing and number of children reflect not only rational economic calculations, such as the opportunity costs involved in having a child (e.g., lost wages, reduced career opportunities), but also the social influences of friends, family members, coworkers, classmates, neighbors, fellow congregants, and others with whom they have close personal ties. These social relationships produce messages to the individual or the couple about the joys and problems of parenthood, and how these vary according to family size and the timing and spacing of children. The messages also involve the morality of having children – ranging from "any child is a blessing from God," to "having

Yemeni child brides.   *Child brides are common in much of the developing world. Excluding China, one in three girls is married before the age of 18 in developing countries, and one in two in the UN-designated least developed countries. In 2010, 67 million women in the age range of 20–4 were married before the age of 18, with 8 million being married before the age 15 (United Nations 2012f: 22). The Yemeni girl in the photo on the left is named Tehan (aged 8). She reported to the UN that in the early days of her marriage to Majed (she was 6 and he was 25 when they married): "Whenever I saw him, I hid. I hated to see him." The young wife's former classmate Ghada (on the right), also a child bride, is pictured with her husband outside their home in Hajjah.*
Photo: Stephanie Sinclair (TooYoungtoWed.org)

more than one or two children will add to environmental destruction and ultimately worsen the lot of humanity," to "you can (or can't) be a good mother and have a career." Finally, the messages include the economic impacts of parenthood and practical matters such as the use of and access to birth control. A wealth of social science research confirms the importance, and often the primacy, of intimate social ties in determining childbearing decisions, as well as how these ties regulate the speed of behavioral change in the formation of new family patterns. (Classic compilations of this research include Coale and Watkins 1986 and Leete 1999; more recent reviews of the empirical research can be found in Bernardi 2003, Bernardi and Klärner 2014, and Scommegna 2014.)

More formally, social scientists have identified four overlapping, key mechanisms linking social interaction within intimate circles to a couple's childbearing desires, intentions, and actual births:

(1) *Social learning* produces behavioral change when observations of and discussions within an individual's most important social networks modify his or her views on the feasibility and the consequences of having a child (or another one); the learning can take place indirectly from observation or more directly from conversations.

For example, Watkins and Danzi (1995) interviewed 72 older Jewish and Italian immigrant women (most in their mid-80s) about the child-bearing decisions they had made in early adulthood after arriving in the US cities of New York, Philadelphia, and Providence. All of these women ended up having significantly fewer children than their parents had had, and all viewed their fertility decline as initiated and facilitated by their "gossip networks." Through these networks women learned the benefits of having fewer children in the urban society to which they had immigrated, as well as methods of birth control. Regarding the latter, they learned about – and then communicated to each other – the details of abstinence, withdrawal, condoms, diaphragms, and abortion (as might be performed by a doctor, midwife, friends, or even self-induced). As women learned from their doctors, midwives, and husbands, they would use this information and add it to the knowledge base of their friendship circles, which often formed around card playing. Here are a few samples from the women Watkins and Danzi interviewed:

> I had an abortion in 1928. I had just started teaching and I didn't want a child. My husband made all the arrangements. His friends knew about these things. (Edna B., Jewish, b. 1902)

> A friend of mine got married before I did and she said to me, "Be careful, Helen, you better take precautions," because she got caught right away. We used birth control, condoms. We heard about it from her. (Helen C., Jewish, b. 1907)

> My sisters and my sister-in-law had abortions. I had a sister-in-law who had five abortions. She used to go to different doctors on the QT. My sister had about three because she had six children already, she didn't want no more. Word of mouth, and she would find [an abortionist] doctor. (Lucy I., Italian, b. 1910)

> [I learned about condoms from a friend, whose husband used condoms], so we did. She was my mentor – and had a lot of finesse. Her husband had been in the service and knew. We knew about diaphragms, but condoms seemed the most common [suggesting that she or her husband consulted others along the way]. (Edith, Italian, b. 1923)

> [Did your parents tell you about condoms?] Oh no. [Then how did you learn about them?] Well you know how girls talk. (Lena B., Jewish, b. 1909)

(2) *Social pressure* is put on individuals in explicit, as well as in less obvious, ways. For example, a child might have grown up hearing the common and blunt refrain from their mother or father that "I will not support you if you have a child out of marriage." But the pressure might be more subtle, rooted in the desire to please, comply, avoid conflict, or fit in. For example, "you might see that your parents are growing older, know that they want to become grandparents, and not want to disappoint them. Or, all of your friends are having children and you are slowly being left behind, feeling out of step with your social group" (in the words of social demographer Laura Bernardi, as quoted in Scommegna 2014: 2).

Recognizing that they are still far from the norm in contemporary society, couples who are childless by choice often seek to avoid the social pressure to have children by leaving behind relationships where they feel the most pressure and seeking out new relationships where the pressure is either minimal or actually reverses the cultural norm and is supportive of the choice to remain childless. In the pre-Internet era, this was often done by moving interactions away from family and from friends with children, to single people or those with children but who were also sympathetic to those who chose not to have them. Indeed, this was a common pattern that Veevers (1975: 474) found in her 1970s study of 81 voluntarily childless wives: "Those friends who have opted for motherhood are gradually replaced by persons who are more likely to provide consensual validation for the rejection of the motherhood mystique." (Veevers' finding has been confirmed in other national contexts: see, e.g., Keim et al.'s [2013: 473] study of German women.) In recent years, individuals and couples desiring to remain childless have increasingly turned to Facebook and Internet-based support groups of like-minded people. For example, Basten (2009) uncovered many Facebook groups built around the philosophy of being "childfree by choice" and found this posting to be typical:

> Our cats give me fulfillment and take care of the slight maternal instinct I have. People forget that having children is a choice – not a bullet point in life. I want to keep traveling way too much with my husband, and there's a lot to be said for being "the cool aunt"!! (who gets to go home to a peaceful house at the end of the day and have a martini.)

Images of posters, pins, badges, decals, and photos supporting individuals and couples wanting to remain childless are also quite common. For example, Basten found photos of a yellow pin that reads: "I'm not *childless*, I'm *childfree*." The former implies that a couple or person is explicitly *without* something that should be naturally expected, while the latter implies emancipation from something either by choice or by good fortune – like being care*free* or disease-*free*. The Internet is well suited for the typical heterosexual adult wanting to be childfree for life, as the profile characteristics of this individual include being well educated, financially stable, and living in an urban area (see Basten's [2009: 6–7] review of the literature).[6] The Internet childfree support groups offer relief from the social pressures almost all adults in the developed and developing worlds feel to have children, not only via encouraging on-line discussions, but also by providing the communication foundation to create in-person, face-to-face groups. (Basten found such groups all across the United States, Canada, and India.)

(3) *Social support* involves material, instrumental, and emotional resources that prospective and new parents receive from their close social ties: Material resources can include hand-me-down clothes, toys, and infant/child furniture (cribs, beds, changing tables, and the like), as well as money; instrumental support includes childcare and helping out with housework and shopping; while emotional support centers on compassionate and kind words ("You'd be [You're] a great mom [dad]"). For example, Bühler and Fratczak (2005: 14) found in a study of 1,475 Polish adults between the ages of 18 and 44 that even after controls for the wife's age, family income, religious involvement, and urban–rural residence, those individuals reporting the greatest likelihood of having a second child were also those having received monetary or non-monetary support from their closest social ties – including parents, siblings, and friends – after the birth of their first child. Perhaps not surprisingly, these same individuals scored high in *providing* support to their closest social ties – thus setting up "long-term exchange relationships and investments in personal relationships for future provisions with supportive resources." (Note that Bühler and Fratczak observe similar findings for surveys conducted in several other European countries.)

More generally, an obvious indication of the significant effects of social support on fertility is the differential fertility of women under the age of 45 with long-term partners (through marriage or cohabitation) versus their counterparts who are single. In the contemporary United States, for example, 80% of married women between the ages of 15 and 44 have had at least one child; 63% of cohabiting women have had a child; while 20% of women who have neither been married nor are in cohabiting relationship have borne a child (Martin et al. 2012: 13). Similarly, the average married woman under 45 has 1.9 children; the average cohabiting woman has 1.3; and the average single woman who has neither been married nor is in a cohabitating relationship has 0.4.

(The averages for men under 45 are slightly lower, but form the same pattern: 1.7, 1.1, and 0.1, respectively; see Martin et al. 2012: 17.) Similar patterns exist cross-nationally (see, e.g., Philipov et al. 2006: 298). In short, women with partners (husbands or cohabitants) are much more likely to have children.

(4) *Social contagion* involves the spread of behavior from person to person as they are linked in various kinds of social networks (e.g., via extended families or the workplace). Just as we saw in Chapter 3 that obesity can be contagious, so too can be the decision to have a child. The decision reflects, in part, the factors of social learning and social pressure discussed above, and, in part, the emotional reaction in the presence of the new babies of friends and relatives. In a study of young Italian women, social demographer Laura Bernardi found that they had strong emotional reactions when holding the baby of a close relationship. The women consistently talked about how the holding experience became "the moment things clicked for them and they soon stopped using contraception to try for a baby" (as quoted in Scommegna 2014: 3).

In strong confirmation of social contagion on childbearing decisions, Pink et al. (2014: 113) followed 33,119 female coworkers in 6,579 German firms and found significant "social interaction effects on fertility among women employed in the same firm. In the year after a colleague gave birth, transition rates to first pregnancy double. This effect declines over time and vanishes after two years." The researchers' hypothesis that contagion effects would be found in the workplace because that is where women spend "a considerable amount of their time and are very likely to be exposed to birth events among their interaction partners" was clearly borne out. The researchers interpret the effects of contagion as being largely the result of social learning: "Fertile colleagues exert influence as social models that change previous beliefs about the feasibility and consequences of having a child" (2014: 118). Finally, a longitudinal study of 1,726 US women between 1995 and 2009 revealed similarly strong effects in friendship circles: Balbo and Barban (2014) found that when a woman in her mid- to late 20s has a close friend who has recently had a baby, within two years the woman is much more likely to have her first planned pregnancy than her counterpart with no close friends having had a baby. Moreover, this jump in the chances of having a planned pregnancy was found even after controlling for race, ethnicity, education, social class background, and marital status (married, cohabiting, single). Like the German researchers, Balbo and Barban (2014: 415) interpret their findings as reflective of a combination of social influence and social learning:

[H]aving friends with whom individuals can share their experiences as parents...reduce[s] the uncertainty associated with parenthood. Friends share not only practical information but also their feelings and worries. Moreover, experiencing this unique life transition alone with a peer group likely leads to higher relational costs. Becoming a parent is a real change in lifestyle that strongly affects one's amount and nature of leisure time, including time spent with friends. The opportunity to experience parenthood with friends makes this transition less costly from a relational perspective. With life changes in a social group synchronized or shared, the risk of being left alone or lagging behind diminishes.... [In short,] friends' childbearing can trigger individuals' decisions to have their first baby.

In sum, micro-level studies on childbearing decisions reveal strong, independent effects both of socioeconomic characteristics and of interaction in intimate social circles.

Selected Consequences of Declining Fertility and Rising Life Expectancy

The dramatic fall in fertility and the equally dramatic rise in life expectancy during the course of the past half-century have had far-reaching consequences on the five major social institutions around which all societies are constructed: the family, the economy, the polity, religion, and education. Some of the deeper consequences on the first two of these institutions are examined below, the discussions of which touch upon the last three.

Family Demography: Smaller Families, Shifting Family Structures, and Changing Gender Roles

The second demographic transition – that is, the unexpectedly rapid decline of fertility in developed nations of the world, as well as the equally unexpected rapid decline of fertility in the majority of developing nations – is entwined with changing gender roles and family structures, changes in which causation runs in both directions. What connects all of the multifaceted changes in fertility, gender roles, and family structure is the global diffusion of the core postmodern values presented earlier: that is, the de-emphasis of societal constraints on the individual and a concomitant emphasis on the individual's independence, self-fulfillment, and happiness. The focus on the individual means that his or her traditionally defined roles and statuses have become less prescriptive, and this applies to everyone – regardless of sex, age, ethnicity, race, class, and other background characteristics. One upshot of this rise of individualism is that getting married and having children are delayed and even demoted in importance.

The two-way causation of the decline in fertility with the liberation of women from their traditional gender roles of wife and mother has been acknowledged and confirmed by social scientists for decades: The combination of educating women and allowing them equal access to the many jobs of the paid labor force reduces their desires for early marriage and childbearing, while at the same time having fewer children has freed women to pursue more education and more and better jobs. Educating women not only delays their entry into marriage, but also reduces the age difference between themselves and their spouses (partners), especially in developing nations: When females marry young, they tend to have older husbands; delaying marriage thus allows females "to establish a sense of self, by allowing them a period of life between childhood and adulthood when they can assert their independence." This independence gives them greater power "in decisions that concern them, particularly decisions concerning marriage and whether to practice contraception within marriage" (Locoh 2009: 176).

Figure 4.8 uses the United States as an example of the close connection between the educational and work status of women and their fertility at the national level of analysis, while Figure 4.9 shows the same connection with family structure. The same pattern is found worldwide (see, e.g., Bhrolcháin and Beaujouan 2012): As women become more educated and more represented in the paid labor force, their fertility rates tend to drop, as does the percentage of children born into the traditional, two-parent family structure. More generally, children in the United States and across the world are increasingly more likely to be in living arrangements other than with two married parents, although the overwhelming majority of them are living with at least one biological parent (e.g., in the United States, 94% of children under the age of 18 live with at least one biological parent). Figure 4.10(a) shows how living arrangements for US children have changed since the early 1990s: Though the large majority of children are still living with two parents (68.5% in 2013), this percentage has dropped significantly since the late 1960s (when, in 1968, 85.4% of children were living with two parents). As will be discussed below, the erosion of the two-parent living arrangement for children has a generally deleterious effect on their well-being. However, Figure 4.10(a) reveals that the erosion essentially ended by the late 1990s, and since then about two-thirds of all US children are living with two parents; relatedly, since

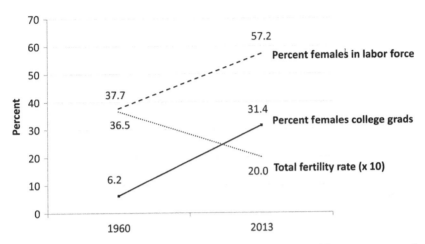

Figure 4.8: As US women have become more educated[a] and better represented in the paid labor force,[b] the US total fertility rate[c] has dropped significantly

Notes: [a] Percentage of females, age 25 and older, with four or more years of college (US Census Bureau 2014b).

[b] Percentage of females, age 16 and older, in the civilian labor force (Bureau of Labor Statistics 2014c).

[c] To maintain the scale on this graphic and thereby more clearly demonstrate the strong relationships among female labor force participation, female education, and fertility, the TFR has been multiplied by 10 (thus, in 1960, the actual TFR was 3.77, and in 2013, it was 2.01). Correlations ($N = 52$ years): female labor force participation and TFR $= -.64$ ($p < .001$); percentage of females with four or more years of college and TFR $= -.45$ ($p < .001$); female labor force participation and percentage of females with four or more years of college $= .89$ ($p < .001$).

Source: Raw data from US Census Bureau (2014c)

2007, there has been a decline and a gradual leveling-off of nonmarital childbearing (Curtin et al. 2014).

Note that race and ethnic background generally correlate with family structure, and much of this correlation is due to socioeconomic differences among race and ethnic groups. Thus, for example, Figure 4.9 shows how the percentage of children born to unmarried mothers has been on the rise in the United States for decades. However, this percentage varies greatly by race and ethnicity: in 2012, 29.3% of the births to non-Hispanic whites were to unmarried mothers (up from 9.5% in 1980), while the equivalent percentage for non-Hispanic blacks was 72.1 (up from 57.2% in 1980), and 53.5 for Hispanics (up from 23.5% in 1980; see Centers for Disease Control and Prevention 2014c). Relatedly,

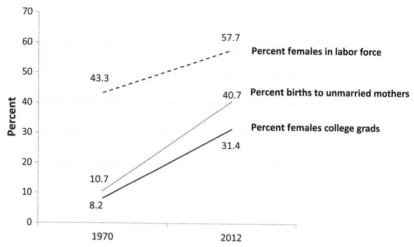

Figure 4.9: *As US women have become more educated and more represented in the paid labor force, they have become more independent and less likely to have their children in the context of marriage*[a]

Notes: [a] Percentage of all live births to unmarried mothers, ages 15–44 (Centers for Disease Control and Prevention 2014c).
[b] Correlations (N = nine five-year intervals): female labor force participation and percentage of births to unmarried mothers = .92 ($p < .001$); percentage of females with four or more years of college and percentage of births to unmarried mothers = .99 ($p < .0001$); female labor force participation and percentage of females with four or more years of college = .86 ($p < .003$).
Source: Raw data from US Census Bureau (2014c)

Figures 4.10(b)–4.10(d) reveal that the rise of the mother-only living arrangement for children has been much more dramatic for blacks and Hispanics than it has for whites.

Most of the children born to unmarried mothers remain with their mothers (86%), and if their mothers do not marry, the chances of the children living in poverty are many times greater than if their mothers do end up marrying – as marriage generally brings a second income-earner into the family, as well as allowing for shared childcare and an increased ability for the mother to work. Figure 4.11 shows the strong relationship between family structure and the chances of children living in poverty: If a child is living with a single mother, or with cohabiting but unmarried parents, he or she has a four-fold increased chance of living in poverty (a 10.9% chance if living with married parents vs a 45.8% chance if living with unmarried, cohabiting parents, vs a 45.3% chance if living with a single mother). This relationship exists more

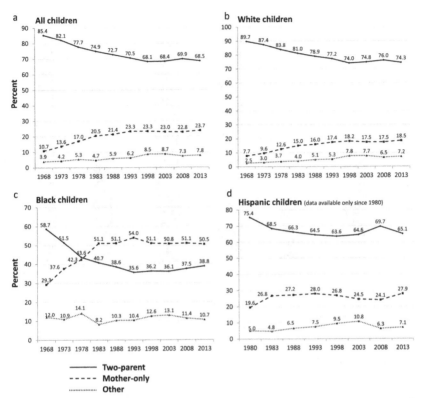

Figure 4.10: Family structures have changed significantly in the past half-century in the developed nations of the world, with an increasing percentage of children living in a mother-only household (the US example)
Source: Raw data from US Census Bureau (2014c)

generally worldwide (Mokomane 2014: 4; OECD 2011 8). Regarding the United States, in particular, most of its peer nations have stronger social safety nets and thus lower rates of child poverty: The average rate of child poverty was 12.4% in the developed nations of the OECD in 2007, while it was 20.6% in the United States; and these rates have remained relatively stable in succeeding years: for example, in 2012, the percentage of children, ages 0–17, living below the poverty line in the United States was 22.2 (see OECD 2009: 35; Vespa et al. 2013: 25).

Aside from reduced fertility, childbearing outside of marriage, and increases in female-headed households, three other indicators of the dramatic changes in family structure and gender role expectations are

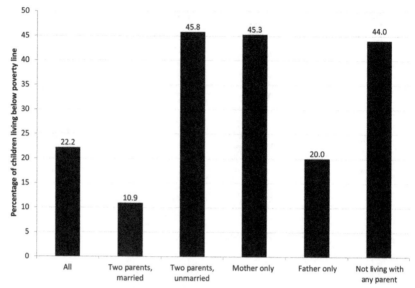

Figure 4.11: The living arrangements of children greatly affect their chances of living in poverty: Children under 18 are much more likely to be living under the federal poverty line if they live with a single mother or with unmarried parents than if they live with two married parents
Source: Raw data from Vespa et al. (2013: 25)

the reduction of the percentage of women marrying, the rising age at which they do marry, and the growing replacement of traditional marriage by cohabitation. Although these changes are taking place at different rates in developing versus developed nations, they are occurring worldwide. For example, Figure 4.12 shows that the proportion of women married before the age of 25 has dropped significantly in both developing and developed nations over the past half-century.

The decline in marriage rates has been heavily offset by the rise in long-term cohabiting couples. For example, in the United States there was a seven-fold increase in cohabiting couples between 1970 and 2010, and the norm has become for a couple to live together before marriage – with this being the case in half of first marriages since 2000 (Copen et al. 2013; Jacobsen et al. 2012: 4–5). Moreover, there is a rise in long-term cohabiting couples treating their cohabitation as a stable relationship, stable enough to have children: for example, in the United States, in 2002, 14% of births among women aged 15–44 occurred within cohabitation, but by 2010, this percentage had risen to 23 (see Copen et al. 2013).

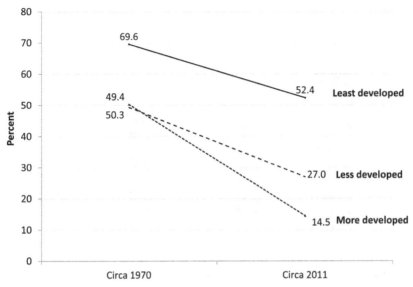

Figure 4.12: *During the last half-century, the percentage of women married before the age of 25 has dropped significantly in nations at all levels of socioeconomic development*
Source: Raw data from United Nations (2014i)

This replacement of marriage by cohabitation is especially widespread in developed nations (OECD 2011), though there are cultural differences. More particularly, in many Western and Northern European countries, long-term "cohabitation tends to be an alternative or substitute for marriage, reflected in the increasing number of couples who remain together without marrying, [while]…in the United States, cohabitation tends to be more of a prelude to marriage" (OECD 2011: 18; cf. Covre-Sussai 2013: 31). In the developing world, cohabitation varies even more strongly by culture – especially with regard to the power of religion in everyday life. In the Islamic nations of the Middle East and Northern Africa, cohabitation is rare as unmarried unions are strongly frowned upon, while the same is true in most of Asia (especially in East Asia, where Confucianism imbues many aspects of national cultures). However, in much of Sub-Saharan Africa, cohabitating couples and polygamy have long been culturally accepted, with the care for children spread across the extended family (the practice of *confiage* – the placing of one's children in the care of others; see Locoh 2009). Cohabitation in Latin America is similar to that in many developed nations, including the United States, in that it has two very different driving forces: For the

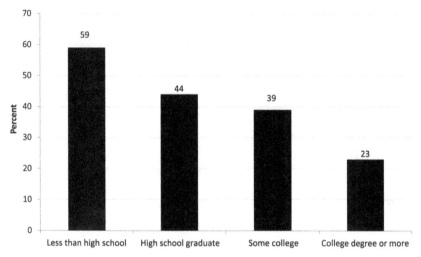

Figure 4.13: Percentage of heterosexual cohabitating (unmarried) couples with at least one child under the age of 18: The education level of the female partner strongly predicts whether the couple has a child
Source: Raw data from Jacobsen et al. (2012)

more prosperous, the key force is postmodernity and the release of women from traditional gender roles to pursue greater education and more rewarding careers, while for the less prosperous, the key force is poverty, with cohabiting individuals being drawn together to combine resources, but also being unsure of their economic ability to sustain the long-term commitment implied by formal marriage (see, e.g., Covre-Sussai 2013). Figure 4.13 speaks to these forces: In heterosexual cohabitating couples involving a college-educated woman, fewer than one in four couples have children under the age of 18, while for cohabiting couples where the woman has less than a high school education, more than one in two couples have children under 18. When college-educated women decide to have children, they are much more likely to have the economic security that makes them more confident in moving from cohabiting with their partners to marrying them (Jacobsen et al. 2012: 4).

Throughout much of Europe, Northern America, and Latin America, the power of religion has waned in the structuring of everyday life and there has been a growing acceptance of cohabiting (unmarried) couples, of children born out of wedlock, of same-sex marriages (or civil unions), and of single-parent heads of households – all influenced by the spread of the postmodern values of social tolerance and the preeminence of individual self-fulfillment and happiness over the sacrificing of these to the needs of the group (e.g., the family, the community, the tribe, or the religious organization; cf. Covre-Sussai 2013; OECD 2011). And in those areas where religion still holds sway, such as the Islamic Middle East and the *Bible Belt* of the southeastern and south central United States (where Protestant fundamentalism and evangelicalism are prevalent), rates of cohabitation and *multi-partnered fertility* (a parent having children from different partners) are comparatively low (see, e.g., Carlson and Furstenberg 2006; Lehre 2000; Wilcox 2008).[7]

Ultimately, the idea of "family" has broadened dramatically in the past half-century. From its traditional sense of a married couple with children living independently as a *nuclear family*, or such a couple living within the context of an *extended family* that includes close relatives (e.g., grandparents, siblings), it now encompasses "young couples with children, young couples with no children, single-parent families, couples whose children have left home, and elderly family members. Consideration also [has] to be given to the evolving structure of modern families that has emerged from recent trends in divorce, second marriages[,]... co-habitation, same-sex partnerships, and reconstituted [*blended*] families" (OECD 2011: 5). New family forms that do not involve young children are increasingly socially accepted and gaining in prevalence. However, even though also more socially accepted and increasingly found, new family forms where children find themselves living with a single parent or with a parent cohabitating with a nonparent pose many challenges for both the individuals involved and the greater society – as these family structures are linked with poverty and all of poverty's attendant problems (e.g., poorer health, poorer academic performance, increased addiction, increased incarceration, and premature death; also refer back to Figure 4.11). Societal-level solutions involve increasing the social safety net (e.g., cash transfers to the poor; universal access to healthcare; inclusion programs in public education), but there is also a growing general awareness of the advantages of two-parent households for children, and indeed in the United States the prevalence of these is no longer on the decline (refer to Figure 4.10; for a discussion of government policies that encourage marriage and relationship stability, see Wherry and Finegold 2004).

The Economic Fall-Out of an Aging Population in the Context of Declining Fertility

As noted earlier this chapter, a country with a TFR of less than 2.1 is below the *replacement level of fertility*. As of 2015, 83 countries, representing nearly half of the world's population, were below replacement fertility. Among the most affected regions are Europe (a TFR of 1.6), Northern America (1.8), and East Asia (1.5, which includes China, Japan, and South Korea). In 2013, half of the nations in the developed world reported to the UN that their national fertility policies were focused on increasing their population growth – and, in contrast, none of the world's four dozen least developed nations had such policies, and just 10% of developing nations had them (United Nations 2013h: 54). The major concern of nations with below-replacement-level fertility rates is the economic burden their aging populations are now placing on their working adults. Some 400 million people were born worldwide in the two decades following World War II (1946–65), the so-called *baby boomers*, and this generation has either reached retirement age, or will do so in the coming two decades. Moreover, they have reached the age when their healthcare needs are greatest. Finally, their retirement and healthcare costs will extend for much longer periods of time than in previous eras, as the baby boomers are the longest living generation in human history: Consider that in 1900, life expectancy in developed nations like the United States was less than 50, while by 2013, after climbing steadily throughout the twentieth century, it had reached 78 for both sexes, and 82 for females (see Chapter 3; see, also, Population Reference Bureau 2014). Because the generation following the baby boomers will be living as long or longer, the age distribution of the world's population is undergoing a dramatic shift. In 1950, 8% of the world's population were 60 or older (some 200 million people); by 2013, this percentage had risen to 11.7 (841 million); and by 2050, the percentage will reach 21.1 (2 billion). The numbers are just as staggering for those 80 and older: In 1950, they comprised 0.6% of the global population (about 15 million people); by 2013, 1.6% (110 million); and by 2050, 4.0% (400 million). By 2025, the population over 60 will be growing 3.5 times as rapidly as the total population (2.8% compared to 0.8%; see Beard et al. 2012: 5; United Nations 2013k: xii). This rise in the older population – which is affecting developed nations now, but will affect most developing nations in the coming few decades – is dramatically illustrated in Figures 4.14 and 4.15.

Taking the United States as an example, Figure 4.16 shows the huge change in the number of contributors to the old-age retirement trust fund of the federal Social Security system compared to the number of beneficiaries since 1950. It is clear that the current generation of working adults is under a much heavier burden than were their counterparts from previous generations: in 1950, there were 16.5 workers to every one retiree; by 1960, this had dropped to 5.1; then to 3.7 by 1970; and as of 2015, this ratio stood at 2.8. As of 2021, the Social Security trust

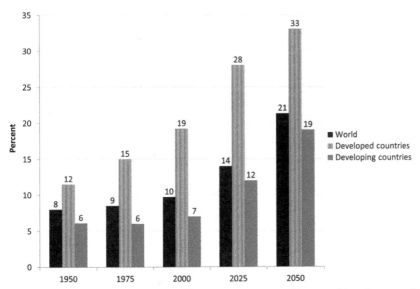

Figure 4.14:   Percentage of the population aged 60 or older: world and national level of economic development, 1950–2050
Sources: Raw data from United Nations (2002: 11 and 2013i)

fund will be running at a deficit; its reserves will keep it in the black until 2035, at which time benefits will have to be significantly reduced or contributions significantly increased. In the words of the trustees of the Social Administration's Old-Age and Survivors Insurance Trust Fund, the impending collapse of the fund is a product of "the retirement of the baby-boom generation...increas[ing] the number of beneficiaries much faster than the numbers of workers increases, as subsequent lower-birth-rate generations replace the baby-boom generation at working age" (Social Security Administration 2013: 3, 55–6).

The US situation is replicated throughout the developed world (United Nations 2013k), plus in selected developing countries – the most promi-nent of which is China. China will see an increase in the proportion aged 60 years or over, from 12.4% in 2010, to 28.1% by 2040; indeed, this increase will be the fastest of all of the world's nations and will concomi-tantly lead to one of the world's heaviest age-dependency burdens (Feng et al. 2014: 25; United Nations 2013k: 14). This rapid change in its structure is due, in part, to China's economic development, which encour-ages lower fertility rates and increased life expectancies in all national contexts; but it is also due, in part, to its aggressive One-Child Policy (officially adopted in 1979; see the preceding discussion in this chapter). China now has 150 million young adults with no siblings, and social

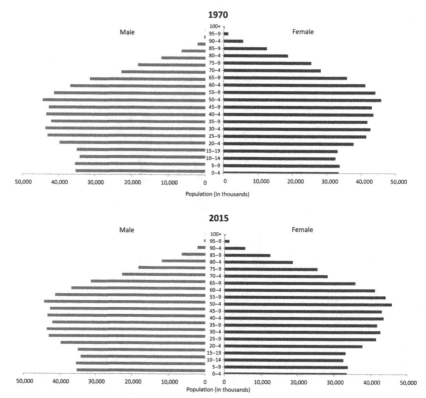

Figure 4.15: Population pyramids for developed countries, 1970 versus 2015
Note: Compared to 1970, notice the very small base of young people in 2015, who will be expected to support the much fatter sections of the pyramid as they grow older – an expectation that cannot be maintained at current retirement and benefit levels of the over-60 population.
Sources: Raw data from United Nations (2016a, 2016b)

demographers have labeled their forthcoming difficulties with taking care of the much larger preceding generation as the *4:2:1 problem*: As is the case in most developing countries, adult children in China are responsible for taking care of their aging parents and grandparents; thus one child is facing the responsibility of caring for the needs of his or her two aging parents and his or her four aging grandparents. The problem is compounded because in the growing urban areas of China, Western values emphasizing the nuclear family over the extended family have taken hold, and rising numbers of only children are leaving their parents' home upon marriage. Moreover, many of these couples coming from one-child backgrounds are increasingly imbued with the postmodern

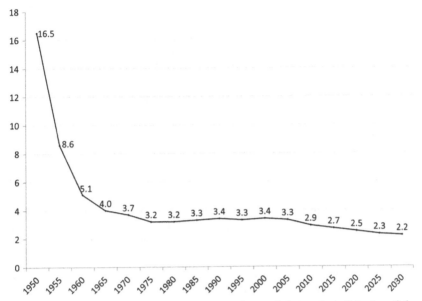

Figure 4.16: The ratio of contributors (working adults) to beneficiaries of the Old-Age and Survivors Insurance Trust Fund of the US Social Security System, 1950–2030

Note: The continually declining ratio will bankrupt the system by 2035 – the low number of current contributors compared to the much higher numbers of previous generations cannot keep up with the costs of the retirement system.

Source: Raw data from Social Security Administration (2013: 55–6)

values discussed earlier in this chapter and choosing to develop their individual potential and happiness at the expense of not having children of their own.

The traditional family structure in China has been a modified form of the extended family, with the oldest son and his wife living with the son's parents, and other children moving out. This *stem family*, as social scientists have labeled it, is still common, but the tradition that pushes parents toward investing heavily in a son who will eventually care for them has been convulsed, such that the only child available might be a daughter. Parents with their only child being female "have little choice but to invest in [her], leading to breakthroughs in gender differences in individual achievements and post-marriage relations,...[and] nowadays the only daughter, especially in urban areas, will not be neglected because of her gender, but will be treated as well as would have been the case had she been a boy" (Feng et al. 2014: 21–2). The traditional system of a wife moving into her husband's parents' household has changed to where it is now just as likely for a husband to move in with his wife's parents. All of these changes – from childless couple-only families, to the stem family involving a daughter remaining at home and bringing her husband into the family – have had the social consequence of increasing the education and power of women in Chinese society. But they have also set up the impending collapse of the traditional care system for aging adults: There simply aren't enough children to support the rapidly growing population of older (60+) Chinese adults.

At the micro level of analysis, an increasing number of parents are decreasing "their reliance on their children supporting them in their old age" and are increasing their savings and wherewithal "to support themselves independently" (Feng et al. 2014: 22). At the macro level, the Chinese leadership has become highly proactive in recent years to prepare for the disjunction between its rapidly growing aged population and its diminishing population of younger working adults. China's efforts in this area are reflective of the recent efforts of its counterpart nations in the developed world that also have below-replacement-level fertility rates. These efforts include the following:

(1) *Continually rethinking and retooling its One-Child Policy.* For example, it frequently relaxes the Policy by allowing for more exemptions: allowing a married couple where each partner is an only child to have a second child; allowing rural couples having a daughter to have a chance of getting a son with the birth of a second child; allowing rural couples in poor areas to have a second child so as to help with the support of the family; giving more control to local governments in enforcing or relaxing the one-child mandate according to local needs, including taking into consideration an increased number of aging adults that on the horizon might be seen as overwhelming the smaller generation of younger working adults. In all, there are 22 exemptions to the One-Child Policy, with more likely to come (see Gu et al. 2007: 130–4). At least some observers believe that the Policy has run its course and that "the question... is not whether, but when, the One-Child Policy will be phased out" (Feng et al. 2012: 126).

(2) *Increasing the frequency and accuracy of its population forecasts.* As of 2014, China's government has only had its national decennial census upon which to base forecasts for the housing, healthcare, and other material needs of its aging population. According to Chen Xiaohong, vice-minister of China's powerful National Health and Family Planning Commission (NHFPC): "That could hardly meet the government's need to understand population dynamics and to make forecasts

to better guide decision-making and public service management...[and] planners would find it helpful to have detailed data at hand for more accurate and practical decision-making" (as quoted in Shan 2014). Thus, starting in 2015, the NHPFC began gathering large-sample quarterly and yearly data on population dynamics, much the same way that virtually all developed nations have done for decades.

(3) *Raising the age of retirement.* As have many of its counterpart nations in the developed world with rapidly aging populations in the context of smaller younger generations, China is raising its age of retirement. When famed social scientist Jared Diamond was 46, he arrived at New Guinea village to begin doing field research. When the local people learned his age, "they gasped out '*setengah mati!*,' meaning 'half-dead,' and they assigned a teen-aged boy to walk constantly beside [him] to ensure that [he] would not come to grief." In short, in rural New Guinea, "where relatively few people reach the age of 60, even 50-year-olds are regarded as old" (Diamond 2012: 211). And so it is in many developing societies where death rates were traditionally high in the not so distant past: An individual in his or her 50s is considered quite old. Such is the case in China, where the retirement age is 60 for men, 55 for female civil servants, and 50 for other female workers. However, by 2012, two-thirds of China's provincial governments' retirement trust funds were running in the red, and the national government is predicted to raise the retirement age for all workers to 65. As is often the case – for example, in the United States, the retirement age for full benefits is currently being gradually changed from 65 to 67 (Social Security Administration 2014a) – the switching to a higher retirement age in China is to be gradually phased in (e.g., one proposal is to add one year to the retirement age for every two calendar years, starting in 2016; see Zhang 2012; Zuo 2014). To help resolve their own disjunctures between the growing size of their aged populations and the diminished sizes of their working populations, between 2008 and 2012, 61 national governments raised their statutory retirement age, while 89 national governments altered their pension systems to keep them running in the black (e.g., by reducing benefits or cost-of-living adjustments; note that 47 nations reported that they adjusted both their retirement ages and their pension funds; see United Nations 2013h: 6). Not surprisingly, raising the age of retirement and reducing benefits is not popular with much of the general public, especially those within a decade or two of retirement. For example, in China, when asked in a national survey about the new proposal to raise the retirement age, 54% were opposed versus 26% in support (with the remaining 20% undecided; see Zuo 2014). As one of the interviewees responded: "Where can a person aged 55 to 65 find a job? Even if he

gets a job as a doorkeeper or street cleaner, who would pay for his pension and health insurance?" (Wang Lishi, a public servant in Jiangsu province). Similar results are found whenever the US public is polled on the issue. As survey analyst Guy Molyneux assessed these findings: "For the public, cutting benefits is the problem, not the solution" (as quoted in Orr 2011).

(4) *Increasing funding of the social safety net.* During the 1960s and 1970s, China became famous for its barefoot doctors and rural coopera- tive medical insurance system. For urban areas, health insurance was government funded. However, the moves to open up the economy in the late 1970s included the abandonment of these safety nets for the popula- tion, which especially affected older individuals – as they tend to have more numerous and more serious health problems. In recent years, and in response to its aging population, the government now requires employ- ers and city employees to make monthly payments into municipal-level insurance pools. Per earlier discussions on the One-Child Policy, Chinese governance allows for considerable variation in the implementation of national policies at the provincial, prefecture, and local levels of govern- ment; thus there are wide variations in what is provided for and the extent to which family members are covered. However, as of 2011, well over 300 million workers and urban residents had recovered some level of medical insurance – representing about half of the total urban popula- tion (Banister et al. 2011).

Similar efforts to increase funding of the social safety net, especially as it protects the elderly, have been implemented in recent years by many national governments. For example, in the United States, the basic federal program for medical care of the 65-and-over population is Medicare. The greater need for the funding of this program – which is expected to cascade from 50 million recipients in 2014 to 80 million by 2030 – has resulted over the past few decades in periodic adjustments to the payroll taxes that fund it. For instance, the base tax rate of 2.9% has incorpo- rated a progressive feature since 2007, with those making more paying at a higher tax rate. Thus, for basic funding, the payroll tax was raised in 2013 to 3.8% on earnings above $200,000 for individuals and $250,000 for couples. Similarly, for selected medical services, Medicare enrollees are required to make a monthly insurance payment, which is adjusted upward as earnings increase – as of 2014, from a minimum of about $105 for the poorest enrollees (individuals with annual incomes less than $85,000) to about $320 for the most prosperous (individuals annual incomes over $214,000). Relatedly, the funding for the retirement part of the social safety net has seen similar upward adjustments in the tax rate: For example, in 1990, only the first $51,300 of an individual's income had the 12.4% tax applied to it, but by 2014, the first $117,000 was taxed.[8]

(5) *Encouraging migration.* Because migrants tend to be young and motivated by economic inducements, and thus more likely to work and pay taxes, many nations, including China, have been encouraging either international migration to their countries or in-migration within the country's borders to provide a better balance between employment needs and available workers. In China, there is a history of severe restrictions of *in-migration*: that is, unlike most nations, an impoverished rural or small-town resident cannot simply pull up stakes and seek his or her fame and fortune in the city. Migrants who move without government permission are denied access to basic services to themselves and their children, including healthcare, housing, and schooling. As poignantly described by Chen Guidi and Wu Chuntao (2006: 199), two well-known chroniclers of the daily life of Chinese peasants:

> Anhui is a large and populous province, an excellent source of labor. By 2000...there were 10 million surplus laborers in the Anhui countryside, 40 percent of the rural labor force. Agriculture had become a losing enterprise. The peasants had toiled on the soil for untold generations and had looked on the soil as the source of life itself, but the soil had become a burden. Thus an army of peasants turned their backs on the soil and marched into the city.
>
> In the city, however, all of the benefits of the urban residents such as the newly invented "basic insurance," "medical insurance," and "housing benefits," and so on were beyond the peasants' reach. Since the "residence permit" forbade them permanent status in the city, the vast army of incoming peasants were doomed to remain migrants in the city. (Note: In 1958, the national government introduced urban residence permits; they were issued only to those already living in cities, so it became nearly "impossible for peasants to settle in the city with full legal rights" [Chen and Wu 2006: 176].)

However, with the realization that the aging urban labor force needed an increasing larger number of fresh replacements, most provincial governments, including that of Anhui, have begun easing the acquisition of the residency permits required by rural migrants to qualify for the social safety net programs (Bao et al. 2011: 565; Chen and Wu 2006: 203). A time-series empirical analysis of the effects of this easing process reveals that it is having the desired effect of encouraging in-migration to urban areas from the countryside (Bao et al. 2011).

Regarding encouraging international migration *to* China, this was until very recently an almost impossible policy to imagine. Historically,

China has been an exporter of young adults to the growing economies of Southeast Asia, Europe, the United States, and Canada. For most of the past 200 years, the bulk of these workers have been hired into low-paying jobs that native populations could not fill, either because they lacked the numbers or because they preferred better-paying, less arduous work. However, in recent years, emigrants from China have been increasingly well educated and have migrated to economies like that of the United States that have unfilled, high-paying jobs in selected high-tech engineering and science sectors. This phenomenon is part of a combination of three major forces that have created needs in China for immigrant workers; the other two are: (a) the need for well-educated liaison workers who can negotiate Chinese factories into the global economy by connecting them to multinational corporations (these workers are called "seagulls" by the Chinese); and (b) the unintended effect of the One-Child Policy on the sex ratio – whereby the birth of males has been prioritized, including by the illegal abortion of female fetuses, with the result being an estimated 115 males for every 100 females in the current under-25 population (*World Factbook* 2014). The upshot: In recent years, an estimated 2 million migrants come to China annually for work, with as many as 10% of them planning to stay, while "foreign brides" from Laos, Myanmar, North Korea, and Russia have immigrated, illegally, by the tens of thousands. The need for selected highly skilled workers to enhance integration into the global economy and for young women to rebalance the sex ratio has forced China to begin developing its first-ever set of migration policies geared toward handling immigrants who intend to stay permanently, as opposed to its traditional policies meant to handle temporary visits by international students, tourists, and workers representing foreign firms. Since China has no real tradition of handling immigrants, this process has, not surprisingly, moved forward with great difficulty at a snail's pace, as even countries accustomed to handling foreign immigration, such as the United States, have difficulty in crafting coherent immigration policies that are politically popular. (To wit, the United States has been struggling, unsuccessfully, for more than two decades over how to handle its estimated 11 to 12 million undocumented immigrants.) To attract well-educated seagulls and foreign investors, the national government instituted a *green card* system in 2003, whereby these kinds of individuals can apply for permanent residence. The system was revised in 2012 and again in 2014, with the latter revision easing the requirements to obtain a green card. While green cards are aimed at attracting high-end talent to make China more competitive in the global market, a *blue card* system has begun in at least one province, Yunnan, to attract foreign brides. To bring these immigrant women out of the shadows of their illegal presence, blue-card acquisition gives them legal status and a degree of security – including access to medical care and schooling for themselves and their children.[9]

In summarizing the major importance of encouraging immigration to counteract the economic burdens that an aging population places on its younger generation of working adults, a US Council on Foreign Relations taskforce on immigration policy concluded that:

> Even countries seen as new economic rivals to the United States, such as China and Korea, face significant declines in their working-age populations and are becoming more interested in attracting immigrants themselves. *The Task Force finds that, though immigration will not substantially arrest the aging of the American population, openness to immigration means that the United States will face fewer of the economic and social pressures that will mount as a growing number of Americans retire and are supported by a smaller working-age population.* When the United Nations examined global demographic trends in 2000, it found that the United States was one of the few countries admitting enough migrants to expand its working-age population. (Alden et al. 2009: 13; italics in original)

Age Dependency Ratios: Are Those Traditionally Defined as "Old" Really That Old?

Not all observers consider the national aging of a population in the context of a low fertility rate as overly problematic. On the contrary, they see this situation as a boon for humanity and contend that the smaller generation of the current era will lead to a higher quality of life.

There are four major reasons for this optimism. First, worker productivity is closely tied to level of education and training. Moreover, because technology has increasingly replaced human effort for low-level work (to wit, assembly lines in factories once staffed by people are now often serviced by robotic devices), educated individuals have much lower rates of unemployment. A smaller younger generation allows a society to concentrate more resources on the schooling of each individual. Moreover, with fewer siblings, parents and grandparents can transfer more of their income and wealth to each younger person – income and wealth that can increase their opportunities for longer and better schooling. For example, an empirical analysis of schooling in Germany, an archetypical nation experiencing an aging population combined with a decreasing fertility rate, leads to the prediction that its university-educated population will nearly double in the next four decades – from the current quarter to nearly half of the adult population (Kluge et al. 2014: 5).

Second, the same case can be made for healthcare. With fewer young people, society, in general, and individual families, in particular, are able to concentrate more medical and health-related resources per person than when the younger generation is larger. Healthier individuals contribute more to the economy and tax the social safety net less.

Japan is an example of these first two processes in action: The productivity of its highly educated workforce has led to a *per capita* economic growth that has been the fastest growing in the world since 2000. (Despite the fact that its *overall* economic growth has been sluggish by international standards; in short, at the national level, the economy looks somewhat dour, but as experienced by *individuals*, it is leading to increasingly higher levels of prosperity.) Its youth rank in the top five of the standardized tests in mathematics, reading, and science that the OECD periodically gives to 15-year-olds in 65 countries (most of these being highly economically developed; see OECD 2014). And even though Japan is spending more on education per student than it ever has, its overall spending in this area has fallen as the size of its student population has fallen. Regarding health, it has the highest life expectancy in the world (84 years); and despite it having the oldest population in the world, the robust physical and mental well-being of its people, including the very oldest, is one of the reasons it spends half of what the United States does on healthcare – even though Japan has a universal healthcare system and the United States does not. (Japan spends 8% of GDP on healthcare, compared to 16% for the United States; see Coggan 2012; Pearce 2014.) More generally, individuals living in developed countries, as well as selected developing countries, can expect not only longer life, but also a longer proportion of their lives spent in good health. For example, empirical extrapolations of the German population reveal that the typical man will spend 80% of his life in good health by 2050, compared to the current percentage of 63. Moreover, recent studies of long-term care expenditures in developed nations reveal that these expenditures "tend to be concentrated at the end of life, during the two years prior to death. This suggests that the increases in life expectancy are not necessarily related to soaring health care costs" (Kluge et al. 2014: 6).

Third, analyses of the carbon emissions produced by those over 60 compared to their younger counterparts reveal that older individuals have lifestyles that reduce these emissions. Part of the explanation is their reduced travel involving work and school-age children. An analysis of German carbon emissions shows that its aging population will reduce these by 20% between 2014 and 2050 (Kluge et al. 2014: 6). Relatedly, as the larger older generation dies off and is replaced by the younger smaller generation, fewer people will mean less stress on the environment regarding food production and preserving the amount and quality of fresh water (the neo-Malthusian view – see Chapter 1).

Finally, many observers point out that the current situation has a large self-resolving component: As the current smaller generation ages, it will replace the larger aged population of the preceding generation: "While it is certainly true that the current and expected changes in age structure will have a negative impact on, for example, public finances, in the medium term, we expect to see much milder consequences in the long run" (Kluge et al. 2014: 2).

Observers emphasizing the positive effects of the increased-age/decreased-fertility situation agree that national communities must think more imaginatively on how to handle it. The traditional solution, of having many younger working adults to care for the fewer numbers of their parents' and grandparents' generations, needs to be set aside in favor of more creative solutions. Indeed, they question the operational definitions of the age-related *dependency ratios* as defined by the UN (2014j) and widely promulgated by demographers; these ratios are meant to assess the degree to which the working adults of a population are burdened by the very young and the very old. Consider, for example, the

Age dependency ratio

$$= \frac{\text{Population} < \text{age 15} + \text{population} \geq \text{age 65 in year}_i}{\text{Population in year}_i \text{ of population Ages 15–64}} \times 100$$

where i is a particular year.

Thus, for example, for the United States in 2014, the

$$\text{Age dependency ratio} = \frac{61,801,455 + 46,179,004}{210,911,644} \times 100 = 51.2$$

This ratio is often disaggregated by the components of the numerator, and thus the

Youth dependency ratio

$$= \frac{\text{Population} < \text{age 15 in Year}_i}{\text{Population in year}_i \text{ of population Ages 15–64}} \times 100$$

and the

Old-age dependency ratio

$$= \frac{\text{Population} \geq \text{age 65 in year}_i}{\text{Population in year}_i \text{ of population ages 15–64}} \times 100$$

Thus, for example, for the United States in 2014, the

$$\text{Youth dependency ratio} = \frac{61,801,455}{210,911,644} \times 100 = 29.3$$

and the

$$\text{Old-age dependency ratio} = \frac{46,179,004}{210,911,644} \times 100 = 21.9$$

Figure 4.17 displays the old-age dependency ratios for the developed versus developing worlds as they have changed since 1950, as well as their predicted changes through 2050. By the traditional definition of the old-age dependency ratio, the coming decades look bleak for the global community, especially for economically developed nations. However, optimistic interpreters of this ratio contend that the notion of "old age" starting in one's 60s should be discarded as it does not describe the contemporary realities of modern medical and public healthcare systems keeping aging adults physically and mentally robust – often well into their 80s and even early 90s. They contrast a country like Sweden, where nearly two-thirds of the population aged 60–4 participate in the paid labor force, with a country like Germany, where just a little more than a third in this age group are participating, as demonstrating the potential of a society to begin extending the working lives of individuals (Kluge et al. 2014: 4).

Indeed, in the long and broad view of human history, the notion of "retirement" from work has largely been unknown. As summarized by Jared Diamond (2012: 234, 239):

> Formal retirement from the labor force...became common only in the late 19th century. Until then, people just worked until their bodies or minds wore out. Now retirement is almost universal as a policy in industrial countries, at an age ranging from 50 to 70, depending on the country....The problem for society as a whole is to use older people for what they are good at and like to do, rather than...stupidly imposing policies of mandatory retirement at some arbitrary age (as remains regrettably widespread in Europe).

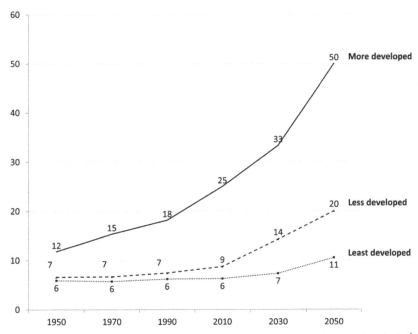

Figure 4.17:   Old-age dependency ratios[a] for least, less, and more developed[b] nations: 1950–2050

Notes: [a] Old-age dependency ratio = (population ages 65 and older/population ages 15–64) × 100; inverting this ratio, the data reveal that in 1950 there were about 8 working adults under the age of 65 for every individual 65 and older in more developed countries; by 2010, this inverted ratio had fallen to 4, and by 2050 it will be 2.
[b] See Chapter 1 for the UN's operational definitions of least, less, and more developed countries.
Source: Raw data from United Nations (2013k: 24)

In the words of Dr Margaret Chan, Director of the WHO, nations that recognize the potential of their older populations will reap "a sizeable *'longevity dividend,'* and will have a competitive advantage over those that do not" (as quoted in Beard et al. 2012: 3). An important key to realizing this dividend will be the retooling of public policy to encourage the employment of older workers. This would involve:

(1) catering to older employees' desire for flexible roles and schedules; (2) investing in worker wellness programs to enhance attendance and productivity and avoid unnecessary healthcare and turnover costs as the workforce ages; and (3) taking advantage of the new core business opportunities that will accompany population aging, such as designing

and marketing consumer products and services that are customized to the physical needs, the financial capacities, the interests, and the channels of influence that characterize the "silver generation." (Beard et al. 2012: 7)

Main Points and Key Terms

1　A society in which the average woman bears just one or two children during her lifetime tells us that females are under little cultural or social pressure to have many children. This lack of pressure often reflects a high level of economic development, ensuring that almost all children make it to adulthood. In contrast, if the average woman is having four or more children, it indicates she is under pressure to produce many children, as the society has a low level of economic development and thus incurs many premature deaths.

2　The total fertility rate (TFR) is the preferred measurement of a society's fertility rate: it has the intuitively pleasing interpretation of indicating the number of children a female can expect to have during her lifetime, and it adjusts for age differences that exist among different populations – thus allowing for comparisons across time, social groups, and geographic areas.

3　The replacement level of fertility is operationally defined as a 2.1 TFR in developed countries: one child to replace the female; one to replace a male; and a tiny fraction (0.1) to account for childhood deaths and women who never bear children. Because of a higher infant mortality rate, the replacement level of fertility in developing societies is generally higher (e.g., 3 or 4, depending upon the level of development).

4　Although many developing nations in Africa, Asia, and Latin America were able to sidestep much of the otherwise-required level of economic development that occurred in Western Europe and Northern America to bring down their death rates, socioeconomic development is still a strong predictor of fertility. A key mechanism driving high fertility levels in very poor nations is the high infant mortality rate, which encourages a "be fruitful and multiply" cultural orientation.

5　Government programs can have significant effects in bringing down fertility, though they have been less successful in reversing fertility rates that have become too low. China's One-Child Policy is the preeminent example of the power of government to lower fertility.

Pro-natalist programs are popular in many developed nations, almost all of which have TFRs well under the replacement rate of 2.1. These programs include generous tax deductions for children, paid parental leave, and assistance in providing childcare; however, they have generally produced little or no success.

6 At the individual level of analysis, important predictors of fertility include age of marriage and socioeconomic status. Women who marry young, or have their first child at a young age regardless of marital status, have a longer opportunity to have many children and tend to do so. Well-educated women tend to have fewer children; in part, this is because of the opportunity costs of having a child (e.g., being less able to take advantage of high-paying jobs that can accompany high levels of education); and, in part, this reflects greater access to and understanding of birth control (and thus preventing unwanted pregnancies).

7 Another important set of individual-level predictors of having a first or subsequent child revolve around belonging to an intimate social circle where others are having children. The social interactions in such a circle invoke mechanisms encouraging the desire to have a child – these mechanisms including social learning, social pressure, social support, and social contagion.

8 Economic development frees women from having to bear many children, and opens up opportunities for education, for participation in the paid labor force, and for personal development. In turn, the cultural emphases on traditional gender roles and families have been altered dramatically – in the rising prevalence and cultural acceptance of nontraditional family forms. This cultural change is captured in the notion of the second demographic transition.

9 The rise of new family forms that are conducive to individual development stands in stark contrast to the phenomenon of child brides that is still common in much of the developing world. Excluding China, one in three girls is married before the age of 18 in developing countries, and one in two in UN-designated least developed countries. Child brides are especially encouraged by a distorted sex ratio: that is, when there not enough women in their 20s or early 30s for the number of men in this age range wanting to marry.

10 As of 2015, 83 countries, representing nearly half of the world's population, were below the replacement level of fertility. The consequence is a small younger generation that will feel mounting financial pressures in supporting the larger generations of their parents and grandparents. Some observers view this situation as ultimately a boon for humankind as fewer children means greater investments can be made in each one – resulting in better health,

better education, better economic productivity, and a better ability to develop and sustain a healthy environment. Key to this boon actually being realized will be a cultural redefinition of what it means to be old (it does not mean being less productive) and of significantly raising the age of retirement.

Review Questions

1 What is the key advantage of using the *total fertility rate* instead of the *crude birth rate* when doing cross-national comparisons?

2 What does a high versus a low *total fertility rate* tell us about a particular country?

3 What is the operational definition of the *replacement level of fertility*? Would it be the same for developing versus developed countries? Why or why not?

4 What is the key intervening variable that connects level of economic development with fertility? What empirical evidence is there that confirms this?

5 China's One-Child Policy contributed to the decline in its total fertility rate. However, some observers contend that the Policy was not the only major reason for this decline, perhaps not even the most important. What evidence supports this contention?

6 What kinds of interventions have developed nations used in recent decades to increase their total fertility rates? How successful have these interventionist programs and policies been?

7 Discuss at least two of the interpretations used to explain why there is a strong inverse relationship between socioeconomic status and fertility at the micro level of analysis. Which of these seems most important to you?

8 Discuss two of the social forces accounting for the persistence of child marriage in developing countries. Do these forces appear to be on the wane?

9 What postmodern values can been used to account for falling fertility worldwide?

10 Some social scientists contend that a national population experiencing a large cohort of its population moving into "old age" in the context of falling fertility rates such that there will be fewer working adults to support the retirement and healthcare costs of the older cohort is actually a blessing in disguise. What lies behind this contention?

Suggested Readings and Online Sources

The same readily available data sets on-line that provide health- and mortality-related statistics at the national level of analysis also include fertility-related statistics (e.g., adolescent fertility rates, crude birth rates, total fertility rates, and the use of birth control). See these sources at the end of Chapter 3.

Individual countries have national offices that keep track of fertility data. For example, in the United States, the Centers for Disease Control and Prevention annually publishes a large number of *National Vital Statistics Reports*, with topics including fertility, marriage, and divorce. These reports often provide detailed breakdowns of the data by a variety of social background characteristics, including age of mother/age of father, education, ethnicity, race, and poverty status. These reports sometimes also include international comparisons.

Hans Rosling's *Gapminder* videos cover many aspects of fertility, including cross-national comparisons on the impact of religion on fertility (2012). Rosling's persuasive and evidence-based *TED Talk* demonstrates that macro-level differences in religion among nations (e.g., Christian vs Islamist vs Confucianist/Buddhist) explain very little about their huge drops in fertility over the past half-century. Instead, the factors emphasized in this chapter are the critically important determinants in explaining fertility decline – including poverty, the education of women and their entry into the paid labor force, and government-encouraged and ready access to modern means of birth control. The influence of religion on fertility is highest where religious communities are dense and segregated from the larger society, with a classic example being the Muslim-Arab population of Israel. (This population's fertility rate is much higher than that of the Jewish population of Israel; Arabs tend to be segregated into smaller towns, while Jews are dispersed across rural, small-town, and urban environments.) In this kind of social situation, the power of traditional religious values emphasizing the family formation and the power of the family in organizing everyday life become translated into strong community-based pressures for women to play out traditional gender roles of marriage and childbearing (see Calvin Goldscheider's classic 1999 article, "Religious Values, Dependencies, and Fertility: Evidence and Implications from Israel"). A similar situation exists in much of rural India and is dramatically presented in the NOVA video originally produced for public television, *World in the Balance: The Population Paradox* (2004). In Part I of this video, an Indian woman who almost died while giving birth to her eighth child is interviewed. Healthcare workers tell her that another pregnancy may well kill her. Nevertheless, her husband and mother-in-law want her to try for another son – a highly prized asset in traditional Indian culture.

A key reason for the differences among ethnic, racial, and religious groups in fertility emphasized in this chapter is the differences in their socioeconomic standing. Another key reason, the differences in their age structures, is examined in Jeffrey S. Passell, Gretchen Livingston, and D'Vera Cohn's *Explaining Why Minority Births Now Outnumber White Births* (2012). These authors observe that minority populations in the United States are younger than whites, "so are more likely to be having and raising children."

Vanessa L. Fong's *Only Hope – Coming of Age under China's One-Child Policy* (2004) presents a wealth of survey and ethnographic research on the economic, emotional, and social effects of the One-Child Policy on the generation of "singletons" that has come of age in China. Ironically, the distorted sex ratio in China that many observers blame on the One-Child Policy has not made marriage for many of the single daughters of the growing middle class any easier. (In general, when men outnumber women by a significant margin, almost all women end up marrying.) In her *Leftover Women: The Resurgence of Gender Inequality in China*, sociologist Leta Hong Fincher (2014) finds the national state-sponsored media campaign in China to encourage women to marry, at seemingly all costs, quite degrading. Chinese social policy analysts recognize that resulting *bare branches* (a common term for single men in China) are problematic for Chinese society, as young, single men are more likely to be involved in alcohol and drug abuse, as well as criminal behavior, compared to their married counterparts (see Monica Das

Gupta, Avraham Ebenstein, and Ethan Sharygin's *China's Marriage Market and Upcoming Challenges for Elderly Men*, 2010; also see Valerie Hudson and Andrea M. den Boer's *Bare Branches: The Security Implications of Asia's Surplus Male Population*, 2004).

The problem of child marriage in developing countries is given critical examinations in *Child Marriage* (Council on Foreign Relations 2013), *Marrying Too Young: End Child Marriage* (United Nations 2012f), and *This Old Man Can Feed Us, You Will Marry Him: Child and Forced Marriage in South Sudan* (Human Rights Watch 2013). This is one of the many women's fertility, health, and welfare issues monitored by both the UN (*UN Women*, 2016c) and the WHO (*Women's Health*, 2016).

The importance of intimate social circles in encouraging or discouraging individuals' and couples' decisions on the timing and level of childbearing is succinctly and clearly presented in Paola Scommegna's *Family, Friends Help Shape Childbearing Choices* (2014).

The myriad of new family forms that have arisen in the developed world, as well as in much of the developing world, are given in-depth treatment in H. Elizabeth Peters and Claire M. Kamp Dush (eds), *Marriage and Family: Perspectives and Complexities* (2009). After laying the groundwork with a thorough discussion of historical and cross-cultural perspectives on family forms, this work examines the most common of contemporary forms – including single-parent, long-term cohabitation, blended families (remarriage where children live with a biological parent and a step parent), and gay unions with children. The OECD provides a thorough analysis of trends in family forms in its *The Future of Families to 2030: A Synthesis Report* (2011), while the UN tracks comprehensive indicators on marriage, divorce, and family forms with its periodically updated *World Marriage Data* report (e.g., 2014i). One of the best summaries of *second demographic transition theory*, which sees the new family forms as critical to the worldwide dramatic drop in fertility rates, and which sees these new family forms as an outgrowth of postmodern values emphasizing individual development and fulfillment, can be found in Ron Lesthaeghe's *The Unfolding Story of the Second Demographic Transition* (2010).

The debate on whether aging populations in the context of falling birth rates are ultimately a burden or a boon for national populations receives sophisticated treatment in John R. Beard, Simon Biggs, David Bloom, et al.'s *Global Population Ageing: Peril or Promise?* (2012), while comprehensive crossnational data, projections, and analyses on aging populations can be found in the UN's *World Population Ageing 2013* (2013k). Empirical extrapolations of data on the current German population, which fits the classic profile of an aging population in the context of low national fertility, lend support to the optimistic view that in the short run this situation will burden working adults and national economies, but in the moderate term (two decades from now), the situation will increase the quality of life; see Fanny Kluge, Emilio Zagheni, Elke Loichinger, and Tobias Vogt's "The Advantages of Demographic Change after the Wave: Fewer and Older, but Healthier, Greener, and More Productive?" (2014). The major nonprofit HelpAge International (2016) strongly supports the position that aging populations result in a net benefit for society.

5

Migration

The story of human coexistence is always also the story of migrations. Over the course of time probably only a small minority of people have remained settled in one and the same place for many generations.
Ludger Pries (1999)

International migration ranks as one of the most important factors in global change. There are several reasons to expect the [current] "age of migration" to endure: Persistent inequalities in wealth between rich and poor countries will continue to impel large numbers of people to move in search of better living standards; political or ethnic conflict in a number of regions is likely to lead to future large-scale refugee movements; and the creation of free trade areas will facilitate movements of labor, whether or not this is intended by the governments concerned. But migration is not just a reaction to difficult conditions at home: It is also motivated by the search for better opportunities and lifestyles elsewhere.... Some migrants experience abuse or exploitation, but most benefit and are able to improve their lives through mobility.
Stephen Castles et al. (2014)

We need to stress that the "age of migration" is also an age of mass internal migration, especially in those countries that are less developed, but rapidly developing. [That said,]...the basic drivers of mobility are the same for both internal and international migration.
Russell King et al. (2008)

Types of Migration

Migration has been a fundamental demographic process throughout human history, and as prefigured in the previous four chapters (e.g., in the discussions of population implosions and of the old-age dependency ratio), it has never been more so than in the current era.

Most generally, migration is defined as the movement of people across a significant boundary, usually a political boundary. It implies a distinct kind of movement in that the people moving do so with the intent of taking up permanent or semi-permanent residency in their places of destination. This intent may lie anywhere in between being fully voluntary, such as individuals moving from one place to another to improve their standard of living, and being fully involuntary, such as was experienced in the nineteenth century by the Cherokee and several other Native American tribes of the southeastern United States, who were militarily forced to vacate their traditional homeland and move to Midwestern Oklahoma Territory under the auspices of the US Indian Removal Act of 1830. Demographers further refine the concept of migration by recognizing four major distinct types (each of which has a variety of subtypes):

(A) *Immigration* = coming to a new country.
(B) *Emigration* = leaving a country.
(C) *In-migration* = coming to a new locality or region within the same country.
(D) *Out-migration* = leaving a locality or region within the same country.

Each of these major types can involve one or more subtypes, depending on the migration example at hand:

(a) *Population transfer* involves a government forcing a large group out of a geographic area based on ethnicity or religion (this subtype is sometimes labeled *forced migration* or *involuntary migration*).
(b) *Impelled migration* involves individuals moving not because a government is forcing it upon them but because of dire circumstances: for example, civil war, religious persecution, crop failure, or an economic depression. (This subtype is sometimes labeled *reluctant migration* or *imposed migration*.) International agencies refer to these migrants as *refugees* if they cross an international border, or as *internally displaced persons* if they remain in the country.
(c) *Step migration* comprises a series of short migrations from a place of origin to a final destination.

(d) *Chain migration* involves a series of migrations within a family or particular ethnic or religious group.

(e) *Migration fields* comprise a cluster of chain migrations from a region of origin into particular neighborhoods or towns.

(f) *Return migration* involves the voluntary return of immigrants (or in-migrants) to their place of origin. (This subtype is sometimes called *circular migration.*)

(g) *Seasonal migration* encompasses moving for a short period of time, usually counted in weeks or months, in response to work opportunities (e.g., migrant farm workers) or lifestyle choices (e.g., retirees in the northern snowbelt areas of the United States heading south to Florida during the winter).

(h) *Unauthorized (or undocumented) migration* involves entering or leaving a country without governmental authorization or documentation. (In a few cases, e.g., post-1958 China, it can also involve internal migration from rural to urban areas.) Because many civil liberties and immigrant rights groups consider the word "illegal" as an epithet that increases hostility toward the immigrant population as a whole, and especially toward those migrants who have not gone through the legal process for entering a county, the once common term *illegal migration* is now increasingly being referred to as *unauthorized migration* or *undocumented migration* by US government agencies and many prominent research centers, while in the European Union it is now deemed *irregular migration.*

(i) *Transmigration* involves migration in which the migrants ("transmigrants") maintain multiple and close ties between their places of origin and places of destination.

The various types and subtypes of migration will be illustrated in the forthcoming examination of the macro- and micro-level reasons motivating people to move.

The Demographic Balancing Equation

The total population of the world increases or decreases to the degree to which births and deaths are in balance. When births are greater than deaths, the world population grows; and, in the opposite direction, when births are fewer than deaths, the world population falls. The rate of population growth or decline depends on the degree to which births outnumber deaths, or vice versa, as well as on the life expectancy of the population.

However, within any given geographic area smaller than the entire planet, population change depends not only on the balance between births and deaths, but also on the balance between immigration and emigration. The fastest-growing areas are those with high birth rates, low death rates, and high rates of immigration – all of which can coalesce to the point of *overpopulation*, in which population size overwhelms available resources, including food, water, housing, and economic infrastructure. And, conversely, the fastest declining areas are those with low birth rates, high death rates, and high rates of emigration – which, if unchanged, lead to the eventual extinction of the society. These facts are expressed in the *demographic balancing equation*:

$$\text{Population size}_{time2} = \text{Population size}_{time1}$$
$$+ \left(\text{Births}_{between\ time1\ \&\ time2} - \text{Deaths}_{between\ time1\ \&\ time2}\right)$$
$$+ \left(\text{Immigration}_{between\ time1\ \&\ time2} - \text{Emigration}_{between\ time1\ \&\ time2}\right)^{*}$$

*where in-migration and out-migration can be substituted for immigration and emigration, respectively

This equation has two key components that contribute to population change: first is the *natural increase* of the area's population – that is, the difference of Births – Deaths during the two time periods; and second is the *net migration* experienced by the area – that is, the difference of Immigration – Emigration (or In-Migration – Out-Migration). Thus, the balancing equation is sometimes expressed as:

$$\text{Population size}_{time2} = \text{Population size}_{time1} + \text{Natural increase}$$
$$+ \text{Net migration}$$

For example, applying the balancing equation to the population change in the United States between 2000 and 2010 results in the following:

$$308,891,000 = 281,422,000 + 18,621,000 + 8,848,000$$

where: 308,891,000 = population in 2010
281,422,000 = population in 2000
18,621,000 = natural increase 2000–10 (births – deaths)
8,848,000 = net migrants 2000–10 (immigrants – emigrants)[1]

The demographic balancing equation is critical to understanding the cultural, political, and socioeconomic effects that are associated with migration for places of both destination and origin. This topic is examined in the final section of this chapter.

The *Push* and *Pull* Forces Explaining Why People Move

There is a vast scholarly literature on migration. Even a cursory look at this literature reveals hundreds of variables linked to geographic mobility. However, a relatively small number of factors, a dozen and a half or so, are consistently emphasized as causative in motivating people to pull up stakes and move. And although entwined with each other in complex and overlapping ways, these factors can analytically be subdivided into the macro and micro levels of analysis. Some of these factors *push* people from their current place of residence (e.g., the closing off of employment opportunities), while other factors *pull* people toward new places (e.g., the opening up of employment opportunities; cf. the classic formulations of Ravenstein 1885, 1889). Finally, while the scholarly literature has two distinct traditions – one focusing on geographic mobility within a country (*internal* migration), and another on *international* migration – the factors used to explain mobility are generally similar in both traditions, and often identical. Figures 5.1a and 5.1b provide heuristic sketches of the major variables driving geographic mobility.

Macro Factors (Figure 5.1a)

The following discussion highlights the first three macro factors displayed in Figure 5.1a (natural environment; structural economic change; large-scale political changes), the discussions of which will offer illustrations of the importance of the last four factors (governmental programs; transportation and communication improvements; similar ethnic community in area of destination; and the ascendency of achieved status attainment).

Natural Environment.   Throughout human history, a key set of motivators for people to make a significant geographic move has involved either natural or human-induced changes to the local environment. Modern humans trace their origins to east Africa some 200,000 years ago. As their survival skills, use of technology, and social organization slowly grew in sophistication, they become increasingly able to harvest local flora and fauna, allowing for higher survival rates and spasmodic but eventual increased population size. When the population grew to the point of outstripping local food sources, a significant part of it would

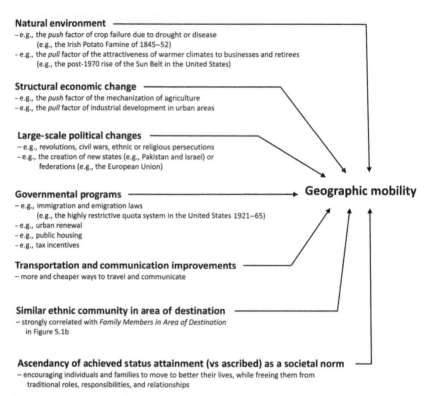

Figure 5.1a: Macro-level factors driving geographic mobility

move on to the next valley, the next mountain, or the next area of shore-line in search of new sources. When the total human population was an estimated (at a mere!) 10,000 in number, it began migrating out of east Africa about 70,000 years ago (National Geographic 2014a). Available paleontological and linguistic research, along with the tracing of DNA back through the generations, gives us a good sense of the ensuing migration streams (National Geographic 2014b). One stream headed west, populating west Africa; another stream north, then west, to populate north Africa; and a third stream due south, populating south Africa. A major fourth stream headed north and then east, crossing the Bab-al-Mandab Strait, which separates modern-day Yemen from Djibouti. (The Red Sea was much lower during this period, and island-hopping across it during low tides via wading or crude rafts was possible.) Many in this stream headed south, then east and north, successively populating India, Asia, and eventually (by 50,000 BCE), using small boats to island-hop, Oceania (modern-day Australia, Melanesia, Micronesia, Polynesia, and

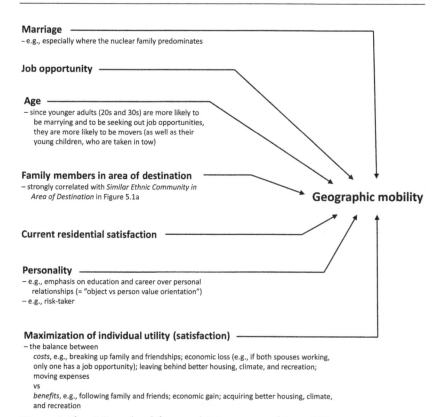

Marriage
– e.g., especially where the nuclear family predominates

Job opportunity

Age
– since younger adults (20s and 30s) are more likely to
  be marrying and to be seeking out job opportunities,
  they are more likely to be movers (as well as their
  young children, who are taken in tow)

Family members in area of destination
– strongly correlated with *Similar Ethnic Community in
  Area of Destination* in Figure 5.1a

Geographic mobility

Current residential satisfaction

Personality
– e.g., emphasis on education and career over personal
  relationships (= "object vs person value orientation")
– e.g., risk-taker

Maximization of individual utility (satisfaction)
– the balance between
    costs, e.g., breaking up family and friendships; economic loss (e.g., if both spouses working,
    only one has a job opportunity); leaving behind better housing, climate, and recreation;
    moving expenses
    vs
    benefits, e.g., following family and friends; economic gain; acquiring better housing, climate,
    and recreation

Figure 5.1b: Micro-level factors driving geographic mobility

New Zealand). Around 50,000 BCE, humans in the Middle East headed
north, then east and west, populating the European continent; they were
soon joined by others living in south-central Asia. Finally, around 20,000
years ago, when the Bering Sea was 300 feet lower than today, Asian
hunters in the far northeast used the Bering Land Bridge to cross into
North America. As they exhausted local food sources, bands would
break apart into smaller groups. Some of these break-out groups progres-
sively headed south and east. By 14,000 BCE, humans were living in
modern-day eastern Canada and the United States, and by 12,000 BCE,
they were all the way down to southern Chile. Figure 5.2 shows these
the major routes of humanity's first set of major migrations, all of which
trace their roots back to east Africa.

Natural disasters and epidemics rooted in diseases borne by area
flora and fauna have been consistent motivators for people to move,
either within internal political borders or across national borders. The

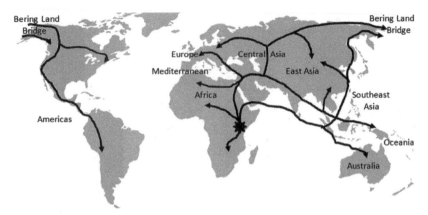

Figure 5.2: Migration routes out of east Africa
Note: All of humanity traces its roots back to east Africa, circa 200,000 BCE.
About 70,000 years ago, humans began migration streams heading in directions
that would lead to the populating of India, Southeast Asia, and Oceania within
20,000 years. A second wave of Middle Eastern and south-central Asian migrants
began populating Europe about 50,000 BCE. A final wave of northeast Asians
trekked across the Bering Land Bridge around 18,000 BCE, and reached southern
Chile by 12,000 BCE.

chronicle of any people residing in a particular geographic area will
reveal multiple and diverse examples of *impelled migration* created by
weather- and disease-related environmental forces. Four illustrative
examples – of the tens of thousands in recorded human history – include
the following:

1   *The Black Death pandemic.* The mid-fourteenth-century Black
    Death pandemic, discussed in Chapter 2, which devastated the popu-
    lations of the Middle East and Europe, motivated large portions of
    local populations to move well beyond the 10 to 20 miles that his-
    torians estimate was the typical degree of mobility that an individual
    in that era might experience during his or her lifetime (Kendall et al.
    2013). Sometimes the plague worked indirectly to create geographic
    mobility: for example, the loss of life of the working-age population
    would destroy the local economy and survivors would move on to
    find more work, often in nearby cities. However, at other times, the
    effects were direct – as in the case of individuals vacating cities to
    flee from the disease: for example, in "the summer of 1348, the Black
    Plague hit Britain, and by the fall it had reached London. It spread
    quickly throughout the city leading to mass migration out and high
    mortality within" (Emery 2013).

A primary source of knowledge about population movements in the distant past involves the creative use of the tools of physical anthropology. In the case of the impact of the Black Death on migration, human dental and bone remains have been studied via the analysis of their levels of strontium and oxygen variants (isotopes); the variants differ by geographic area and are passed on to humans through food. Thus, if individuals have spent an extended period of their lives in one area and then moved to another, where they die soon thereafter, the strontium and oxygen ratios in their tooth enamel and bones will be different than the levels expected if they were from the area where they had passed away (Emery 2013; Kendall et al. 2013).

2   *The Irish Potato Famine.* The Irish Potato Famine, which unfolded between 1845 and 1852, was rooted in the dependency of the Irish peasantry on two key food sources: cabbage and potato. These vegetables were eaten directly and also used as food to raise pigs. In the years immediately before 1845, "the Irish peasantry, although poor and oppressed by alien landlords, were a healthy, well-fed nation" (Cartwright 1972: 229). In 1845, however, a devastating form of blight, *phytophthora infestans*, hit the potatoes in local areas, and by 1846 it had ravaged the entire country and devastated most of the national crop. During the next half-decade, at least one million people died (from starvation – and the diseases that the malnourished are susceptible to, especially dysentery and cholera), and at least another million emigrated to Canada, England, Scotland, South Wales, and the United States. At the start of the famine, the population of Ireland was estimated at 8.2 million, but by the famine's end, it had dropped by a quarter to 6.5 million (Smith 1992: 411).

3   *Hurricane Katrina.* Hurricane Katrina shattered the US Gulf coast in late August of 2005. At least one and a half million people fled their homes as the storm approached, with the largest share in the metropolitan New Orleans area. On the day before the storm hit, 80% of the 455,000 residents of New Orleans left the city, in accordance with a mandatory order from Mayor Ray Nagin. The majority of those not evacuating were found among the poor and the disabled, many of whom had no means of transportation. The non-evacuation problem was exacerbated because many of these individuals lived in the lowest lying areas of the city – areas, as everyone was soon to realize, that lacked adequate storm-protection levees and sea walls. (Much of New Orleans lies at sea level or below and is protected from flooding by such barriers between the land and the water – the Mississippi River and large lakes, all at the edge of the Gulf of Mexico.) This phenomenon is actually quite common.

That is, in natural disasters, "the most vulnerable people are often the ones forced to move either because they live in marginal low-lying or steep-slope areas with greater exposure to hazards, or they have poor-quality housing and thus subject to greater losses" (Bremner and Hunter 2014: 4).

Many of Katrina's refugees fled to bordering states, but many others went even further north, west, and east – ending up in 45 different states (according to a major federal study of the refugees; see Groen and Polivka 2008: 39). A quarter of the New Orleans evacuees had not returned by 2010, at which time the likelihood of their eventual return was considered almost nil by most analysts. Much of the rental housing in the city was destroyed and never rebuilt; and by 2013, rents for the remaining and rebuilt housing were averaging 40% higher than they were before Katrina (Lewis 2013).

4   *Global warming and climate change.* Hurricanes, droughts, and floods have increased threefold since the mid-1980s. In 2008, extreme weather events – hurricanes, tsunamis, and floods – displaced an estimated 20 million people. However, gradual and cumulative changes in the environment linked to climate change have had, and are anticipated to have, even greater effects. For example, between 1985 and 2014, twice as many people were affected by droughts as by storms, 1.6 billion versus 718 million.

Between 2015 and 2050, hundreds of millions of people – perhaps as many as a billion – are expected to become *environmental migrants* (International Organization for Migration 2015). The majority of these individuals will be victims of either coastal flooding – caused by erosion and sea-level rise – or farmland droughts and desertification (destroying livelihoods and systems of food production). Environmental scientists have connected the rising numbers of floods, droughts, and desertified areas to global warming and associated changes in the climate – and have linked a large part of these changes to human population growth and increases in greenhouse gases produced by the burning of fossil fuels (see, e.g., IPCC 2012, 2015; Melillo et al. 2014; Min et al. 2011; Pall et al. 2011; Peterson et al. 2012).

In sum, throughout human history, large numbers of individuals have been forced – or enticed, in the examples of seeking richer farmlands or less inclement weather – to move because of environmental factors. However, these factors have been displacing people at an accelerating pace over the past three decades, and will continue to do so for the foreseeable future. Indeed, since the 1990s, in any given year millions of

A hurricane's devastation.   On August 29, 2005, Hurricane Katrina devastated *much of the Gulf coast areas of Alabama, Mississippi, and Louisiana. New Orleans was especially hard hit with flooding, as its levees and sea walls gave way to the storm's surge. As depicted in this photo, four days after Katrina hit, the bulk of the city was still suffering from high flood waters.*

Out of the city's 455,000 people, 80% evacuated, but as of 2010, more than 111,000 had not returned – and by that point were never expected to do so. (As of 2015, the population stood at 379,000.) Over the tri-state area, 1.5 million people fled their homes, and more than a year later "about 410,000 had not returned to their homes ... and of these, approximately 280,000 had not even returned to the counties in which they were living prior to the storm" (Groen and Polivka 2008: 39).

Photo credit: Gary Nichols (US Navy)

individuals have been, or can expect to be, displaced by acute and chronic changes in the environment. For example, during the mid-1990s, Myers (2002) estimates that the prevalence of people moved either temporarily or permanently owing to environmental conditions was 25 million. Among the major population dislocations he cites were the droughts in Eritrea, Kenya, Somalia, and Sudan (10 million people fled the area, with only 5 million returning); 6 million environmental refugees in China, being forced to abandon their farmlands and move to neighboring towns and cities owing to shortages of agricultural plots; and hundreds of thousands of Haitians who suffered from the loss of crops owing to poor farming practices, including planting on steep slopes that suffer constant erosion during the rainy season. ("In former times, some

Chronic long-term strain	Medium-term pressures	Forced displacement
e.g.: – soil degradation – declining land availability – poor agricultural practices	e.g.: – severe drought – recurrent livelihood failure	e.g.: – tsunami – extreme flooding – earthquake
Effect: *Gradual out-migration over time*	Effect: *Large out-migration, but some are unable to leave*	Effect: *Almost all people leave temporarily*

Figure 5.3: The continuum of environmental pressures contributing to migration
Source: Adapted from Bremner and Hunter (2014: 5)

of [these Haitian refugees] were driven by political oppression and government corruption. But for most, the predominant factor has [become] environmental, and to that extent these people deserve to be called environmental refugees." Myers 2002: 610.) By 2010, as many as 38 million people per year were being "forcibly displaced by climate-related events (mainly floods and storms)"; moreover, "drought, the main category of slow-onset disaster," was affecting another 100+ million people, although how many are being forced to move is not clear (European Commission 2013: 10). Figure 5.3 summarizes the continuum of environmental pressures that contribute to human migration.

As a final note, the same environmental variables that *push* individuals out of particular geographic areas serve to *pull* individuals into other particular areas when the flipsides of these variables are taken into consideration. Thus, for example,

- individuals moving out of drought areas seek new destinations where water is plentiful (e.g., in the 1930s, the panhandles of Texas and Oklahoma, as well as abutting sections of New Mexico, Colorado, and Kansas, experienced such severe drought that the area became known as the "Dust Bowl," which resulted in tens of thousands of farm families leaving – with many being pulled toward the fertile soils and more water-abundant farmlands of central and southern California);
- those living in flood zones are motivated to move to areas of higher ground, especially after experiencing the devastation of flood waters more than once (e.g., after massive flooding of the Missouri and Mississippi Rivers in 1993, not only did thousands move out of the low-lying areas abutting the rivers, but the entire towns of Valmeyer, Illinois and Rhineland, Missouri were relocated);
- as energy costs rise and heating bills do so concomitantly, individuals and businesses are drawn to areas with milder temperatures (e.g., this

was one reason for the rise of the Sunbelt states that began in full force during the 1970s, especially in the southeastern and southwestern areas of the United States);

- older individuals who have grown tired of dealing with snow and cold weather are drawn to warm states such as Arizona and Florida (and even further south into Mexico and the Caribbean) – with some of them being circular migrants, living in their snowbelt homes in northern US states and Canada during the summer and in their sunbelt home during the winter months (this subculture of migration has become so large and so well understood that these migrants have become known simply as *snowbirds* – with those in the greater culture understanding all that is implied by this label).

Structural Economic Change. Throughout human history, major changes in the system of economic production have impelled major movements of human population. As described in Chapter 2, the rise of agriculture around major river systems spawned the first permanent human settlements 12,000 years ago; and by 2,000 BCE, major urban areas were developing in China (along the Yellow and Yangtze Rivers), the Indian peninsula (along the Ganges and Indus Rivers), the Middle East (along the Tigris and Euphrates Rivers), Egypt (along the Nile), and in parts of Meso-America (Mexico/Central America) and South America (along various smaller river systems).

Technological advances lie at the heart of economic changes. The new technologies of the late eighteenth- and early nineteenth-century Industrial Revolution – including iron plows, seed drills, and threshing machines – greatly boosted agricultural production. Indeed, enough food was produced to feed not only the agrarian populace but also the growing urban populations congregating around the textile and other factories that were arising by the thousands in Canada, the United States, and Europe. Dramatic improvements in transportation, including steam-powered rail engines and ships, linked rural areas where food was produced to the urban areas consuming it.

Rural-to-Urban Migration.   The effects of industrialization were monumental and included the greatest single type of migration humanity was to experience, right to the present day: As technological advances increased production and decreased the need for human labor in the countryside, massive numbers of people moved from rural to urban areas in search of work in the industrializing urban economies. These economies were built first on manufacturing, and since the mid-twentieth century, have increasingly been based on services, information processing, wholesale and retail sales, and leisure activities.

Although in many ways more technologically advanced than Europeans (e.g., in weaving and iron and steel production), Asia was significantly behind Europe and Northern America in the industrializing process, with Japan beginning heavily to promote industrialization and the building of the material (e.g., railways, canals, roads, and bridges) and socioeconomic (financial, educational, and regulatory) infrastructures to support it in the 1870s – some 100 years after the process was underway in the West. Yet, although China, India, Pakistan, and much of East and Southeast Asia would be almost another 100 years behind, they were able to transform their economies much more quickly than their European and Northern American predecessors. Hong Kong, Singapore, South Korea, and Taiwan realized such spectacular rates of economic growth and per capita wealth in the 1970s and 1980s that they collectively became known as the "Four Asian Tigers." Among many other nations experiencing major industrialization in the past several decades, Brazil, Indonesia, Malaysia, Mexico, the Philippines, Russia, South Africa, Thailand, and Turkey stand out.

The contemporary mega urban centers that have arisen throughout the developing world in the past half-century are reflective of the huge change-over from largely agricultural to heavily industrial (and associated financial, information, and marketing services) economies. These centers have grown their populations largely through internal migration from their nations' rural, village, and small-town agriculturally dominated areas. Prominent examples include Jakarta, Indonesia (with a current population estimated at 29,959,000; up from 2.7 million in 1960!), Delhi, India (24,134,000; from 2.3 million in 1960), Seoul-Incheon, South Korea (22,992,000; 2.8 million in 1960), Manila, Philippines (22,710,000; 2.3 million in 1960), Shanghai, China (22,650,000; 6.8 million in 1960), Karachi, Pakistan (21,585,000; 1.9 million in 1960), Mexico City, Mexico (20,3000,000; 5.5 million in 1960), São Paulo, Brazil (20,272,000; 4.0 million in 1960), Istanbul, Turkey (13,187,000; 1.5 million in 1960), Bangkok, Thailand (14,910,000; 2.2 million in 1960), Buenos Aires, Argentina (13,913,000; 6.6 million in 1960), and Lagos, Nigeria (12,549,000; 0.8 million in 1960). (Population estimates are from Demographia 2014 and United Nations 2014k.) Worldwide, 160.8 million people lived in cities of at least 300,000 people in 1960 (about 5% of the total world population of 3 billion); by the end of 2014, this figure had ballooned to an astonishing 2.2 billion (31% of the world's 7.2 billion people); and by 2030, the number is expected to be 2.9 billion (35% of the estimated world population of 8.3 billion). In a major analysis of internal migration, the UN Expert Group on Internal Migration concluded that this massive "urbanization has been driven by the... transition from low productivity agriculture to more productive mechanized agriculture that has produced labor surpluses in rural areas. [And because] cities attract businesses and jobs, they become magnets for migrants seeking better opportunities" (United Nations 2008: 3).

Rural-to-Urban Migration Spurs International Migration.   Massive rural-to-urban internal migration, especially in developing nations, has also spawned international migration. Even though migrants from rural areas benefit from their move to urban areas (e.g., average income is higher in urban vs rural areas; urbanites also have better access to education, healthcare, transportation, communication, clean water, and proper sanitation), the rapid rate of influx of people has overwhelmed urban economies and infrastructures (and continues to do so). Although employment opportunities are much greater than in rural, village, and small-town areas, there simply are not enough jobs. Moreover, large cities

> are prone to suffer from environmental contamination stemming from traffic congestion, the concentration of industry, and inadequate waste disposal systems. Cities also tend to make demands on land, water, and natural resources that are disproportionately high in relation to their land area or their population, whose high average income results in high consumption. Although the concentration of population and economic activity in cities is at the root of these problems, persistent disparities among city dwellers imply that poor people bear the brunt of the negative aspects of urbanization. Because income inequality in the cities of developing countries is stark, the numbers involved are large and growing. (United Nations 2008: 4)

One upshot is that many internal migrants to urban areas end up seeking employment opportunities and a better life by crossing international borders. Archetypical examples in recent history include Mexican emigration to the United States and Italian emigration to the United Kingdom.

Many rural Mexicans begin their *multi-step migration* journeys by moving from their small villages to larger provincial towns – which often become " 'saturated' with excessive numbers of rural migrants" (King et al. 2008: 8). The next step is often a move to Mexico City or to one of the major border cities (where US multinationals have established vast numbers of export assembly operations – *maquiladoras* – on the Mexican side since the passage of the trade-liberalizing *North American Free Trade Agreement* [NAFTA] in 1993), including Juárez, Matamoros, Nuevo Laredo, Reynosa, and, Tijuana. Finally, drawn by higher wages, more and better work prospects, and the opportunity to live closer to family members who have already relocated to *"el otro lado"* (translated as "the other side" – a common phrase by which Mexicans refer to the United States), the next step is to emigrate to the United States. Having family members who have legal status in the United States – are citizens or hold green cards that the federal government issues to those on a legal path to citizenship – offers several advantages. These members often give material and emotional assistance in the relocation process, and they provide one of several legal pathways to citizenship. Having a close relative sponsor the immigrant is one of the three most common ways to acquire a green card.[2] First preference is given to spouses and minor children of a US citizen; next in line are unmarried children aged 21 and older; then married children and their spouses; and, finally, brothers and sisters.

However, except for the first category (spouses and minor children), waiting times are long (counted in years), and if employer sponsorship cannot be found, many Mexican migrants cross the border without authorization. Because the long, 1,500-mile border between the United States and Mexico makes entering the country relatively easy compared to trying to enter via a seaport or airport, Mexico now accounts for just over half of the estimated 11 to 12 million unauthorized immigrants currently living in the United States (Pew Research Center 2014b) – the overwhelming majority of whom are working in low-level services, agriculture, or construction. (Most employee-sponsored legal immigrants are in high-tech, high-prestige job areas, not in low-level service and related low-prestige work.) As these migrants are critical to the functioning of many local and regional economies, what sanctions they should receive has been one of the most important political debates in the United States over the past two decades, a debate that reached a critical junction in the fall of 2014, when the administration of President Barack Obama took executive action to protect as many as 5.4 million unauthorized immigrants from deportation – the majority of whom (3.25 million) were from Mexico (Pew Research Center 2014c; note that as of the fall of 2015, Obama's executive action was being challenged by 26 US states in the federal court system and was likely to be nullified – see Parser 2015).

The Economic Foundations of International Migration.   As of 2014, the UN classified 232 million individuals as "international migrants" – those living for one year or longer in a country other than the one in which they were born (this total includes refugees and unauthorized migrants). The overwhelming majority of these individuals had migrated for economic reasons, either escaping a decline in their standard of living rooted in large-scale economic change (e.g., the mechanization of agriculture

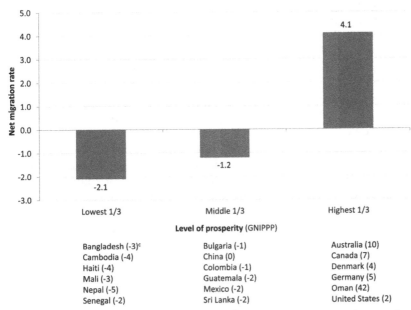

Figure 5.4:   Net migration[a] and prosperity,[b] with selected national examples
Notes: [a]Net migration rate = (Immigrants – Emigrants) per 1,000 population. Because most countries do not keep records on emigration, and because estimates of unauthorized immigration are generally crude, the calculation of net migration is done indirectly: *Net migration rate* = $((($Population size$_{year2}$ – Population size$_{year1}$) – (Births – Deaths for the year))/Population size at mid-year) $\times$ 1,000. For a technical discussion on the messiness of estimating net migration and the net migration rate, see United Nations (1970: Chap. iv).
[b]GNIPPP per capita is gross national income in purchasing power parity (PPP) divided by mid-year population (see Figure 3.3, note b).
[c]Net migration rate in parentheses.
[d]Correlation = .55 (p < .0001); N = 179 countries.
Source: Raw data for 2013, from the Population Reference Bureau (2014)

and being pushed from the farm to find work in the city, often in another country) or desiring to improve their standard of living – even though considered relatively well off by local standards (this is especially true of well-educated and skilled workers). Several key social facts point to the importance of the economic bases for migration:

1   The majority of international migrants, more than two-thirds (69%), end up in highly developed, high-income countries, especially the United States. Per Figure 5.4, the richest third of the world's nations have much higher net migration rates than the poorest third. Indeed,

the average country in the richest third gained a net of 41 immigrants per 10,000 population in 2013, while the average country in the poorest third lost a net of 21 emigrants per 10,000 population that same year. Conversely, and relatedly, those countries that are in the top third of the world for the proportion of their populations being very young, and thus whose economies struggle to produce enough employment for their youth as they begin their work careers in their late teen years and early 20s, have a net migration loss (losing, on average, 17 people per 10,000 population to emigration in 2013), while those countries that are in the bottom third for the proportion of their populations being very young, and thus whose economies have more job openings than their low numbers of young people are able to fill, experience a net migration gain (gaining, on average, 26 new people per 10,000 population via immigration; see Figure 5.5).

2   At the same time, the majority of international migrants, more than three-quarters (76%), come from developing (low- or middle-

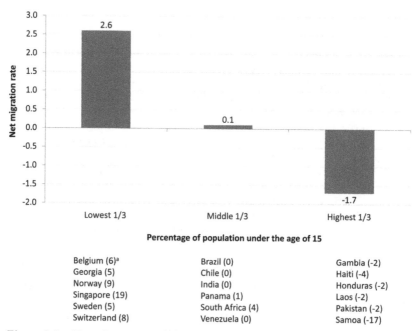

Figure 5.5:   Net migration and the percentage of the national population under the age of 15, with selected national examples

Notes: [a]Net migration rate (Immigrants − Emigrants) per 1,000 population in parentheses.

[b]Correlation = −.25 ($p < .0001$); $N = 210$ countries.

Source: Raw data for 2013, from the Population Reference Bureau (2014)

Table 5.1:   Top 10 countries of destination and of origin for international migrants in 2013 (in millions)

Top 10 countries of destination		Top 10 countries of origin	
United States	45.8	India	14.2
Russia	11.0	Mexico	13.2
Germany	9.8	Russia	10.8
Saudi Arabia	9.1	China	9.3
United Arab Emirates	7.8	Bangladesh	7.8
United Kingdom	7.8	Pakistan	5.7
France	7.4	Ukraine	5.6
Canada	7.3	Philippines	5.5
Australia	6.5	Afghanistan	5.1
Spain	6.5	United Kingdom	5.0

Note: Most immigration to Russia is the result of Russians living in the former states of the USSR returning to Russia.
Source: Adapted from Pew Research Center (2013a: 12, 15)

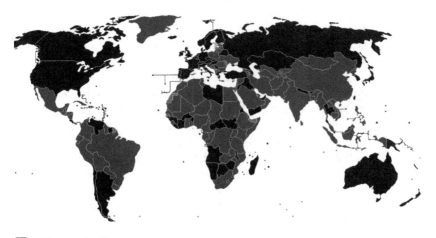

■ Positive net migration
■ Zero or negative net migration

Figure 5.6:   Global map of net migration, 2015
Source: Global map adapted from Wikimedia Commons (2015)

income) countries, with India, Mexico, and China being especially prominent in recent decades. Table 5.1 shows the top 10 countries of destination and of origin for the international migrant population as of 2014, while Figure 5.6 displays a global map of net migration.

3   A large proportion of international migrants send money to family members back home. Known as *remittances*, these funds have been on the rise in recent decades (e.g., despite the global recession of 2008/9, remittances tripled between 2000 and 2013 – to over $500 billion), and, moreover, they are largely sent from migrants living in high-income developed countries to their families in their developing low- and middle-income countries of origin. In 2013, the share of all remittances received by middle-income countries (such as China, India, and Mexico) was an estimated 71%; the share to low-income nations (e.g., Liberia and selected other Sub-Saharan African nations) was 6%; and the share to high-income nations was 23% (see Pew Research Center 2013a: 5, 18).

Economic-based migration often leads to *return* (or *circular*) *migration*, either because migrants fail to realize their monetary/lifestyle expectations or because they have indeed realized these expectations and have returned to their country of origin – a place where they feel more comfortable with the language and culture, and a place where they can now better afford to live (e.g., being able to buy land or set up a business; or having gained the work experience that makes them more attractive to employers). This phenomenon has generally been part of the history of migration. For example, an estimated 40% of English and Welsh migrants to the United States returned back to their home countries between 1861 and 1913, while a similar percentage of Italian migrants to Argentina, Brazil, and the United States returned to Italy in the early twentieth century (see Baines 1995 and Nugent 1992, as cited in Skeldon 2013: 2). More recently, tens of thousands of migrants to the United States from India return home each year – giving up the notion (if they ever had it) of permanent settlement there. After Mexicans (29%) and mainland Chinese (5%), Indians constitute the third largest immigrant group in the United States (1.9 million, representing about 5% of the 40.4 million US residents who were foreign-born in 2011; see Whatley and Batalova 2013). Many return home because they have acquired job skills in the United States that make them very competitive in the Indian labor market; others return to care for aging parents; and many do so because they "feel a sense of belonging like nowhere else" (Jones 2015; see also Gupte and Jadhav 2014; Semple 2012).[3]

Unauthorized Migration, Temporary Visas, and Transmigration Reflect Economic Motives.   The current high level of unauthorized immigration to the United States and Western European nations is indicative of the economic forces behind migration. For example, an estimated 11 to 12 million unauthorized migrants now reside in the United States (largely from Mexico and Central America; see Pew Research Center 2014b, 2014c), while as many as 3.8 million live in the developed nations of the European Union (largely from Eastern Europe, as well as North and West Africa; see Morehouse and Blomfeld 2011: 6–9). (Both the United States and the EU apprehend/deport roughly a half million unauthorized immigrants a year; see European Commission 2015; Gonzalez-Barrera and Krogstad 2014.) Many of these migrants circulate between living in their country of destination when work is available and returning to their country of origin when it is not. Seasonal migratory work in agriculture and tourism are classic examples.

The rise of unauthorized migration has been accompanied by a rise in temporary work visas in developing countries – acknowledging the need for workers, but fearful that if given permanent residency, immigrants will overwhelm the destination country either economically or culturally or both. For example, in recent years, the United States has accepted about 1 million immigrants annually for permanent residency, while admitting nearly 3 million temporary workers and their families (Foreman and Monger 2014: 1; Monger and Yankay 2014: 1); in Australia, the comparable numbers are 213,000 for permanent residency and 500,000 for temporary status; and in Canada the numbers are 280,000 and 380,000, respectively (Skeldon 2013: 3).

In the age of the Internet, social media, mobile phones, and relatively inexpensive and fast long-distance travel, *return, circular, temporary,* and *seasonal* migration have spawned a newly identified form of migrant: the *transmigrant.* Examples of transmigrants can be found in virtually every country in the contemporary era. Transmigrants develop cultural identities that do not coincide closely with their places of destination. Through modern means of communication and transportation, they are able to maintain close ties to their places of origin – ties that involve personal finances, cultural practices, self-identities, and the ebb and flow of daily life. Archetypical examples include:

- large numbers of Filipino households involved in constant exchanges of the funds and resources between the Philippines and common destination countries like the United States and Canada;
- middle-class Caribbean immigrants living in US East Coast cities who send their children to private West Indian schools for at least part of their educations – "where the curriculum reflects both Caribbean and US experiences, preparing children to live a transnational existence" (Schiller et al. 1999: 74–5); and
- Mexican circular, seasonal, and even permanent migrants who move more or less smoothly between their communities of origin in Mexico

and their communities of destination in the United States (see, e.g., Lozano-Ascencio et al. 1999).[4]

European Migration Illustrates the Effects of Structural Economic Change. As a final note on the importance of the economic basis for migration, the historical case of Europe is particularly instructive. From 1600 to 1925, it was an exporter of its peoples, primarily to Northern America (a million a year in the early 1900s) – though also sending significant numbers to South America, Asia, and Africa. But since the 1950s, it has become an importer of people (e.g., in 2010, the European Union absorbed 1.2 million permanent migrants – with France, Germany, Spain, and the United Kingdom being the major countries of destination; see Skeldon 2013: 3).

In the seventeenth and eighteenth centuries, much of the emigration was motivated by mercantile ventures in which commercial joint stock corporations – like the Dutch West India Company (founded 1621) and the East India Companies of the English (1600), Dutch (1602), Danes (1616), French (1660), and Swedes (1731) –

> hired European merchants, military officers, and officials to emigrate [so as] to profit from, conquer, and govern their many and often vast colonies.... [T]he cumulative number of Europeans [emigrating] could be substantial: In the seventeenth and eighteenth centuries, the Dutch East India Company [alone] sent one million Europeans (many of them emigrants from German states) to Asia, especially to Indonesia. (Fisher 2014: 66)

With the spreading abolition of serfdom in Europe (unintentionally contributing to the rising importance of *achieved* social positions of the individual, as opposed to the social positions *ascribed* to him or her at birth), along with legal enclosures of rural lands that had once been village common lands, the less prosperous of Europe increasingly looked to North America to find sustainable livelihoods, and they financed the cost of passage across the Atlantic by selling themselves as *indentured laborers*. Indeed, in the eighteenth and early nineteenth centuries, two-thirds of the Irish, English, Scotch, French, and German immigrants to North America paid their way through indentureship (Fisher 2014: 67).[5] An indentured laborer would sell him/herself to a ship's captain to pay for passage; and the ship's captain would, in turn, sell the laborer to buyers in the ports of destination. Buyers included small and large farm owners (tobacco farms in Virginia and the mid-South were common places for many indentured laborers to end up) and small and large businesses (e.g., retailers, wholesalers, importers, exporters, and craftworks).

As technology-driven increases in food production and improvements in private and public sanitation unfolded during the nineteenth and early twentieth centuries (see Chapters 2 and 3), national populations grew and outstripped the capacity of European economies to provide employment (in part because of the economic depressions created by repeated warfare, including the Napoleonic Wars of 1799–1815; in part, because of the Potato Famine, discussed earlier in this chapter, which struck not only Ireland but much of Europe in the late 1840s and early 1850s). One consequence: Emigration from Europe continued to grow throughout the nineteenth century. Indeed, by the 1880s and 1890s, and into the first two decades of the twentieth centuries, as many as a million immigrants a year were arriving in the Americas from Europe – 20 million to the United States alone (with the peak year being 1907, when 1.3 million entered the country legally). Some sought out farm lands in the plains of the United States, Canada, Argentina, and Brazil; others sought work in the copper, gold, lead, and silver mines that dotted the landscape between the Rocky Mountains and the Pacific coast; and many more took employment in the thousands of factories that sprang up in towns and cities throughout the Northeast, Mid-Atlantic, and Midwest regions of Northern America. From the early 1800s to the early 1900s, an estimated 9.5 million Eastern Europeans, 7.5 million Britons (including 4.5 million Irish), 5.5 million Germans, 4.2 million Italians, and 2 million Scandinavians migrated to the United States and Canada. And after Brazil abolished slavery in 1888, the demand for replacement workers motivated more than a million and a half Italians alone to emigrate there (Fisher 2014: 89).

World War I (1914–18), the Great Depression of the 1930s, World War II (1939–45), and highly restrictive anti-immigrant legislation passed in the United States in the early 1920s all conspired to reduce immigration dramatically from Europe to the Americas, especially to the United States. Nevertheless, until the mid-1960s, the US *Immigration Act of 1924* assured that the relatively small amount of immigration it did experience would favor Europeans (Figure 5.7a). The Act created a quota system restricting entry to 2% percent of the total number of people for each nationality as of the 1890 national census. This formula favored immigrants from Western Europe, and all but prohibited immigration from Asia (as the fear of the large number of Chinese entering the western United States to work in mines and on railroad construction had led to the 1882 *Chinese Exclusion Act*, which barred the further immigration of Chinese laborers). Europeans lost their favored status, however, with the passage of the 1965 *Immigration and Nationality Act*. This legislation got rid of the nationality-based quota system, meaning that Europeans now had to compete for green card status with Asians, Africans, and Latin Americans – where the majority of U.S. immigrants now come (see Figure 5.7b). At the same time, however, post-1965 Europe was robustly rebounding from the devastations to its societies and national economies of the 1914–45 era. One consequence was an historic turnaround in which its rates of immigration began outstripping its rates of emigration (i.e., net migration was positive). The shift

> was first evident in the 1950s in an area extending northwards and eastwards from France and Switzerland, then the countries of most intense immigration, including Belgium, Germany, and Sweden. By the early twenty-first century most of the countries of southern and western Europe, as well as Turkey, had become areas of net immigration. Only a small number of countries extending from the Baltic Republics to the northern frontier of Greece experienced net emigration, which was mostly directed to western and southern Europe. The Russian Federation, too, had undergone the shift from emigration to immigration with the return of many ethnic Russians from the republics of the former Soviet Union. (Skeldon 2013: 4)

Large-Scale Political Changes. Throughout recorded human history, large-scale political changes have either coerced people to move or highly motivated their voluntary decision to do so. In some cases, governments have forced the *population transfer* of a particular ethnic or religious group from one region to another; and in other cases, the chaos and dread associated with civil wars, insurrections, revolutions, and persecutions have created a situation of *impelled migration,* in which individuals, families, and groups flee their homes in search of safe havens – often involving the crossing of national borders. The following briefly developed examples, one historical and one contemporary, illustrate the importance of this macro factor in explaining geographic mobility. Note that such examples could readily be drawn exclusively from almost any and all of the individual histories of the world's current 195 countries.

(1) *The Africa to the Americas slave trade.* Between 1501 and 1866, an estimated 12.5 million African men, women, and children were forcibly removed from their villages in Africa and sold into slavery for shipment to the Americas – where half were put to work on sugar plantations, while the rest were forced to do all manner of indoor and outdoor physical labor, but especially other hard field work on cocoa, coffee, cotton, rice, and tobacco plantations located in North America, the Spanish Americas (Spanish-speaking Central and South America), Brazil, and various Caribbean islands possessed by the British, Danes, and French.

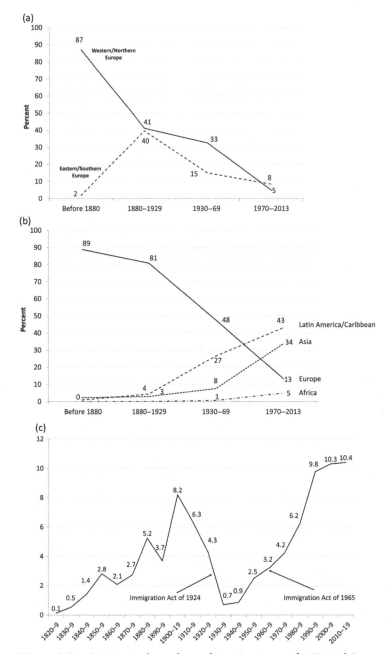

Figure 5.7: Origins and numbers of immigrants to the United States
(a) Percentage of immigrants to the United States by region of Europe
(b) Percentage of immigrants to the United States by region of origin
(c) Total number of immigrants to the United States (in millions), 1820–2019
by decade
Notes: [a] The 2010–19 estimate is based on 2010–14 immigration totals.
[b] Total number of legal immigrants from 1820 to 2019 = 85.8 million.
Source: Raw data from US Department of Homeland Security (2014)

Under conditions of untold misery, 1.8 million died en route, and the carefully maintained ship manifests of this valuable "cargo" revealed that 10.7 million actually disembarked (Voyages Database 2009).

Africans sold into slavery were abducted from their villages mainly by other Africans with whom they were regularly at war – and this practice had been well established for at least a century before the post-1500 *trans-Atlantic slave trade* began (with three major slave trade markets involving the selling of Sub-Saharan Africans and shipping them across [1] the Indian Ocean to India, [2] the Red Sea to Middle East states, and [3] the Sahara Desert to Northern African states; note that slaves were also traded among Sub-Saharan African communities, with this form of slavery being similar to the European practice of indentured servitude, in which slaves had some rights of and hope for release). The Americas slave trade became so huge, however, that victorious clans, tribes, and kingdoms developed into small "empires" based upon it, including the Kingdom of Benin (modern-day Edo, Nigeria), Dahomey (modern-day Benin), and, among many others, the Ashanti Confederacy (including parts of modern-day Ghana and Ivory Coast).

The captured Africans – two-thirds of whom were young, strong men – were sold at armed trading posts that dotted Africa's western and southeastern coastlines. The nations sponsoring the largest number of slave ships from these posts included Portugal (responsible for transporting 5.1 million slaves to the Americas), Britain (2.7 million), France (1.2 million), and Spain (0.9 million) – with ships from the Netherlands (Holland), the United States, and Denmark transporting most of the remaining slaves. Table 5.2 displays the key destination points of the trans-Atlantic slave trade during its dreadful 350-year history.

The legacy of the Atlantic slave trade is complex and manifold. Nunn's (2007) sophisticated econometric analyses of historical data reveal that those African nations suffering the greatest losses to the slave trade have yet to truly recover from its devastations. His conclusions are echoed in Manning's (1990: 124) summary observation of his historical research on the slave trade: "Slavery was corruption: it involved theft, bribery, and exercise of brute force as well as ruses. Slavery thus may be seen as one source of precolonial origins for modern corruption." Because neighboring villages would attack each other to capture slaves, relations between villages

> tended to turn hostile. As a result, ties between villages were weakened, which in turn impeded the formation of larger communities and broader ethnic identities. [And...]because of this process, the slave trades may be an important factor explaining Africa's high level of ethnic fractionalization today. This is significant for economic

Table 5.2:   *Trans-Atlantic slave trade disembarkation regions, 1514–1866*

Ship's national flag	Key destinations	Number of slaves disembarked

Portugal (& Brazil)	Brazil
	  – Amazonia
	  – Bahia
	  – Pemanbuco
	  – Southeast Brazil
		5,099,816

Great Britain	British Caribbean
	  – Jamaica
	  – Barbados
	  – Antigua
	  – St Kitts
	  – Grenada
	  – Dominica
	  – British Guiana
	  – St Vincent
	  – Montserrat/Nevis
	  – Trinidad/Tobago
		2,733,323

France	French Caribbean
	  – Saint-Domingue
	  – Martinique
	  – Guadeloupe
	  – French Guiana
		1,164,967

Spain (& Uruguay)	Spanish Americas
	  – Cuba
	  – Puerto Rico
	  – Central America
	  – Spanish Americas
		884,923

Netherlands	Dutch Americas
	  – Dutch Caribbean
	  – Dutch Guianas
		475,240

United States	Mainland United States
	  – Northern United States
	  – Chesapeake
	  – Carolinas/Georgia
	  – Gulf states
		252,653

Denmark	Danish West Indies	91,734
TOTAL		10,702,656

Source: Raw data from Voyages Database (2009)

development given the established relationship between ethnic frac-
tionalization and long-term economic growth. (Nunn 2007: 4)

Figure 5.8 confirms Nunn's fundamental conclusion of the significant
inverse relationship between the historical total number of slaves exported
from a nation and its contemporary prosperity.

In the United States, the African American descendants of the slave
trade still lag economically, as a group, far behind the descendants of
white European immigrants. For example, even since the passage of the

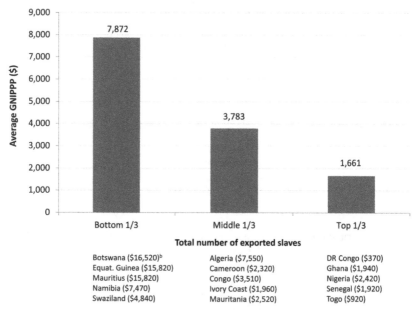

	Total number of exported slaves	
Botswana ($16,520)[b]	Algeria ($7,550)	DR Congo ($370)
Equat. Guinea ($15,820)	Cameroon ($2,320)	Ghana ($1,940)
Mauritius ($15,820)	Congo ($3,510)	Nigeria ($2,420)
Namibia ($7,470)	Ivory Coast ($1,960)	Senegal ($1,920)
Swaziland ($4,840)	Mauritania ($2,520)	Togo ($920)

*Figure 5.8: The strong inverse relationship between the historical level of slave
exportation[a] and contemporary prosperity, with selected national examples*
Notes: [a] Total number of exported slaves (includes all four major slave markets:
the Trans-Atlantic, Indian Ocean, Red Sea, and Trans-Saharan).
[b] GNIPPP per capita for 2013 is in parentheses; it is gross national income in purchasing power parity (PPP) divided by mid-year population (see Figure 3.3, note b).
[c] Correlation = −.46 ($p < .001$); N = 49 countries. Note that, per Nunn (2007),
the variables are related proportionately (a percentage change in total exported
slaves produces a percentage change in GNIPPP); as such, the correlation here
is based on the natural logarithm of the total number of exported slaves and the
natural logarithm of GNIPPP. Angola is an outlier, as it exported the greatest
number of slaves, 3.61 million, and its current GNIPPP of $5,490 ranks it 13th
highest out of the 49 African nations in the data set; thus, from the graph, we
would expect it to have a GNIPPP closer to $2,000 than to $5,500.
Sources: Raw data for GNIPPP from the Population Reference Bureau (2014);
for total slaves exported from Nunn (2007: 13)

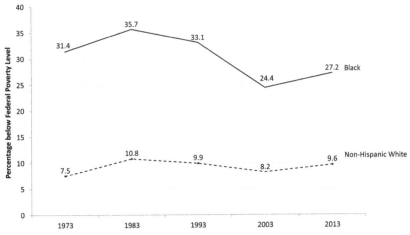

Figure 5.9:   US poverty rate by race, 1973–2013
Source: Raw data from DeNavas-Walt and Proctor (2014: 46–7)

Civil Rights (1964) and Voting Rights (1965) Acts, which were meant to eliminate discrimination based on race, color, religion, and national origin, black poverty rates still cling to about three times that of their white counterparts (see Figure 5.9; regarding the obdurate nature of solving the problem of black poverty, see the somewhat dated but still relevant 1998 classic of Massey and Denton on the problem of "American Apartheid"). And although many more Brazilians claim mixed racial ancestry than do contemporary US Americans, the descendants of black slaves in Brazil, the nation receiving the largest number of African slaves (some 5.1 million; see Table 5.2), have a legacy comparable to their counterparts in the United States: higher rates of poverty, unemployment, and morbidity, and lower life expectancies and levels of education (see, e.g., Telles 2006, 2012).

(2)   *The Syrian Civil War.* In the spring of 2011, coming on the heels of anti-government protests in Algeria, Egypt, and other Arab states, nationwide demonstrations against the nondemocratic regime of President Bashar al-Assad were met with violent suppression. As with other demonstrations that were part of what became known as the *Arab Spring*, Syrian protestors were heterogeneous in social backgrounds and in specific demands for change, but they were united in believing that the current regime was unresponsive to a depressed economy, rising food prices, high unemployment, widespread poverty, and extreme inequalities in wealth. Although these had been more or less ongoing problems for decades, a growing proportion of the younger-adult population were

becoming educated and, through mass media and international travel, were able to compare the material benefits they were receiving to what the educated were receiving in the developed world. They also were being schooled on strategies for change, as provided, for example, by Turkey – where the regime had become more responsive to an educated population by opening up the political process (free elections, encouragement of party formation) and by opening up the economy – in part, by attacking corruption and by reforming the legal system. Finally, they were being schooled on tactics via social media coverage of the street demonstrations and demonstrators' organizing efforts in Tunisia and other places where protests were on the upswing.

Violence begets violence. The government's use of force in response to street demonstrations sparked the rise of a variety of armed opposition groups – some secular, some religious, most organized around religious, tribal, and clan ties. Generally speaking, government forces came largely from Alawite (a small but powerful sect of Shi'ite branch of Islam) and other Shia groups, while rebel groups had Sunni Islamist roots. Among the better-armed rebel groups were the Free Syrian Army (formed by deserters of the Syrian military, most of them being Sunni); the Islamic Front (formed from strongly religious Islamist groups wanting to replace the nonsectarian government with an Islamist state governed by religious [sharia] law); and the Islamic State of Iraq and the Levant (known as ISIL or ISIS).[6]

The rebel groups fought not only the Assad regime, but also each other. As of 2015, the most powerful of these groups had become ISIS, which controlled significant amounts of territory in northern Syria and western and northern Iraq. The group considers itself a Sunni caliphate (an independent state governed by a supreme religious leader, a caliph, whose administrators are religious authorities that govern through sharia law). Although the Syrian military and several of the rebel groups have reputations for brutality, ISIS has distinguished itself by the ruthlessness of the violence it has perpetrated against Shia Muslims, uncooperative Sunni Muslims, and a host of minority ethnic/religious groups – including Armenian Christians, Assyrians, Chaldeans, Druze, Mandeans, Shabaks, Turkmens, and Yazidis. Indeed, Amnesty International's investigation of its abuses led to the conclusion that ISIS "has carried out ethnic cleansing on an historic scale and...has systematically targeted non-Arab and non-Sunni Muslim communities, killing or abducting hundreds, possibly thousands, and...forcing more than 830,000 others to flee the areas it has captured" in just a one-month period alone in the summer of 2014 (Amnesty International 2014: 4).

ISIS and two other radical Islamist groups, Ahrar al-Sham ("Islamic Movement of the Free Men of the Levant") and Jabhat al-Nusra ("Support Front for the People of Syria"), have received several thousand recruits from radicalized sympathizers from abroad. (All three groups have roots in Al-Qaeda, but ISIS lost Al-Qaeda's sanction in 2014. For the complex and ever-changing relationships among these and other rebel groups, see Cockburn 2015; Lister 2014.) The sympathizers are recruited by increasingly sophisticated social networks that communicate through social media and face-to-face in Muslim-majority nations and in the large Muslim neighborhoods that now exist in major metropolitan areas throughout Europe and in Muslim-majority nations – most notably Morocco, Saudi Arabia, and Tunisia. As of 2015, about 3,000 of the estimated 12,000 foreign recruits were from Western countries, with Australia, Belgium, France, Germany, and the UK most heavily represented. The recruits have been linked to 81 different countries, with most joining the most extremist groups.

> One reason for this is the chronic failure of mainstream rebel forces to fight effectively and work together, which has led to a multiplicity of small groups operating locally and joining alliances as a way to maintain their influence rather than build a force capable of taking on the Syrian army. By contrast, the more extreme groups, especially those with a high number of foreign fighters, are better resourced, fight harder, are more disciplined, and better motivated. This gives them an advantage, both against government forces and when competing for recruits or territory with other rebel groups. (Barrett 2014: 10; also see Agence France-Presse 2015)

Hundreds of these recruits eventually returned to their native countries, where many of them brought even more radicalized beliefs than they had when they left, as well as terrorism tactics and new connections with others like themselves. The fear that their return would spark new acts of terrorism put European and other developed nations on increased alert. Indeed, during 2015 there were many attacks, as well as many more thwarted planned attacks, in Belgium, France, Germany, and elsewhere that were linked to Islamic immigrants who either had supported the recruitment of other immigrants, or had gone themselves, to fight for Al-Qaeda and other radical jihadist groups in Iraq and Syria (see, e.g., Associated Press 2015a, 2015b; Reuters 2015a, 2015b). As of early 2015, Germany alone reported that 600 German residents had joined ISIS and other similar groups in Syria and Iraq, with some returning fighters having been put on trial and others having been prosecuted for providing support (Reuters 2015b). The murder of 12 staff members of the controversial *Charlie Hebdo* magazine, which had become infamous for publishing offensive cartoons picturing icons of Islam, resulted in Muslim immigrant communities in Europe "being viewed with increasing suspicion in both France and Germany, with their significant Muslim populations, and even in the UK" (Wyatt 2015).[7]

All told, between the summer of 2011 and the summer of 2015, some 200,000 Syrians lost their lives in the civil war and another 6.5 million were forced to flee their homes to escape its violence.[8] Some fled to nations where they had friends and relatives, including the United States, Canada, and many European nations; but these countries have generally not had open-arm policies that would welcome large numbers of these refugees, so most Syrians fled to camps set up in the neighboring nations of Lebanon (1.1 million *registered* Syrian refugees, but there were many that went unregistered – some 500,000 in Lebanon alone), Turkey (1.1 million registered refugees), Jordan (623,000 registered), Iraq (232,000 registered), and Egypt (138,000 registered). The refugees quickly began taxing the resources of their host countries. And in January 2015, Lebanon's Interior Minister, Nohad Machnouk, announced that his country was officially done accepting any more Syrian refugees: "We have enough. There's no capacity anymore to host more displaced" (as quoted in BBC News 2015). At the same time, so many refugees have been in their host countries for so long that the host governments have begun to grant them some limited rights and basic services. Though living conditions are still generally deplorable, Turkey has taken the lead in this area, offering refugees temporary work permits, as well as basic institutional services in its five major refugee camps – including schools, health clinics, and community centers (Rantac 2014).

Refugees from Syria in the Zaatari refugee camp in Jordan, June 2014
Source: © Dominic Chavez/World Bank

By the late summer and early fall of 2015, the strains on many of the camp refugees had reached a level of severity that began motivating hundreds of thousands of them to take dangerous land and sea routes to seek asylum in Europe. A common path involves a trek through Turkey to coastal points on the Aegean Sea; taking often overloaded and poorly maintained boats and rubber rafts to Greece; and migrating northward through Macedonia and Serbia, then though Hungary or Croatia, and eventually through Austria and into Germany – the most common destination (receiving an estimated 800,000 refugees in 2015, most from Syria, but also significant numbers fleeing war-torn Iraq and Afghanistan; see Dearden 2015). The migrants often pay everything they have to human traffickers, some of whom are humanitarian in motive but many others of whom are unscrupulous and taking advantage of people in dire straits. The human deluge forced European nations to rethink their generally unwelcoming asylum/refugee policies, and in September 2015 the EU moved to apportion 120,000 refugees among its member countries. The deluge of refugees forced this EU decision, and media reports on it largely focused on the negative reactions of many national leaders and of their citizens (the general sentiment being that their countries do not have the economic resources and infrastructures sufficient to handle such large numbers of migrants arriving in such a short time span; see, e.g., Akkoc 2015; Chan 2015; and Dearden 2015).

Per the start of this section, the political histories of almost every one of the current 195 countries recognized as sovereign states by the UN could have been used to illustrate how large-scale political changes can result in forcing large numbers of individuals to move, either fleeing from internal violence and civil war, or fleeing from being forcibly moved by the government in acts of "ethnic cleansing" or "purification." Forced migrations are especially prone to occur when

> the "Us" group of actors considers itself to be a community of descent and parts of its actual or claimed territory are inhabited by population groups who do not belong to this "Us" group or titular nation. Security arguments (prevention of separatist movements or repulsion of [the greedy] ambitions of a neighboring state) play as much a role in this as revenge for suffered injustice or the redistribution of assets, societal resources, and opportunities. (Sundhaussen 2010: 2)

More generally, internal violence and human rights abuses between and among various ethnic and religious groups are generated (1) when inequalities become consolidated with them (e.g., being identified as a member of Group 1 gives an individual and his or her fellow group members greater access to money, prestige, and political power, while membership in Group 2 gives an individual and his or her fellow group members lesser access to these resources), *and* (2) where there are few or no democratic means for redressing inter-group inequalities. Indeed, Figure 5.10 reveals the strong inverse relationship that exists between the level of political freedom and the level of internal violence that nations experience (as measured by deaths due to internal war and conflict – what the World Bank labels as "battle-related deaths"; see World Bank 2014a, 2015). During the first decade of the twenty-first century,

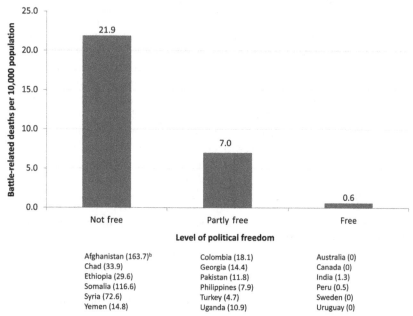

Figure 5.10: The strong relationship between political freedom[a] and battle-related deaths from internal war, with selected examples (2000–12)

Notes: [a]Political freedom ratings of not free, partly free, and free are based on a complex, composite index of a nation's levels of political rights and civil liberties. Twenty-five indicators are used and include the following constructs: (1) freedoms of expression, assembly, association, education, and religion; (2) the fairness of the legal system, including the independence level of the judiciary; (3) the freeness of economic activity; (4) the degree of equality of opportunity for women and minority groups; and (5) the reputability of elections, as judged by international monitoring organizations (see Freedom House 2014a, 2014b).
[b]Battle-related deaths from internal war per 10,000 population in parentheses; it is comprised of civilian and military deaths in battle-related conflicts experienced between warring parties within a country between 2000 and 2012 (World Bank 2014a, 2015).
[c]Correlation = −.22 ($p < .001$); N = 199 countries.

29% of the world's nations experienced such battle deaths; however, 54% of the 50 nations that are considered to be nondemocratic ("not free," according to the rankings of the international nonprofit organization Freedom House) experienced such violence, which falls to 46% of those 59 nations considered transitionally between a nondemocratic and democratic polity ("partly free" on the Freedom House ranking), and finally to just 7% of those 89 nations deemed to have a high level of democracy (labeled as "free" by Freedom House; see Figure 5.10).

The Increasing Scale of Politically Induced and Forced Migrations. Although always part of human history, the scale of politically induced migration reached unprecedented levels over the past century – with as many as 80 million Europeans alone being displaced by political upheavals (Sundhaussen 2010: 1). Indeed, in Central, Southeastern, and Eastern Europe,

> there is hardly a nation or ethnic group whose members were not in one or another form and to one or another extent forced to leave their home during the course of the 20th century. They were forcibly resettled, expelled, or fled because they belonged to a particular nation or nationality or were allotted to it, regardless of individual incrimination. (Sundhaussen 2010: 19)

Huge dislocations created in the years leading up to, during, and immediately after World War I (involving the forced or impelled migration of several million Armenians, Bulgarians, Greeks, Macedonians, and Turks) and the break-up of Yugoslavia into successor states from 1991 to 1999 (involving the forced and impelled migrations of over 4 million Bosnians, Croats, and Serbs) provided bookends for the huge forced migrations of ethnic minorities that occurred under National Socialism in Germany (1933–45) and Stalinism in the former USSR (1922–53). Both regimes alternated between mass executions and forced migrations to handle their minority populations. The National Socialist regime is most famous for the mass execution of European Jews (with 6 million either being executed or having died of starvation and disease in concentration camps), but it also executed or forcibly relocated what totaled to millions of Roma (Gypsies), Poles, Ukrainians, Byelorussians, and other Slavs. Stalin executed or forcibly relocated millions of USSR minority group members – Chechens, Germans, Korean, Poles, and Tatars (destination points included Siberia and the former Soviet states of Kazakhstan, Kirghizstan, Tajikistan, and Uzbekistan). Less commonly known was the massive deportation of Germans from former German states in the east that were given to Poland, as well as of German speakers who had lived for generations in several Eastern European states – including Czechoslovakia, Hungary, Romania, and Yugoslavia. The German forced migrations have been characterized as "the largest single movement of population in human history...[involving] between 12 and 14 million civilians, the overwhelming majority of them women, children and the elderly....From the beginning, this mass displacement was accomplished largely by state-sponsored violence and terror" (Douglas 2012: 1; also see Douglas 2013).

Since the 1980s, the UN has been monitoring the number of displaced persons created by large-scale political upheavals, such as the case of Syria discussed above. (Technically, the UN operationally defines *refugees* as those fleeing calamity and who cross a national border, while it defines those fleeing calamity but staying with national borders as *internally displaced persons*.) More generally, refugees and displaced persons are divided into broad categories: those displaced by environmental calamities (like the case of Hurricane Katrina, which was discussed earlier), and those displaced by internal violence (as in Syria). As with environmental migrants noted earlier in this chapter, the number of internally displaced persons due to political violence and human rights violations has been on a general rise since the UN and its partner organization the Norwegian Refugee Council (NRC) began record-keeping. (From year to year, the curve dips and rises, but the overall general trend is upward.) The NRC tallied 16.5 million such persons in 1989; 19.5 million in 1998; 25.3 million in 2004; and, in the most recent year for which data are available, 33.3 million in 2014 (see Albuja et al. 2014: 9–10; Ferris 2014: 5). In 2013, the NRC reported 22 million internally displaced persons due to environmental calamities (e.g., floods, droughts, hurricanes, earthquakes) – double the number of 40 years earlier (and with all estimates predicting steadily increasing numbers for the next 40 years; see Yonetani et al. 2014). Moreover, these two major sources of impelled migration often overlap, making the lives of those forced to move especially onerous: "In 33 out of 36 countries affected by armed conflict between 2008 and 2012, there were also reports of natural hazards forcing people to flee their homes. [Thus,] measures to reduce disaster and displacement risk related to natural hazards may also reduce the risk of conflict driven by insecure livelihoods" (Yonetani et al. 2014: 10).

As a final note, in a relatively smaller number of cases, the political changes promoting geographic mobility involve a dramatic turn in government policy on migration, such as what happened to create the exodus of many East Europeans from their socialist states after the 1989 fall of the "Iron Curtain" (see Dietz 2002), and as occurred since the 1980s after the 28 nations of the European Union began allowing individuals to cross borders freely to pursue employment opportunities (see Gelatt 2005; see also, the discussion and Figure 5.7c earlier in this chapter on the major 1965 legislation in the United States that opened up its borders to large-scale international migration from Africa, Asia, and Latin America).

Micro Factors (Figure 5.1b)

The individual-level (micro) factors influencing geographic mobility are, as was noted earlier, entwined with each other, and with the various macro factors sketched in Figure 5.1a, in complex and overlapping ways. They could be illustrated with any one of the myriad of historical examples of major semi- or fully voluntary migrations, as well as with most smaller migrations in which the migrants have had a degree of choice in whether – and where – to move. The example chosen here is the recent influx of Somalis into the US state of Minnesota, which provides a classic example of *chain migration* – in which prospective migrants learn of opportunities and receive advice, and sometimes material assistance, "by means of primary social relationships with previous migrants" (Macdonald and Macdonald 1964: 82). The previous migrants are from the same family, neighborhood, or religious organization. A clustering of chain migrations from a region of origin into a set of particular neighborhoods or towns constitutes a *migration field* – and this is what has occurred in Minnesota over the past two decades. (For the classic development of this concept, see Allen's [1972] analysis of the migration field of French Canadian immigrants to southern Maine during the late nineteenth and early twentieth centuries.)

The political turmoil and violent unrest that occurred in Somalia off and on between 1990 and 2015 motivated, and often compelled, more than a million of its estimated 10 million citizens to seek a better life elsewhere – most settling temporarily in nearby countries (including Djibouti, Kenya, Ethiopia, Burundi, and Yemen) and slowly and cautiously returning as they felt safe (e.g., in 2014, 120,000 returned home; see UNHCR 2015b; also see UNHCR 2014, as well as Centers for Disease Control and Prevention 2008). However, in the early 1990s, a few hundred families and individuals gained official refugee status in the United States and were resettled – under the auspices of the federal Office of Refugee Resettlement – in several Minnesota cities (including Minneapolis, St Paul, Mankato, and Rochester), as well as in Washington DC and selected cities in several other states (prominently including Atlanta, Georgia, and Columbus, Ohio). The Minnesota immigrants were particularly successful. They initially received help from local charitable groups, including Lutheran social services and Catholic charities. Despite their lack of English, they were able to find jobs in low-level service (e.g., daycare centers, retail, taxi services) and manufacturing (e.g., meat- and poultry-processing) that were being eschewed by many native Minnesotans. They were pleased to find quality public schools, many of which eventually created bilingual classrooms that featured a Somali-speaking aide for the regular teacher. They were at first surprised, and then delighted, to find they could worship openly the Sunni version of Islam that many of them devoutly follow. With the majority being near or below the poverty line, they qualified for food stamps. They also qualified for Medicaid if they could not receive health insurance from their places of work. They had no fear of an invading militia from a competing clan assaulting their daughters and wives, forcing their sons and husbands to serve it as soldiers, or of being outright murdered.

Because the initial immigrants were refugees from a war-torn country, communication back home was neither quick nor fluid, as is the case for migrants who are fully voluntary (who can readily make a cell phone call or send a text message or email back home; see the concept of *trans-migrant* discussed earlier in this chapter). Nevertheless, however haltingly, they were eventually able to begin getting the word out to their family, friends, and neighbors left behind or who had resettled in other areas that – despite its cold climate – Minnesota was a place of opportunity. Indeed, Minnesota soon became the consistently top state in the United States regarding the number of Somali immigrants it received each year, and by the end of 2013, as many as 90,000 of them and their progeny were living there – concentrated heavily in neighborhoods and suburbs in and around the Twin Cities of Minneapolis/St Paul (see Condon 2006; Darboe 2003; Dunbar 2010; Minneapolis Foundation 2004; Minnesota Historical Society 2015; Toppo and Overberg 2014; and US Census Bureau 2013e).[9]

As is typical of migration chains and fields, immigration of a group into an area begets more immigration of that group into that area. Thus, one humanitarian nonprofit organization that monitors and lends assistance to the Somali community, Arrive Ministries of Minnesota (2015), observes that "Somalis originally came to Minnesota because of the good economy and low unemployment. More recently they have come because there is a recognized community here – Somali shops, businesses and restaurants." For example, Nur Ali and his wife, Mahado Mohamed, were living in a Kenyan refugee camp when they first heard about the success of Somalis in Minnesota. Nur, Mahado, and their five children were originally resettled in Connecticut. But while living in Hartford, they heard from a fellow Somali that "all recent arrivals head to Minnesota, home of 'Little Mogadishu' " (Koumplilova 2014). Mohamud

Noor, head of the Confederation of Somali Community in Minnesota, observes that "you tend to go somewhere you can connect.... Before people even arrive from Africa, they know they are [eventually] coming to Minnesota" (as quoted in Koumplilova 2014).

The Links of Age, Gender, and Education to Migration

Though, historically, many immigrants at the beginning of a migration chain have been young men, who after securing employment later brought over their wives, children, and other family members, Somalis arriving in Minnesota are more reflective of modern migration trends – which find many migrants moving as families, and the number of women equaling, or even slightly outnumbering, the number of men. The historical gender change in geographic mobility reflects the rise of gender equity throughout the developed world, and increasingly in selected developing countries. The increased movement of families reflects less restrictive immigration regulations, allowing spouses and children of authorized immigrants to move as a unit (e.g., as is the case when the immigrant has received a visa or green card based on his or her specialized job skills), as well as the increased comfort and safety of modern means of transportation (compare a six-week trans-Atlantic voyage on a relatively small sailing ship to a modern jumbo aircraft making the same trip in a matter of hours).[10] Regarding age, however, there has been a consistent age-migration curve describing the relationship between these two variables throughout history. As exemplified in Figure 5.11, those in their 20s and 30s are most likely to be movers, reflecting changes in their life-cycle activities (marriage, seeking educational and employment opportunities) and their overall generally good health (making them, along with their employability, good candidates for refugee resettlement). These individuals often have very young children, so children under the age of 10 are the second most common age group to be movers.

Although, as a group, Somali immigrants are less educated and poorer than native Minnesotans (e.g., in 2010, one estimate was that 82% were living near or below the federal poverty line; and 68% lacked a high school diploma – compared to 8.4% of other Minnesotans; see Dunbar 2010), there is some evidence that the Somali migrants to the state coming from other US states (as opposed to those directly resettling from Africa) tend to be better educated and have more resources (as of 2008, roughly two Somalis were entering Minnesota from another US state to every Somali entering as a resettled refugee directly from Africa – and this ratio appears to have been on the rise ever since; see Remington 2008; Yusuf 2012: 64–5). This is generally reflective of those in

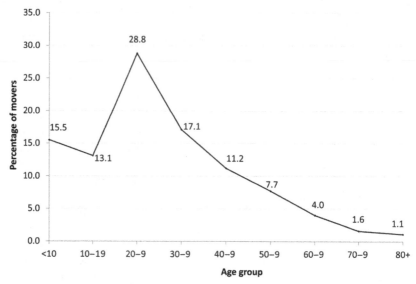

Figure 5.11:   Empirical example of the age–migration curve: individuals who moved in the United States, 2012–13

Notes: The curve is fairly stable, worldwide, across time and across geographic areas: Adults in their 20s and 30s, along with their young children whom they take in tow, are most likely to be movers.

[a] Of the total US population in 2013, 11.7% (35.9 million) of the 307.2 million people aged 1 and older moved; 64.5% moved from one residence (e.g., house or apartment) to another residence within the same county; another 19.4% moved to a different county within the same state; 13.3% moved to a different state; and 2.9% moved abroad. National probability sample surveys of movers reveal their top reasons for moving are (1) housing-related (e.g., moving to a better neighborhood or a larger home accounted for 48% of the movers); (2) family-related (30%, most often related to a change in marital status – getting married, divorced, or separated); and (3) job-related (19%, e.g., taking a new job, being transferred by one's employer, retiring, or falling victim to unemployment; for a more detailed breakdown of these percentages, see Ihrke 2014).

[b] Females were slightly more likely to be movers than males, with 50.9% of all movers being female.

Source: Data calculated from US Census Bureau (2015a)

developed nations who make significant moves: that is, those who move long distances (e.g., in the United States, from one state to another, as opposed to from one residence to another within the same city or county) tend to be better educated and thus have more job opportunities and greater financial resources to make an actual move (for the United States as an example of this phenomenon, see Figure 5.12).[11] Even that part of

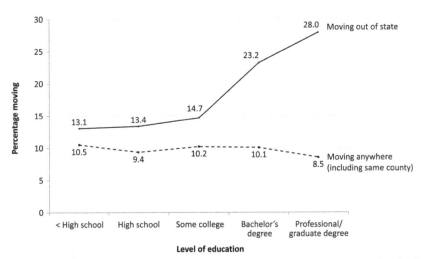

Figure 5.12: Empirical example of the positive relationship between level of education and long-distance geographic mobility: individuals who moved in the United States, 2012–13, by level of education

Note: Although educational level does not predict the probability of moving, college graduates are significantly more likely than those with less education to be long-distance movers – reflecting, in part, their greater opportunities for employment across the nation and, in part, their greater resources for being able to make such a move. Gans (1982: 89–90) argues that the "object" value orientation of the well educated also make them more willing to pull up stakes and move away from friends and family, in contrast to the "person" value orientation of the less educated: "[There are two value-based] kinds of individualistic modes of behavior, *object-oriented* and *person-oriented*. The distinction between them can be described by differences in aspirations. Object-oriented individualism involves striving toward the achievement of an 'object.' This may be … a material object, such as a level of income; a cultural object, such as a style of life; or a social object, such as a career or status position. … Person-oriented individualism also strives, but not for object goals. Here, the overriding aspiration is the desire to be a person within a group; to be liked and noticed by members of a group whom one likes and notices in turn … ; person-oriented people develop their aspirations within a primary group in which they are members, and which they are not interested in leaving."
Source: Data calculated from US Census Bureau (2015a)

international migration that reflects individuals from less developed nations voluntarily moving to developed nations to seek better employment and lifestyle opportunities reveals that the movers are not the poorest of the poor, as it takes a level of resources to move oneself, or one's entire family, from one nation to another. (Compare the discussion earlier in this chapter on the impact of structural economic changes on migration – to wit, those countries contributing the greatest numbers of emigrants are UN-designated *developing* nations, not *least developed* nations; in part, this is because the developing countries include many with large populations, but, in part, it is because the individuals in these nations tend to have more resources, however meager they might appear to be to those living in the developed world, than their counterparts in least developed nations.)

Migration and Its Impacts, Including the Problem of Assimilation

Selected Economic and Political Impacts

When an area experiences a significant amount of immigration (or in-migration) or emigration (or out-migration), the impacts can be roughly divided into those that are positive and those that are negative. An area with a surplus of unemployed individuals can experience a boon if these surplus individuals and their families move away. Thus, for example, as the farmlands of the Midwestern United States opened up in the nineteenth century, many European farmers trying to live off of increasingly smaller plots of land were drawn to the Midwest. These "smallholders who migrated could get larger plots of land than they had farmed back in Europe. As the Midwest filled up and Europe became less crowded, plot sizes gradually equalized. Eventually, farmer Schmidt in Germany was as well off as farmer Schmidt in Iowa" (Collier 2013: 49–50). Moreover, historically and even more prominently in the modern era, immigrants succeeding in destination areas help their areas of origin by sending back remittances to relatives in their homeland (see the discussion of remittances earlier in this chapter; also the evidence presented in Dayton-Johnson et al. 2009).

Beyond economics, migrants from poorer, nondemocratic countries can positively affect their homelands when they migrate to more prosperous, democratic countries and are exposed to democratic ideas. This exposure has been empirically shown to promote greater democracy in the homeland. For example, during the Senegal elections of 2012, Senegalese migrants living in the United States and France were surveyed, and it was discovered that through regular phone calls "most of these migrants were urging their relatives to register to vote, and nearly half were recommending whom to support" (Collier 2013: 185; cf. Dedieu et al. 2013). In a similar vein, for the 2009 elections in Mali, Chauvet et al. (2013) found that emigrants from the country who had returned home from nations with democratic regimes were, in general, more likely to vote than their nonmigrant counterparts; importantly, many nonmigrant neighbors of the return migrants modeled themselves on the migrants and were thus more likely to vote; finally, and perhaps most importantly, this modeling effect occurred with both better educated *and* less educated neighbors. Inspired by these findings, Oxford University international migration specialist Paul Collier (2013: 187) effuses: "This is really encouraging. Not only do return migrants bring back new norms of democratic participation learned in the high-income societies, but they are also catalysts for change among the uneducated, who are otherwise hardest to reach."

At the same time that an area of origin is sometimes helped by emigration, if the area of destination has need for workers, it, too, will experience benefits with the influx of immigrants. Not only will individuals fill open jobs, but their families will create demand for goods and services, and if the immigrant workers are doing so legally, they will be paying income taxes to support government services – including critical national programs such as social security for the retired and medical care for the infirm. Indeed, as noted in Chapter 4, openness to immigration means that a nation experiences fewer of the economic and social pressures that mount as a growing proportion of the population ages and enters retirement in the context of the generation behind them being smaller (as is almost universally the case in the developed world) – with fewer workers paying taxes to support the healthcare and social needs of the older generation. The United States is a prime example of a nation being economically saved by large-scale immigration from the combination of an aging population and a declining birth rate (Alden et al. 2009: 13; Frey 2014: 2).

Of course, the effect can run in the opposite direction too: Areas experiencing heavy emigration may be losing their younger workers, leaving jobs unfilled and taxes lost (including taxes that would support the costs of an aging population). Thus, for example, Dayton-Johnson et al. (2009: 149–50) observe that the outflow of skilled workers can deprive "developing countries of their human capital and results in *brain-drain* with serious consequences on the delivery of key services like education or health care, and on economic productivity." A classic example is the massive loss of the educated population of Haiti over the past few decades. It is estimated that this country of 10 million has lost 85% of its college-educated population since 1990 – people with the skills to innovate and adapt new technologies to help the economy grow. Countries similarly experiencing an overall social and economic impairment from the emigration of its best educated individuals include Afghanistan, Guinea-Bissau, Laos, Liberia, Malawi, Sierra Leone,

Zambia, and Zimbabwe. (Docquier and Rapoport [2012] have identified 22 such countries, with most of them being in Sub-Saharan Africa, and all of them being small and poor.)

At the same time, areas experiencing heavy immigration may find immigrants competing with natives for jobs, and in some cases finding new jobs offered at lower wages because immigrant workers are willing to take them (with the "lower" wages being much higher than anything they experienced in their home countries or areas of origin). Thus, for example, a variety of recent studies in the United States and the United Kingdom reveal that large influxes of individuals who are poor and lack education can hurt low-wage native workers (those below the 20th percentile; see., e.g., Dustmann et al. 2013; Khatiwada et al. 2006; Ruark and Graham 2011). Indeed, the case study of Somalis in Minnesota speaks to this problem: even though Somali immigrants took tough jobs that many native Minnesotans were shunning, including in poultry and meat-processing, Remington (2008: 5) observes that these processing firms "have implemented a strategy that entails new immigrants relocating to rural areas, closing unionized plants, re-opening non-union plants, and lowering wages to a level that attracts only immigrant workers." More generally, Collier (2013: 111–12) explains that studies showing deleterious effects of immigration on native workers, especially those in the lower reaches of social class system, fit the basic principles of economics:

> [T]he immigration of workers would be expected to reduce wages and increase returns on capital. As a result, indigenous workers would be worse off and indigenous wealth owners would be better off. As to government-provided services, the existing stock of public capital – schools, hospitals, roads – would be shared among more people and so per capita provision would deteriorate. Poorer people receive more of their income from work and less from wealth and more of their overall well-being from government-provided services. Hence, the prediction from first principles of economics is that immigration benefits those indigenous people who are wealthy but makes poorer indigenous people worse off. [In short,] the working classes lose from competition with workers willing to accept lower pay, [as well as from] competition with immigrant families using social services.

That said, when the negative and positive effects of international migration are combined, the balance most often shows a net gain for countries of both origin and destination. In their review of the relevant empirical literature, Dayton-Johnson et al (2009: 151) observe:

It is increasingly accepted that international migration can help reduce poverty and contribute to economic growth in the migrants' countries of origin. According to a World Bank study an average increase of 10% of emigrants in the total population of a developing country is associated with a 1.6 percentage point reduction in poverty (using an international poverty line of USD 1 per day). Moreover economic analyses show that an increase in temporary migration in developed countries, including low qualified migrants, could produce gains amounting to USD 150 billion each year, equally shared between developed and developing countries. Meanwhile, a 10% increase in the share of remittances in Gross Domestic Product (GDP) is associated with a reduction of poverty by 1.2%.

Collier (2013: 113, 203) does not dispute this conclusion, but also warns that it based on the limited range of currently observed variations in immigration and emigration, which tells "us little about what would happen if migration continued to accelerate. For that, we would be safer to retreat to the economic first principles [noted above]: the wages of most indigenous workers would drop considerably and remain lower for many years," while the poorest 10% of high-emigration nations, like Haiti, would experience even greater negative effects of the brain drain.

Because of the fear of competition for jobs with the native population, because of the fear of excessive pressure they put on public amenities (education, healthcare, welfare benefits, etc.), and because of the fear that they will debilitate the national culture (and its particular mix of values and norms), a large influx of migrants to a new area stirs political controversy. For example, in the United States, national polls consistently show that about half of the native-born population believes that immigrants contribute to crime and about a third maintains that immigrants decrease overall job opportunities for the native-born – even though when asked to evaluate whether "on the whole, immigration is a good thing or a bad thing for the country," two-thirds consistently respond that it's "a good thing for the country today"; and, similarly, two-thirds to three-quarters would support the nation's 11 to 12 million unauthorized immigrants being offered a pathway to citizenship as long as it met certain requirements (e.g., learning English, not having a criminal background; for long-term and more recent trends in public attitudes toward immigration and immigrants, see, Gallup 2015a).

Current US national politics, as well as the politics in states with large immigrant populations, are off and on dominated by discussions on how best to handle immigrant populations, especially the 11 to 12 million unauthorized immigrants that are part of the 45 million immigrants now living in the country. (Note that as of 2012, the five states with the highest proportions of immigrants were California [27% foreign-born], New York [23%], New Jersey [21%], Florida [20%], and Nevada [19%]; see Krogstad and Keegan 2014.) Although there are exceptions (e.g., when President Barack Obama took executive action in the fall of 2014 to protect as many as 5.4 million unauthorized immigrants from deportation), immigrants generally do not fare well as beneficiaries or participants in the democratic political process. And even though they have advocates, especially from nonprofit social welfare organizations (including many that are church-affiliated) and grass-roots political organizations (from the tiny Somali advocacy group the Confederation of Somali Community in Minnesota, to high-profile organizations like the American Civil Liberties Union and the American Immigration Council), they are generally reluctant to vote or otherwise involve themselves with conventional politics.[12] Why so?

- In part, it is because they cannot vote until they become citizens.
- In part, it is because their lack of political involvement and voting prior to citizenship generates habits of daily life that do not include politics – in sociological parlance, they have not been socialized on the basics of participation.
- In part, and also related to the socialization process, voting and other political behaviors are stimulated when an individual interacts regularly with those already involved in these behaviors – and, as immigrants, they lack this form of social capital (doubly so if they do not speak English well, and triply so if they are poor, as the poor, in general, have much lower levels of voting and other forms of conventional political participation than their middle-class-and-above counterparts).
- Finally, in part, it is because they do not want to draw attention to themselves.

Regarding the last of these reasons, it is obvious why unauthorized migrants would not want to draw the attention of public officials, but even authorized migrants, most of whom have a strong desire to fit in and to become at least partially assimilated into – and accepted by – the dominant culture, do not like to put themselves in the middle of controversial topics; being apolitical is an easier path to follow. In Western societies, including the United States, "across all forms of political participation…immigrants…are one group who are consistently found to participate less than the mainstream population" (Ruedin 2011: 6).[13]

When they do express a preference for a candidate or party, and when they do actually vote, immigrants in the United States and Europe tend to favor the left (progressive candidates and parties; see e.g., Bevelander and Spang 2014: 40; Lopez and Taylor 2012; Posner 2012). Thus, for example, in the 2012 US presidential election, Hispanic and Asian voters, the majority of whom are first-generation Americans, overwhelming supported the liberal Democratic candidate Barack Obama over the conservative Republican candidate Mitt Romney (71% of Hispanics voted for Obama, while 76% of Asians did so; see Lopez and Taylor 2012; Posner 2012). In a 2013 Gallup poll of both immigrant and native-born Hispanics, it was found that both groups heavily favored the Democratic Party over the Republican Party by a ratio of 2 to 1 (for first-generation immigrants, 57% leaned Democratic and 25% Republican; for second-generation, 64% leaned Democratic and 30% Republican; see Newport and Wilke 2013; note that the ratio is similar for Asians, 75% of whom are immigrants: 50% identify with the Democratic Party vs 28% for the Republican Party; see Krogstad 2014). Similarly, in a 2012 Pew Research Center survey of Hispanic immigrants who were neither US citizens nor legal permanent residents (to wit, they were unauthorized immigrants), 31% identified as Democrats and just 4% as Republicans.

In the view of many contemporary political observers, Republicans resist making the pathway to citizenship easier for unauthorized immigrants because they fear it will yield a landslide of support for the Democratic Party (see, e.g., *The Economist* 2015; Patten and Lopez 2013; cf. Rydgren 2008 for similar fears of the political right in Europe). Indeed, national immigration reform has been at a standstill in the United States for decades because of the dramatically differing views of Republican and Democratic legislators (Kim and Brown 2014). Ironically, from the viewpoint of conservative and Republican observers, both Asian and Hispanic immigrants and their offspring appear to be voting against their own interests. Despite their great diversity in national backgrounds, Hispanics have, as was noted in Chapter 3, several common traditions, including a generally strong emphasis on the family, as well as a generally strong emphasis on religion (Gaines et al. 1997; Gallo et al. 2009; Marin and Marin 1991). And as those who keep track of contemporary US politics are well aware, greater-than-normal emphases on the family and on religious values are fundamental components of the American brand of conservativism. (Indeed, a 2015 national probability poll of Republicans revealed that the majority, 57%, favored establishing Christianity as the national religion; see Strauss 2015.) Conservative Republican Ronald Reagan, the US president from 1980 to 1988, once famously remarked to one of his campaign advisors: "Latinos are Republicans – they just don't know it yet." By this, he meant that conservative, church-going, entrepreneurial, family-loving Latinos were "being tricked by Democrats" (as quoted in *The Economist* 2015).

Similarly, imbued with the family focus of Confucian values (Smith 1991: 175–7), Asian immigrants generally have a strong sense of family and are, moreover, overrepresented in the upper middle class (with income levels well above the rest of the population). And conservativism and Republicanism are both linked to those with higher levels of prosperity. Why change a status quo that has resulted in you being on top?[14]

Half of all Hispanics living in the United States today, and three-quarters of all Asians, are first-generation immigrants – with significantly lower voter turn-out rates than for both native blacks and native whites (Krogstad 2014; Krogstad and Lopez 2014). For example, in recent midterm elections (the elections between presidential elections, e.g., 2010 and 2012), both Hispanic and Asian turn-out of eligible voters has been just 60% of that of whites (31% for both Hispanics and Asians, vs 49% for whites) and only 70% of that of blacks (31% vs 44%). However, when they do begin to vote in greater numbers, which is the expectation by the third generation, US politics will turn more to the left – more toward multicultural acceptance, more toward strong social safety nets, more toward being immigrant friendly, more toward Democratic candidates. (Note that the offspring of immigrants tend to vote very similarly to their parents; see Newport and Wilke 2013.)

The Problem of Heterogeneity

All things equal...people prefer to be with others who look like them, speak the same dialect, and hold the same beliefs. An amplification of this evidently inborn predisposition leads with frightening ease to racism and bigotry. Then, also with frightening ease, good people do bad things.

Edward O. Wilson (2014)

Some established Minnesotans...feel resentment or competition towards relative newcomers who appear to be surpassing them economically. Others...fear that already scarce resources will be spread even more thinly as services such as job training and English language instruction are provided to new immigrants. And some people are simply intolerant of cultural differences.

The Minneapolis Foundation (2004)

Aside from feeling the resentment and fear from the native population regarding the competition for jobs and the stresses on public services created by a new immigrant group, the group also typically suffers from prejudice and discrimination and troubles associated with cultural assimilation – including difficulty in grasping the concept of race in America because individuals are identified by skin color more often than by nationality (Darboe 2003). For example, the Somali immigrants to Minnesota have found movement into the middle class difficult, with a majority living at or below the poverty line. They have felt the sting of prejudice when trying to improve the quality of their local schools. And even though free to practice Islam, they have felt and experienced anti-Muslim bigotry from classmates, coworkers, neighbors, and public officials, especially since 9/11 and the War on Terror, which is almost synonymous with the war on radical Islam (for narrative examples, see, e.g., Yuen 2009; Yusuf 2012: 48–54). More generally, in a 2011 national probability sample, 48% of US Muslims reported that they had "personally experienced racial or religious discrimination in the past year," on par with other prominent minorities – including Hispanics (48%) and African Americans (45%).[15]

The experience of highly successful Somali immigrant Ahmed Jama provides an illustration of the struggles that immigrants can experience when they begin pushing for equality. Jama and his family moved to Eden Prairie, Minnesota, in 1998. They were "lured by the promise of a growing Somali community, affordable housing, and high-quality schools" (Toppo and Overberg 2014). Jama reported that initially he and his fellow immigrants "never spoke in public; never advocated for our kids. We never advocated for our housing rights or employment rights. We lived in the shadows of society for 15 years." But when he and a few other bold Somalis began showing up at local school committee meetings to support a proposed plan to redraw school boundary lines to more equitably distribute low-income and minority students throughout the city's schools – and ultimately to reduce the achievement gaps among the schools – they were met with a generally "ugly" and "racially inflammatory" response. Jama commented to a journalist covering the school boundary redrawing controversy that local white residents "are not used to blacks, Muslims, scarves. It was a culture shock for them as much as for us. The fear of the unknown was overwhelming."

Although the school plan was ultimately approved, and within three years (2012–14) student achievement rose and the inter-school achievement gap narrowed, Somalis felt a hostile environment, one that was also reflected in a decreasing interest on the part of landlords to maintain the stock of affordable housing (to wit, they increasingly began rejecting subsidized housing vouchers). The upshot: As many as 40% left the city and moved to less prosperous suburbs – adding to the concentration of low-income, black, and immigrant students already in the schools in these communities. By the end of 2014, Jama had decided that he would most likely follow his compatriots who had left Eden Prairie. "I don't know about the future," he reported, "but now it looks like we are at a standstill as far as integration" (Toppo and Overberg 2014; for a variety of rich, narrative examples of the cultural conflicts Somalis have experienced, see Roble and Rutledge 2008 and Yusuf 2012).

While Jama's reaction might be considered moderate in the larger range of possible reactions to the suffering of prejudice and discrimination, other Somalis' reactions have been more extreme. As has been the historical case for a significant proportion of most immigrant groups, some have decided to return to their home country and to bear the dangers of its periodic internal wars rather than to risk suffering more hostility and feelings of alienation by staying in Minnesota or the greater United States. And others, especially teenagers and young men, have reacted by leaving the United States and returning to Somalia to join the region's main radical jihadist group, al-Shabaab (an affiliate of Al-Qaeda), or by retreating to neighborhoods where they reside in high numbers and form turf-based street gangs (where they find refuge from the hostility of the native-born, including native-born blacks, with whom they feel little affinity, as well as from other immigrant groups; see Roble and Rutledge 2008: 182; Shane 2015; Temple-Raston 2015; Yuen and Aslanian 2013; Yusuf 2012: 48–54).

More generally, immigrant groups take multiple generations to achieve success to the degree that their national background is no longer strongly predictive of their socioeconomic standing. In the United States, white European immigrant groups in the nineteenth and early twentieth centuries were met with high levels of prejudice and discrimination, from both the native population and other immigrant groups, but within two to four generations they were generally well incorporated into American society. The speed and success of incorporation for these groups, as has been the cross-national case for most all immigrant groups in the modern era, initially depended upon the degree of their linguistic and cultural differences from the majority population – which was, in the US example, predominantly white, English-speaking, and Christian (with a Protestant majority). First-generation non-Protestant, non-English speakers (e.g., Italians, Eastern Europeans) generally had tougher experiences than their Protestant, English-speaking counterparts from England, Scotland, and Wales. Regardless of national origins, however, the second generation found that learning English and attending US schooling contributed to their economic success. Success was enhanced by finding public-sector jobs (e.g., as garbage men, police officers, fire fighters, and city hall desk-workers) and developing various entrepreneurial enterprises (from ethnic-based grocery stores to pubs to funeral homes). Such success prompted them to gradually move out of ethnically segregated neighborhoods to find better housing, better schools, and more services at the outer edges of cities and into surrounding suburbs. Increased "positive" contact with the native population and other immigrant groups in schools, workplaces, and neighborhoods led to intermarriage among those of different nationalities, and with intermarriage the importance of national background to individual identity and success diminishes greatly. "In sum, there exists a strong positive correlation between the socioeconomic status of an ethnic group and the length of time since its arrival" (Carter 1993: 116).[16]

Given this historical context, both academic and social service organization observers of the Somali experience in Minnesota agree that the immigrant group has been in the United States for a relatively short time. And with the passage of time, these observers have already begun seeing success. For example, John Borden, of the social service agency the International Institute of Minnesota, observes: "Time is probably the single biggest factor [for success]. Everything from signing up for English classes to starting a business eventually becomes a matter of following others' footsteps. They can talk with six of their brothers and cousins who have already done it" (as quoted in Dunbar 2010). Cawo Abdi, a Somali immigrant and sociologist at the University of Minnesota, believes Somalis have not had a harder-than-usual time integrating compared to most other groups. "A lot of what we are seeing with the Somali community is very much what we have seen for other refugees and migrants in the history of migration to the United States. While their children or grandchildren will likely have an easier time integrating, members of the…group's first generation still don't feel like the US is their home" (as quoted in Dunbar 2010).

Although, as noted earlier in this chapter, the legacy of slavery is evidenced in the generally higher poverty and unemployment rates of blacks in America, it is also true that immigrant blacks appear to be on a course that has many similarities with white immigrant groups. Thus, for example, the poverty rate of first-generation immigrant blacks in 2012 was 21%, while it was 14% for the second generation. A similar success story exists for immigrant Hispanics (23% of the first generation were in poverty in 2012, vs 16% of the second generation). And though immigrant Asians have not seen the same significant drop in poverty rates, their rate for the first generation was initially much lower than that of immigrant blacks and Hispanics, and has stayed so (12% for both the first and second generation; note that poverty data are from the Pew Research Center 2013b). This story of success for recent African, Hispanic, and Asian immigrants has unfolded even though they have had to overcome, and are still overcoming, the legacies of historical discrimination against peoples of color in the United States, as well as continuing contemporary prejudice and discrimination.

Indeed, recent black, Hispanic, and Asian immigrant groups, including those with a sizeable portion who are less educated and poorer, have been following similar steps to collective economic success to those taken by their white European counterparts in the nineteenth and twentieth centuries:

> New migrants invade low-income neighborhoods in search of inexpensive housing and low-skill jobs. Competition between newcomers and native social groups ensues, often accompanied by hostility, mistrust, prejudice, and discrimination. Eventually, groups become segregated in relatively homogenous subareas. With the passage of time (two to four generations), however, segregated ethnic enclaves shrink, as individuals from them enter mainstream America, both occupationally and residentially. Stepping-stones from poor, segregated, inner-city neighborhoods to the mainstream include education, intermarriage, civil service, and ethnic-based economic enterprises. (Carter 1993: 116)

Regarding the stepping-stone of intermarriage, echoing what happened historically to their white European counterparts, intermarriage rates have risen sharply between the first and second generations for the new (post-1965) immigrant groups from Asia, Latin America, and Africa: For Asians, intermarriage with members of a different race or nationality has risen from 10% for the first generation to 24% for the second generation; for Hispanics, this rate jumped from 7% to 27%; and for immigrant blacks, the intermarriage rate rose from 9% to 30% (see Pew Research Center 2013b).

Along with federal legislation barring housing discrimination (e.g., the Fair Housing Act of 1968), rising education levels, incomes, and rates of intermarriage have led to significantly decreasing rates of residential segregation over the past three decades. For example, in 1980, 50% of the black population lived in neighborhoods that were at least 80% black; but by 2010, just 20% were living in such neighborhoods. In 1980, Asian immigrants were highly concentrated in "Chinatowns" and "Little Koreas" in major US cities like Los Angeles and New York; however, by 2010, just 11% were living in a census tract that had an Asian majority (50% or more). Because they are being constantly infused with large numbers of new immigrants, most of whom are not well educated or fluent in English – and thus are drawn to neighborhoods with large numbers of Spanish speakers – Hispanics have not witnessed the same dramatic drops in segregation levels that have been experienced by blacks; nevertheless, less than half, 43%, are currently living in Hispanic-majority census tracts. The equivalent proportion for blacks is 41%. The most segregated racial group in the United States today are whites, almost 90% of whom live in majority-white neighborhoods (see Frey 2014; Glaeser and Vigdor 2012).

Though whites are now the most segregated group in the contemporary United States, their proportion of the total population has been falling since the post-1965 immigration wave began (which has involved mainly Africans, Asians, and Latinos), and in 2011, for the first time in its history, more babies of color were born than white babies. By 2040, whites with a European background will comprise less than 50% of the total population. In the words of distinguished social demographer William Frey (2014: 1–2):

> This milestone signals the beginning of a transformation from the mostly white baby boom culture that dominated the nation during the last half of the twentieth century to the more globalized, multiracial country that the United States is becoming.... [D]emography is truly destiny, [and, as such, current]...fears of a more racially diverse nation will almost certainly dissipate. In many communities, a broad spectrum of racial groups already is accepted by all, particularly among the highly diverse youth population. Moreover, as [my research] illustrates, a growing diverse, globally-connected minority population will be absolutely necessary to infuse the aging American labor force with vitality and to sustain populations in many parts of the country that are facing population declines. Rather than being feared, America's new diversity – poised to reinvigorate the country at a time when other developed nations are facing advanced aging and population loss – can be celebrated.

Regarding immigrant blacks, in particular, Figure 5.13 demonstrates how the stepping-stones into the mainstream of rising levels of education, employment, and income have been increasingly realized; and at the same time, the figure also reveals how immigrant blacks have outpaced native blacks in their socioeconomic progress over the past several decades.

Explaining the Greater Success of Immigrant Blacks and Other Immigrants of Color

Why immigrant blacks have surpassed native blacks so quickly is currently a question of great academic interest to contemporary social scientists, not to mention to blacks themselves. People of color – blacks, Latinos, Asians, Native Americans – have historically faced higher levels of prejudice and discrimination and less than full assimilation into

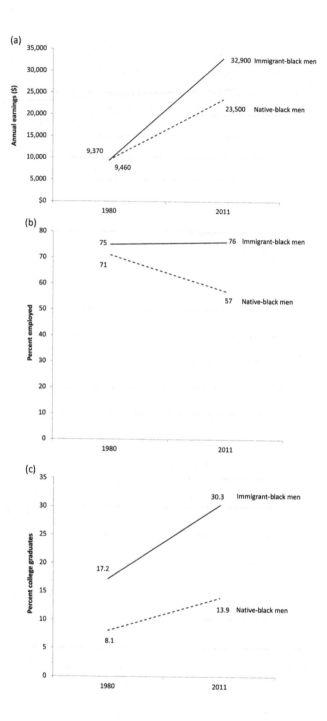

(a)

(b)

(c)

American culture and society compared to white European immigrants. But recent immigrants from Asia, Africa, and Latin America have come closer to experiencing the white immigrant process of assimilation than has been the historical pattern of partial and segmented assimilation for people of color. The broadest interpretation points to the legal and social changes in the 1960s that accompanied the loosening of immigration restrictions from Africa, Latin America, and Asia. These changes "lowered the barriers to minority participation in society and [allowed] schools and workplaces [to become] more integrated." Indeed, "many new immigrants seem to be following the assimilation path of European immigrants nearly a century ago…[and] the achievements of some minorities indicate that minority status alone need not thwart advancement" (Pollard and O'Hare 1999: 43–4).[17] This conclusion is echoed in the findings of a recent major empirical study of second-generation immigrants to the United States:

Figure 5.13: Immigrant-black versus native-black indicators of socioeconomic success, 1980–2011

(a) Earnings: In 1980, immigrant-black men and native-black men had essentially the same personal annual incomes: Immigrant men were earning 99% of what native men were making. By 2011, however, immigrant-black men were earning 140% of their native-black counterparts. Note that both groups were significantly behind white men, who averaged $16,400 in 1980, and $48,500 in 2011.

(b) Employment: In 1980, immigrant-black men and native-black men had essentially the same employment rates: The immigrant men's rate was 106% of that for native men. By 2011, however, the immigrant-black men's rate was 133% of that for their native-black counterparts. Note that both groups were significantly behind white men in 1980, who had an 84% employment rate; by 2011, only native-black men trailed their white counterparts, whose rate of 76% was identical to that for immigrant-black men.

(c) Education: In 1980, the proportion of immigrant-black men with a college degree was 210% of that of native-black men. By 2011, the immigrant-black men's rate had grown to 218% of that for their native-black counterparts. Note that both groups were significantly behind white men in 1980, 22.4% of whom had a college degree; by 2011, only native-black men trailed significantly behind their white counterparts, whose rate of 32.0% was almost the same as that for immigrant-black men (30.3%).

Note: Data are for males, ages 21–65; female data show the same trends, with immigrant-black women significantly outpacing native-black women in earnings, employment, and education between 1980 and 2011.

Source: Data are from the 1980 US Census and the 1-in-100 Public Use Sample of the American Community Survey for 2011, as excerpted from Rauh (2013: 19)

Second-generation Americans – the 20 million adult US-born children of immigrants – are substantially better off than immigrants themselves on key measures of socioeconomic attainment.... They have higher incomes; more are college graduates and homeowners; and fewer live in poverty. In all of these measures, their characteristics resemble those of the full US adult population. Hispanics and Asian Americans make up about seven-in-ten of today's adult immigrants and about half of today's adult second generation. [T]he second generations of both groups are much more likely than the immigrants to speak English; to have friends and spouses outside their ethnic or racial group, to say their group gets along well with others, and to think of themselves as a "typical American." (Pew Research Center 2013c)

Regarding immigrant versus native blacks in particular, among the more popular explanations accepted by *immigrant* blacks – as opposed to native blacks, almost all of whom trace their roots to the American South and slavery – is the differential experience of native-versus immigrant-black interactions with whites. As black author Jacob Conteh (2013), an immigrant to the United States from Sierra Leone, summarizes the differential-experience interpretation:

[There is...]a huge chasm between African-Americans and African immigrants in the United States. That chasm has widened over the years. It has caused deep animosity between many African-Americans and their African immigrant cousins.

The problem stems from deep misconceptions.... Astonishingly, many African-Americans believe that Africans are backward and primitive. Some make crude jokes about Africans or do not acknowledge the great contribution Africa has made to the world.

For their part, many African immigrants buy into the erroneous notion that African-Americans are lazy and violent. They do not appreciate the great sacrifice African-Americans made, through advocating for their civil rights, to lay the foundation for Africans to be able to come to the United States and live in a country where both blacks and whites have equal rights, at least in theory if not always in practice.

The different experiences of the two groups [is the key] to understanding the deep division that exists between African Americans and Africans.... Before migrating to the United States, most Africans have typically dealt with white Americans who went to Africa as Peace Corps volunteers, missionaries, doctors, or teachers. These Americans acted as mentors and guardians to the Africans and developed positive relationships with them. [Thus,] when they come to the United States,... Africans can easily identify with white Americans because they understand each other. Before migrating to the United States, the majority of Africans have had little to no direct negative experiences with whites....

On the other hand, most African-Americans grew up in black neighborhoods where they learned from older generations the history of slavery and the cruelty it inflicted on the black race. Furthermore, they have usually experienced firsthand and in their communities the legacies of racism that still exist in the United States. With this background, many African-Americans are not generally predisposed to trust white Americans, and they look down on those African immigrants who express respect or admiration for white Americans....

Africans...are ready to integrate into the American culture without getting involved in the lingering racial conflicts. They do not typically get involved in the ongoing civil rights struggle – and that has angered many African-Americans....

Most African immigrants to the United States came here for economic advancement. They do not have any political agenda. They are willing to take any job and do not blame the "system" when they fail in their endeavors.

The differential-experience interpretation would lead to the research hypothesis that foreign-born and native-born blacks differ in their attitudes toward minority success, including the need for affirmative action programs. Indeed, attitudinal data from the General Social Survey offer moderate confirmation of this expectation (see Table 5.3).

Some social scientists and black intellectuals give significant importance to the differential-experience interpretation. For example, in reflecting on a study showing that the majority of Harvard black students are immigrants or the offspring of immigrants, famed black Harvard University professor Henry Louis Gates, Jr remarked: "We need to learn what the immigrants' kids have so we can bottle it and sell it, because many members of the African-American community, particularly among the chronically poor, have lost that sense of purpose and values which produced our generation" (as quoted in Rimer and Arenson 2004). And reacting to the same observation – that is, the predominance of immigrant blacks and their children in the United States' most prestigious universities – Harvard sociologist Mary C. Waters, an immigration specialist, notes that immigrant blacks are "more successful than many African-Americans for a number of reasons. [But among them is that] since they come from majority-black countries, they are less psychologically handicapped by the stigma of race" (as quoted in Rimer and Arenson 2004; cf. Waters 2001).

However, other sociologists and black intellectuals argue that the differential-experience interpretation wrongly elevates the cultures of black immigrants over African American culture and results in a

Table 5.3:   Attitude toward affirmative action: native-born versus foreign-born blacks

Attitude toward affirmative action	US-born blacks (%)	Foreign-born blacks (%)
Strongly opposes	30.2	39.5
Opposes	23.7	24.2
Supports	46.1	36.3
All	100	100
	(n = 1,842)	(n = 157)

Notes: Attitude toward affirmative action measured with the cumulated 1993–2012 General Social Survey (2012) item AFFRMACT ("Some people say that because of past discrimination, blacks should be given preference in hiring and promotion. Others say that such preference in hiring and promotion of blacks is wrong because it discriminates against whites. What about your opinion – are you for or against preferential hiring and promotion of blacks?" Response choices: Strongly Support; Support [combined for Table 5.3]; Oppose; Strongly Oppose). As of 2013, foreign-born blacks constituted about 10% of the total US black population – thus the subsample sizes (1,842 vs 157) are dramatically different.

Percentage differences between foreign-born and native-born blacks for the first row (Strongly Opposes: 39.5% – 30.2% = 9.3%) and third row (Supports: 36.2% – 46.1% = –9.9%) are statistically significant (χ^2. = 7.2, p < .028; N = 1,999). Phrased as ratios, foreign-born blacks are 31% more likely than native-born blacks to strongly oppose affirmative programs (39.5 ÷ 30.2 = 1.31) and, on the other hand, native-born blacks are 27% more likely to support these programs (46.1 ÷ 36.3 = 1.27).

blaming-the-victim mentality. Indeed, the relevant social science research supports an alternative interpretation for the great success levels of recent immigrant groups of color: the explanatory power of the starting points of various immigrant groups – when comparing their differing success amongst each other, as well as with native blacks and native whites. In short, groups coming to the United States differ in their overall levels of education and financial resources, and those with greater amounts of these assets – and notwithstanding the Somali refugees of Minnesota, these include many blacks from Africa and the British Caribbean – are quicker to gain prosperity and move into the middle class or above. Thus, for example, about 6% of migrants to the United States from Mexico have a college-level education, compared to 50% of those from Asia (Center for Immigration Studies 2015: Table 27; Pew Research Center 2013b). The result has been "streamlined acculturation and upward mobility into the middle-class mainstream" for a majority of the children of Asian immigrants, while second- and third-generation Mexicans have experienced much slower mobility. (Their mobility is nonetheless arching in an upward direction – into the top half of the working class as skilled workers, e.g., in the building trades, repair services, and maintenance;

and, indeed, "downward intergenerational mobility or even stagnation are unlikely outcomes for the children of Mexican immigrants" [Luthra and Waldinger 2013: 171].) Studies of immigrants to European and other OECD countries also find the educational and financial starting point of an immigrant group to be partly responsible for comparable patterns of differential success (see, e.g., Froy and Pyne 2011: 12; Heath et al. 2008).

Main Points and Key Terms

1   Migration is defined as the movement of people across a significant boundary, usually a political boundary, and it implies that the people moving do so with the intent of taking up permanent or semi-permanent residency in their places of destination.

2   Demographers recognize many different types of migration, the most fundamental being immigration (coming to a new country), emigration (leaving a country), in-migration (coming to a new locality or region within the same country), and out-migration (leaving a locality or region within the same country).

3   Within any given geographic area smaller than the entire planet, population change depends not only on the balance between births and deaths (the natural increase), but also on net migration (the balance between immigration [or in-migration] and emigration [or out-migration]). The demographic balancing equation expresses these facts as: Population size$_{time2}$ = Population size$_{time1}$ + Natural increase + Net migration.

4   Demographers divide the many causal forces motivating people to move into sets of macro and micro factors. Among the most important macro factors are changes in the natural environment (e.g., the onset of a drought), structural economic change (e.g., industrialization), and large-scale political changes (e.g., civil war).

5   Among the most important micro factors motivating people to move are marriage; occupational prestige (with those qualifying for high-prestige jobs having more employment opportunities and thus both greater motivation and financial resources to make a move); age (those in their 20s and 30s, along with their young children, being most likely to move for work, educational, or family formation reasons); and the maximization of individual satisfaction (balancing the costs and benefits a move would mean regarding employment, family relations, health, housing, and recreation).

6   The effects of industrialization on human social organization have been monumental and include the greatest single type of migration: rural to urban. Over the past two centuries, as technological

advances increased production and decreased the need for human labor in the countryside, massive numbers of people moved from rural to urban areas in search of work in the industrializing urban economies. These economies were built first on manufacturing, and since the mid-twentieth century, increasingly on services, information processing, wholesale and retail sales, and leisure activities.

7   Economics motivates much of international migration: Individuals migrate either to escape a decline in their standard of living rooted in large-scale economic change (e.g., the mechanization of agriculture and being pushed from the farm to find work in the city, often in another country) or to improve their standard of living – even though considered relatively well off by local standards (this is especially true of well-educated and skilled workers). As such, two-thirds of international migrants end up in highly developed, high-income countries.

8   Unauthorized migration, a highly contentious contemporary social problem in the United States and the nations of Western Europe, reflects the importance of the economic motives underlying international migration – as the majority of undocumented immigrants are fleeing areas of high unemployment and low wages to take unfilled and generally low-skill jobs in more prosperous areas.

9   On balance, international migration improves the economies of countries of both origin and destination. Emigrants decrease unemployment in the areas they leave, and immigrants tend to have high employment rates – they thus pay taxes that support social programs, and they add to overall economic vitality by way of their purchases of goods and services.

10   New immigrant groups often feel resentment from the native population regarding competition for jobs and the stresses put on public services. Immigrants also often suffer from prejudice and discrimination, and they can struggle to assimilate culturally and politically. However, within two to three generations, increases in intermarriage, education, the landing of civil service jobs, and the building of ethnic-based economic enterprises all work together to lift most groups into the middle class.

achieved social status (standing) (196)
ascribed social status (standing) (196)
Arab Spring (203)
Black Death pandemic (182–3)
brain drain (243 n.3)
brain gain (243 n.3)
chain migration (177)
Chinese Exclusion Act (197)
circular migration (177)
climate change (184)

Review Questions

1 What does transmigration mean, and what does it tell you about the modern world?
2 The demographic balancing equation has five key elements on the right side of the equation sign. Which of these has the least precise measurement? Why?
3 How can changes in the natural environment work to push people away from one geographic area or pull them into another area? Give at least one example from this chapter.
4 What has motivated the massive rural-to-urban migrations that virtually all countries have experienced in recent history?
5 Give at least one example of the kind of evidence that indicates the strong economic foundations for much of international migration.

6   Which kind of country – least developed, developing, or developed – is most likely to experience immigration, and which emigration? Why?

7   Under what conditions is political violence/internal war most likely to erupt between and among different ethnic or religious groups within a society?

8   Why does the age–migration curve look the way it does?

9   Discuss at least two of the reasons underlying the lower levels of political participation on the part of immigrants versus their native-born counterparts.

10   Immigration affects both the area of destination and the area of departure, and it can do so both positively and negatively. Give at least one example of the positive effects that both areas can undergo as a result of the migration, and give at least one example of the negative effects that can unfold in both areas.

Suggested Readings and Online Sources

The UN has a wide variety of print and online sources covering the many cultural, economic, political, and social aspects of migration – as well as providing annual updated data in readily downloadable formats, including Microsoft Excel. Among these sources, the more important include the Migration Section of the Demographic Analysis Branch of the UN's Population Division and the UN's website on *World Urbanization Prospects*. Excellent complements to the UN sources include Demographia.com's *World Urban Areas* and related data-rich reports on its website; the website of the intergovernmental International Organization for Migration (see, especially, its dictionary of *Key Migration Terms* and its *World Migration Report*); and the US Census Bureau (especially helpful is how the demographic balancing equation applies to individual countries – see US Census Bureau 2016a; also see the US Census Bureau's "population clock" website [2016b], which gives net migration data – as well as a host of migration-related data sets and reports). More specific to the 28 nations of the European Union, detailed reports and data on migration can be found at the Migration Policy Institute's website, while comparable information on the 34 nations of the OECD can be found in its annually updated *International Migration Statistics Database*.

The complex relationships of environmental factors with migration, including the impacts of climate change, can be found in the International Organization for Migration's ongoing project *Migration, Environment and Climate Change: Evidence for Policy* and its associated website

Migration, Climate Change and the Environment. The US Global Change Research Program provides a variety of reports and data sets on the effects of climate change on the United States, in particular, while the Population Reference Bureau has many similar reports, data sets, videos, and web-based seminars ("Webinars") on this topic as it affects international populations.

The complex and manifold relationships of migration and structural economic change in the contemporary era are detailed in a series of empirical articles in Denis Ushakov (ed.), *Urbanization and Migration as Factors Affecting Global Economic Development* (2015), while Mike Davis's *Planet of Slums* (2006) provides a sensitive examination of the economic change and political callousness that have produced untold human misery for a large portion of the hundreds of millions of rural-to-urban migrants in the developing world. A more upbeat and wide-ranging conversation on connections of immigration with global economic development can be found in the open-source 2014 Public Radio International interview of Nobel prize-winning economist Amartya Sen and his former student Luis Alberto Moreno (current president of the American Development Bank) at http://radioopensource.org/immigration-and-development-with-amartya-sen/. The interview includes the topics of (a) the movement of poor laborers in developing countries into the fields, factories, and low-level service jobs that are unfilled by the native-born populations in developed countries; (b) the movement of well-educated technical workers from developing nations, including India, into the high end of the US labor market; and (c) the huge impact of remittances on the developing nations to which they are sent by their immigrants to developed nations. (Note that the interview starts at the 6-minute mark of this hour-long recording.)

Detailed data on the numbers and social backgrounds of immigrants to the United States can be found at the Pew Research Center (2016) website on immigration, as well as at the US Department of Homeland Security's annual *Yearbook of Immigration Statistics.* Internal migration rates, as well as detailed survey data on migrants (including their reasons for moving, as well as their background characteristics like age, gender, and level of education), can be found at the US Census Bureau's Migration/Geographic Mobility website. (For a detailed, but highly readable, analysis of the most currently available Census Bureau migration data, see David Ihrke's *Reason for Moving: 2012 to 2013: Population Characteristics* [2014].)

The Pew Research Center has produced a number of detailed reports on the cultural, economic, political, and social impacts of unauthorized immigration in the United States – see, for example, *Five Facts about Illegal Immigration in the US* (2014b). For the European situation, the

Migration Policy Institute and the European Commission's division on Migration and Home Affairs have produced several analyses and policy recommendations for getting a handle on what European governmental and social welfare organizations call "irregular" immigration (as opposed to the terms most commonly used in the United States: "unauthorized," "undocumented," or "illegal").

An excellent print examination of the history of the great migrations, including those involving Europeans coming to the Americas, is Michael H. Fisher's *Migration: A World History* (2014), while an equally illuminating study of contemporary world migration and its positive and negative effects on places of origin and destination is Paul Collier's *Exodus: How Migration Is Changing Our World* (2013). Essential complements to the Collier book include Stephen Castles, Hein De Haas, and Mark J. Miller's *The Age of Migration: International Population Movements in the Modern World* (5th edn, 2014), and Douglas S. Massey, Joaquin Arango, Graeme Hugo, et al.'s *Worlds in Motion: Understanding International Migration at the End of the Millennium* (1998). For the hybrid national identities of many of today's global migrants, see the detailed case studies in Brian D. Behnken and Simon Wendt (eds), *Crossing Boundaries: Ethnicity, Race, and National Belonging in a Transnational World* (2013).

The best available data on the trans-Atlantic slave trade can be found at Emory University's Voyages Database (*Voyages: The Trans-Atlantic Slave Trade Database* 2009) and Neil A. Frankel's website on *The Atlantic Slave Trade and Slavery in America* (2009). Excellent print complements to these sources that include both ancillary data and in-depth historical analyses are David Eltis and David Richardson's *Atlas of the Transatlantic Slave Trade* (2010); James Oliver Horton and Lois E. Horton's *Slavery and the Making of America* (2006); and Hugh Thomas's *The Slave Trade: The Story of the Atlantic Slave Trade: 1440–1870* (1997).

Current and historical data related to the impact of internal and cross-national war on impelled and forced migration are available from the United Nations High Commission for Refugees and the Norwegian Refugee Council. The High Commission's website provides detailed and often-updated profiles of individual countries, including Syria. For excellent examinations of the Syrian situation, in particular, and of the Arab Spring, in general, see Paul Amar and Vijay Prashad (eds), *Dispatches from the Arab Spring: Understanding the New Middle East* (2013); Mahmood Monshipouri's *Democratic Uprisings in the New Middle East: Youth, Technology, Human Rights, and US Foreign Policy* (2014); and Patrick Cockburn's *The Jihadis Return: ISIS and the New Sunni Uprising* (2015).

The plight of Somali refugees worldwide is monitored by the nonprofit Somali Documentary Project (see its Facebook page); one of its best accounts of the often difficult Somali experience of trying to assimilate and succeed in American society is Abdi Roble and Doug Rutledge's *The Somali Diaspora: A Journey Away* (2008). Another good relating of the Somali immigrant experience in Minnesota is Ahmed Ismail Yusuf's *Somalis in Minnesota* (2012).

A variety of Gallup polls on migration are repeated every several years in the United States and selected developed nations. These polls provide a rich source of data on native-born versus immigrants' view of the assimilation experience – including attitudes on whether immigrants contribute to unemployment and crime, on the one hand, and to innovation and economic and cultural vitality, on the other hand (see, e.g., http://www.gallup.com/poll/152660/faces-global-migration.aspx; and http://www.gallup.com/poll/1660/Immigration.aspx). A sophisticated set of analyses of survey data on the effects of educational level, employment status (working vs unemployed), age, gender, level of contact between the native-born and the foreign-born, and nativity (native- vs foreign-born) on anti-immigrant attitudes in the United States and Europe can be found in Joel S. Fetzer's *Public Attitudes toward Immigration in the United States, France, and Germany* (2000). Fetzer finds that older, native-born, unemployed (or under-employed), less educated males, who have few positive contacts with immigrants, are most likely to express anti-immigrant attitudes.

Social anthropologist Rinus Penninx (2005) provides a useful paradigm for assessing the integration of migrants as this process has produced varying degrees of success in Europe. In the best of all possible worlds, integration takes place economically, socially, culturally, and politically. In general, he concludes that most European countries have fallen greatly short of full integration because they have failed to fully embrace *multiculturalism*. A core aspect of this worldview is that immigrants cannot become equal citizens unless the state and society accept that both individuals and groups have the right to be culturally different.

Regarding the complexities of immigrants of color assimilating culturally, socially, and economically into American society, in his 2014 book of the same name, William H. Frey gives an excellent, detailed, and data-rich account of the immigration-fueled "diversity explosion" in the United States that has been underway since the post-1965 relaxation of racist immigration laws that had kept migration from Africa, Asia, and Latin America to a minimum since 1921. Frey's book shows how rates of race- and ethnic-based segregation are on the decline, while rates of intermarriage are on the rise. His interpretations are upbeat, and he sees the new immigrants rescuing older Americans from declining fertility rates and infusing the economy and cultural with new stakeholders and innovators – who move into existing jobs that are unfilled, who create new jobs, and who pay taxes, including those that support Social Security and Medicare.

In his *Getting It Wrong: How Black Public Intellectuals Are Failing Black America* (2006), sociologist Algernon Austin argues vehemently that the notion of immigrant black culture being in any way superior to native-black (African American) culture is not supported by the data. Rather than indicating cultural superiority or inferiority, disparities in educational, employment, and income between immigrant and native-born blacks are due to immigrants being "often special people: They are rarely the average members of their country. They are usually above average in at least one of three things: motivation, skills, or formal education. It is not unusual for them to be above average in all three" (p. 19).

In his thoughtful and empirically based book, *Those Damned Immigrants: American's Hysteria over Undocumented Immigration* (2013), Ediberto Román carefully assesses the argument that unauthorized immigrants hurt the economy, create unemployment for the native-born, and overwhelm the US educational and healthcare system. At the national level, he concludes that the overall effects of unauthorized immigration are small but positive. Although some individual states have had their economies hurt by high numbers of unauthorized migrants, Román shows how this damage could be prevented by selective and relatively inexpensive federal interventions.

Notes

Chapter 1   Overview of Population Study

1   Note that the most recent one-year sample data are available for communities of 65,000+, and the most recent three years of sample data for communities of 20,000+. The one- and three-year samples are more current, but because the number of respondents is smaller than for the five-year period, the accuracy is not as great (see US Census Bureau 2013a).

Chapter 3   Mortality

1   For accessible examples of how life tables are constructed, see Bell and Miller (2005) and Haupt et al. (2011); for a more sophisticated treatment of the topic, see Kinter (2008).
2   For reviews of the various negative consequences of the Green Revolution, see, e.g., Cordain (1999); Foley (2014); Frison et al. (2011); Manning (2014); Pesticide Action Network Asia and the Pacific (2007); Shetty and Schmidhuber (2011); United Nations (2014e); and Zwerdling (2009a, 2009b).
3   For a detailed historical and cross-national account of why grain- and sugar-heavy diets generate obesity, and why Asian versions of grain-heavy diets are less likely to produce obesity because they are almost completely devoid of sugar, see Taubes 2011.
4   For a review of the complex mechanisms giving female biology an advantage over male biology in protecting the individual from cardiovascular disease, see Kolar and Ostadal (2013); for the inverse correlation between size and longevity, see Samaras (2002 [though contrast Paajanen et al. 2010]).

Chapter 4   Fertility

1   Subtotals: 50 *more developed*, 33 *less developed* countries, and no *least developed* countries (calculations based on data taken from Population Reference Bureau 2015).

2   If we assume that life expectancy for the global population will not go much above 90, and if we assume a TFR of what now exists in the more developed world and China, around 1.5 to 1.6, both very reasonable assumptions, then the sophisticated population model of Lutz and Scherbov (2008: 14) arrives at 8.8 billion by 2050, dropping to 8.5 billion by the end of the century, and continuing to drop until population stability is reached at around 2300, at 1.1 billion.

3   For discussions of the complex structure and intertwined controversies surrounding the One-Child Policy, see Cai (2010); Chen and Wu (2006); Feng et al. (2012); Fong (2004); Gu et al. (2007); US Department of State (2004); and White (2006). For shorter discussions, see BBC News (2000); Elliott et al. (2013); Marsh (2012); Pfeiffer (2012); and Public Radio International (2013).

4   For the inverse of effects of earnings on fertility, see Schultz (1994); for the equal power of men and women in developed nations on deciding the number and timing of children, see Stein et al. (2014) and Thomson (1997).

5   For a more general discussion of the growth of postmodern values, see Inglehart's (2000) empirical analyses of the *World Values Survey*. The foundation of this value system is the growing sense of economic security that comes with continued prosperity: When individuals live in a society where fears of mass starvation still exist, their values emphasize the importance of the group over the individual.

6   While growing slowly – e.g., in the United States from 5% in the 1970s, to 6% in the 1980s, to 7% in the 1990s – the voluntary desire to be childless for a lifetime involves only a tiny proportion of the adult population.

7   Covre-Sussai uses the *World Values Survey* to confirm the religion–cohabitation relationship at both the individual and country levels of analysis using the United States and 23 Latin America and European nations; Wilcox uses the *Fragile Families Child Well-Being Study* to confirm the relationship at the individual level of analysis in the United States.

8   For the complexities in the changing of the funding of Medicare and Social Security retirement benefits, see Internal Revenue Service (2014); Portez et al. (2011); Social Security Administration (2014b, 2014c); and Tax Policy Center (2014).

9   Unauthorized immigrants throughout the world are often taken advantage of by employers and criminals, as they cannot turn to government agencies, including the police or the court system, for protection (more on this topic in the next chapter). For China's struggles to handle international immigration and how these compare to similar struggles of nations in the developed world, see *China Daily* (2010a, 2010b, 2014); Haimei (2011); Xienhuanet. com (2012); and Zhang (2014).

Chapter 5   Migration

1   Because about one-quarter of US immigrants come to the country without authorization and are thus hard for Census Bureau enumerators to detect, the estimate of net migration is less accurate than the estimates of births and deaths, which are based on national vital statistics reports. The vagary introduced into the equation by the uncertainty of the exact number of unauthorized migrants produces a slightly different 2010 total population here than that which was actually reported by the US Census Bureau: 308,746,000. Data excerpted from Camarota (2011: 10); Makun and Wilson (2011: 2); and US Census Bureau (2014d, 2014e).

2   The second is to be sponsored by an employer that cannot meet its workforce needs from US citizens. Note that 66% of authorized immigrants arrive via family sponsorship, about 16% because they have special skills to fill high-tech jobs in computing, engineering, and science. Most of the rest, about 12%, are granted refugee/asylee status: e.g., Somalis fleeing their war-torn nation (see Monger and Yankay 2014; US Department of Homeland Security 2014).

3   As most of the return migrants are well educated, the phenomenon has acquired the label *brain gain* – as opposed to its opposite, which has been going for much of the past half-century: the *brain drain*, caused by the emigration of many of the brightest and most talented individuals from developing countries like India and China (see the discussion of the brain drain later in this chapter). Per the discussion in Chapter 4, emerging high-tech super powers like India and China have been easing immigration policies and adding tax and other incentives to get their best-educated émigrés to return home.

4   For many other contemporary examples of the hybrid national identities and sense of belonging of a variety of immigrant groups, see Behnken and Wendt (2013).

5   Per Table 5.1 and the earlier observations on remittances, most migrants come from developing countries that are considered "middle income" by the World Bank, and *not* from the poorest four dozen nations designated by the UN as "least developed," as it takes some degree of personal or familial resources to make a migratory journey, especially one of long distance that can involve crossing international borders. Thus, were a system of indentured labor in place on a large-scale basis today, as it was 200–400 years ago, it is likely the world would see many more migrants from very poor countries.

6   Historically, "the Levant" is the area from southern Turkey to Egypt, hence the ISIL acronym. The key territory in this region is Syria, thus the group is sometimes known as the Islamic State of Iraq and Syria, from which comes ISIS. By 2015, they preferred to call themselves simply "Islamic State" – even though all three labels are routinely used by the media.

7   France has the largest Muslim population in Europe, some 5 million or 7.5% of the population, compared with Germany's 4 million or 5% of

the population, and the United Kingdom's 3 million, also 5% of the population.

8   When the violence that has spilled over into northern Iraq is taken into consideration, several million more can be added to this figure (see Amnesty International 2014; Miles 2014; UNHCR 2015a; United Nations 2014l). Note that in 2015, the United Nations High Commission for Refugees estimated that "10.8 million of Syria's 22 million [total] population was affected by the conflict and in need of humanitarian assistance, including 6.5 million internally displaced; [moreover,] ... the number affected is expected to grow" (UNHCR 2015a).

9   Estimates of the total Somali immigrant population in Minnesota vary widely by source, with community leaders believing that the Census Bureau grossly underestimates the total number (Koumplilova 2014). Somali writer and translator Ahmed Ismail Yusuf (2012: 63) offers insight into one of the reasons behind the high variability in the estimates of the Somali population in Minnesota: Somalis are "hesitant to enumerate who and how many are living at a particular address, fearing landlords may use the information against them." However different these estimates are, data from the federal Office of Refugee Settlement (2015) reveal that the only year in the past two decades that Minnesota did not rank as the top state in the country for receiving resettled Somalis was in 2009.

10   For changes in the gender distribution of migrants worldwide, see United Nations (2015c) and Zlotnick (2003). In 1960, 46.6% of all international migrants were female; by 2013, this had risen to 48.0%. Per the note in Figure 5.11, in developed nations, including the United States, females are actually slightly more likely to be movers.

11   "[W]hereas the supply and demand for unskilled labor can be met within a local labor market, the more highly skilled the occupation, the more likely supply and demand for the skill will extend from local to regional to national levels" (Nam and Philliber 1984: 188; cf. Dahl and Sorenson 2010).

12   Aside from voting, other forms of conventional participation include political discussions, wearing campaign buttons, contacting an official, donating money to a party, signing a petition, attending a political rally, helping out a campaign, or actually running for office. Note that immigrants are even more reluctant to participate in unconventional political activities, e.g., marches, sit-ins, and boycotts.

13   Ruedin's own analyses emphasize the importance of the lack of socialization and of social capital as explanations for low levels of immigrant political participation, in general, and in differences among various particular immigrant groups in their levels of participation. See also Katsiasficas's (2014) similar conclusions regarding low political participation of immigrants in the 28 nations of the EU. For analyses of the similarly heated, complex, and convoluted politics involving the acceptance and treatment of immigrants in Europe, see, e.g., Bevelander and Spang (2014), who also review the political incorporation of immigrants in developing nations – where the rights and participation tend to be even more curtailed than in developed nations.

14   Note that as of 2013, 49% of Asian adults were college-educated versus 28% of the rest of the population, the median annual household income for Asians was $66,000 versus $49,800 for non-Asian households, and the median household wealth of Asians was $83,500, well above the $68,529 median for everyone else (see Pew Research Center 2013d).

15   Note that Muslim immigrants to European countries report similar experiences: In the three countries with the largest Muslim minorities – the UK, France, and Germany – Muslims "are significantly more likely than the general population to say they experienced discrimination in the past year" (Gallup 2015b: 23; for the US and European survey data, see Gallup 2015b).

16   For the continued importance of having positive contacts between immigrants and nonimmigrants as a means of reducing the prejudice of native-born individuals toward immigrants in the United States, see Carter (2008). Compare the similar findings of Hooghe and Vroome (2013) and of Jolly and DiGiusto (2014) for Europe. For a large-scale meta-analysis confirming the general proposition that contacts between individuals of different ethnic, racial, and religious groups can reduce prejudice and thereby increase minority group prosperity and increase intermarriage rates, see Tropp and Pettigrew (2010).

17   Pollard and O'Hare (1999) document the major and burgeoning economic, political, and social successes of immigrants of color during the 1980s, and 1990s (see also Murdock 1998). Documentation of continued immigrant success since 2000 can be found in Austin (2006); Haskins (2007); Luthra and Waldinger (2013); and Pew Research Center (2013c).

References

Aberth, J. 2007. *The First Horseman: Disease in Human History*. Upper Saddle River, NJ: Pearson Education.

Achenbach, P., and M. Jackson. 2014. "What Can Government Do About Falling Birth Rates?" Washington, DC: Woodrow Wilson Center. (Web)

Adler, N., and K. Newman. 2002. "Socioeconomic Disparities in Health: Pathways and Policies." *Health Affairs* 21: 260–76.

Agence France-Presse. 2015. "20,000 Foreign Fighters Head to Syria: US." Feb. 10. (Web)

Akkoc, R. 2015. "Migration Crisis: Desperate Refugees Escape Camps and Start a 110-mile Trek to Austria." *The Telegraph*: Sept. 4. (Web)

Albuja, S., E. Arnaud, M. Caterina, et al. 2014. *Global Overview 2014: People Internally Displaced by Conflict and Violence*. Geneva: Internal Displacement Monitoring Centre, Norwegian Refugee Council. (Web)

Alden, E. (director), J. Bush and T.F. McLarty III (cochairs) 2009. *US Immigration Policy*. Washington, DC: Council on Foreign Relations. Independent Task Force Report No. 63. (Web)

Allen, J. 1972. "Migration Fields of French Canadian Immigrants to Southern Maine." *Geographical Review* 62: 366–83.

Alliance for a Green Revolution in Africa. 2014. *Africa Agricultural Status Report 2013: Focus on Staple Crops*. (Web)

Amar, P., and V. Prashad (eds). 2013. *Dispatches from the Arab Spring: Understanding the New Middle East*. Minneapolis: University of Minnesota Press.

American Community Survey. 2013. *Measuring American – People, Places, and Our Economy*. (Web)

American Psychological Association. 2014. *Stress in America: Paying with Our Health*. (Web)

Amnesty International. 2014. *Ethnic Cleansing on a Historic Scale: Islamic State's Systematic Targeting of Minorities in Northern Iraq.* London: Amnesty International. (Web)

Anderson, B. 2015. *World Population Dynamics: An Introduction to Demography.* Boston: Pearson.

Arias, E. 2004. "United States Life Tables, 2001." *National Vital Statistic Reports* 52: 1–39. (Web)

Arias, E. 2012. "United States Life Tables, 2008." *National Vital Statistics Reports* 61: 1–118. (Web)

Arrive Ministries of Minnesota. 2015. "Somalis in Minnesota." (Web)

Associated Press. 2015a. "US Accuses 6 Immigrants of Helping Islamic State Group." Feb. 6. (Web)

Associated Press. 2015b. "Germany Charges 22-Year-Old with Membership in Islamic State." Feb. 11. (Web)

Austin, A. 2006. *Getting It Wrong: How Black Public Intellectuals Are Failing Black America.* New York: iUniverse.

Baines, D. 1995. *Emigration from Europe 1815–1930.* New York: Cambridge University Press.

Balazs, R. 2014. "Epigenetic Mechanisms in Alzheimer's Disease." *Degenerative Neurological and Neuromuscular Disease* 4: 85–102.

Balbo, N., and N. Barban. 2014. "Does Fertility Behavior Spread among Friends?" *American Sociological Review* 79: 412–31.

Banister, J., D. Bloom, and L. Rosenberg. 2011. "China: Population Aging and Economic Growth." Tsinghua University, Beijing: International Economic Association Sixteenth World Congress. (Web)

Bao, S., Ö.B. Bodvarsson, J.W. Hao, and Y. Zhao 2011. "The Regulation of Migration in a Transition Economy: China's Hukou System." *Contemporary Economic Policy* 29: 564–79.

Barrett, R. 2014. *Foreign Fighters in Syria.* New York: Soufan Group. (Web)

Basten, S. 2009. "Voluntary Childlessness and Being Childfree: The Future of Human Reproduction, Working Paper #5." Oxford: St John's College Research Centre, University of Oxford. (Web)

BBC News. 2000. "China Steps-up 'One-Child' Policy." BBC News: Sept. 25. (Web)

BBC News. 2015. "Syria Conflict: Lebanon Refugee Curb Prompts UN Concern." BBC News: Jan. 5. (Web)

Beard, J., S. Biggs, D. Bloom, et al. 2012. *Global Population Ageing: Peril or Promise?* Geneva: World Economic Forum. (Web)

Behnken, B., and S. Wendt (eds). 2013. *Crossing Boundaries: Ethnicity, Race, and National Belonging in a Transnational World.* New York: Lexington Books.

Bell, F., and M. Miller. 2005. *Life Tables for the United States Social Security Area 1900–2100: Actuarial Study No. 120.* Washington, DC: US Social Security Administration. (Web)

Bernardi, L. 2003. *Channels of Social Influence on Reproduction.* Rostock: Max Planck Institute for Demographic Research. (Web)

Bernardi, L., and A. Klärner. 2014. "Social Networks and Fertility." *Demographic Research* 30: 641–70.

Bevelander, P., and M. Spang. 2014. *From Aliens to Citizens: The Political Incorporation of Immigrants*. Bonn: Institute for the Study of Labor. Discussion Paper No. 7920. (Web)

Bhrolcháin, M., and É. Beaujouan. 2012. "Fertility Postponement Is Largely Due to Rising Educational Enrolment." *Population Studies* 66: 311–27.

Borlaug, N. 2000. "The Green Revolution Revisited." Special Lecture, Norwegian Nobel Institute, Oslo (Sept. 8). (Web)

Boserup, E. 1981. *Population and Technological Change: A Study of Long-Term Trends*. Chicago: University of Chicago Press.

Boslaugh, S. 2013. *Health Systems Around the World: A Comparative Guide*. Thousand Oaks, CA: Sage.

Bostean, G. 2013. "Does Selective Migration Explain the Hispanic Paradox? A Comparative Analysis of Mexicans in the US and Mexico." *Journal of Immigrant and Minority Health* 15: 624–35. (Web)

Brazilian Institute of Geography and Statistics (Instituto Brasileiro de Geografia e Estatistica). 2013a. *The National Household Survey* (*A Pesquisa Nacional por Amostra de Domicílios*). (Web)

Brazilian Institute of Geography and Statistics (Instituto Brasileiro de Geografia e Estatistica). 2013b. *The National Household Survey, 2011*. (Web)

Bremner, J., and L. Hunter. 2014. *Migration and the Environment*. Washington, DC: Population Reference Bureau. (Web)

Brown, J., J.R. Burger, W.R. Burnside et al. 2014. "Macroecology Meets Macroeconomics: Resource Scarcity and Global Sustainability." *Ecological Engineering* 65: 24–32. (Web)

Brown, L. 2009. *Plan B 4.0: Mobilizing to Save Civilization*. Substantially revised edn. New York: W.W. Norton.

Buettner, D. 2009. "How to Live to Be 100+." TED Talk. (Web)

Buettner, D. 2010. *Blue Zones: Lessons for Living Longer from the People Who've Lived the Longest*. Washington, DC: National Geographic.

Bühler, C., and E. Fratczak. 2005. "Learning from Others and Receiving Support: The Impact of Personal Networks on Fertility Intentions in Poland." Rostock: Max Planck Institute for Demographic Research. (Web)

Bureau of Labor Statistics. 2013. *Fatal Occupational Injuries by Selected Worker Characteristics and Selected Event or Exposure, 2012 (Table 4)*. (Web)

Bureau of Labor Statistics. 2014a. *American Time Use Survey Summary*. (Web)

Bureau of Labor Statistics. 2014b. *Earnings and Unemployment Rates by Educational Attainment, 2013*. (Web)

Bureau of Labor Statistics. 2014c. *Labor Force Statistics from the Current Population Survey*. (Web)

Cai, Y. 2010. "China's Below-Replacement Fertility: Government Policy or Socioeconomic Development?" *Population and Development Review* 36: 419–40.

Caldwell, J. 1986. "Routes to Low Mortality in Poor Countries." *Population and Development Review* 12: 171–220.

Camarota, S. 2011. *A Record-Setting Decade of Immigration: 2000 to 2010*. Washington, DC: Center for Immigration Studies. (Web)

Carlson, M., and F. Furstenberg Jr. 2006. "The Prevalence and Correlates of Multipartnered Fertility among Urban US Parents." *Journal of Marriage and Family* 68: 718–32.

Carter, G. 1993. "Social Disintegration in Inner-City Black Neighborhoods of the Frostbelt: The Example of South Providence." *Research in Urban Economics* 9: 115–40.

Carter, G. 2008. "Predicting Black and White America's Attitudes toward Immigrants: A Test and Refinement of Contact Theory Using the TAPIII." Bridgewater State University: New England Sociological Association Spring Conference. Working Paper (Apr. 19).

Carter, G. 2010. "Inequality." Pp. 389–94 in Gregg Lee Carter (ed.), *Empirical Approaches to Sociology*. Boston: Allyn & Bacon.

Cartwright, F. 1972. *Disease in History*. New York: Dorset.

Cartwright, F. 2000. *Disease in History*. 2nd edn. Stroud: Sutton Publishing.

Castles, S., H. de Haas, and M. Miller. 2014. *The Age of Migration: International Population Movements in the Modern World*. 5th edn. New York: Guilford.

Catlin, B., A. Jovaag, and J. Willems Van Dijk. 2015. *2015 County Health Rankings: Key Findings Report*. Madison: University of Wisconsin Population Health Institute. (Web)

Center for Immigration Studies. 2015. *Immigrants in the United States: A Profile of America's Foreign-Born Population*. Washington, DC: Center for Immigration Studies. (Web)

Centers for Disease Control and Prevention. 2008. *Promoting Cultural Sensitivity: A Practical Guide for Tuberculosis Programs That Provide Services to Persons from Somalia*. Atlanta: US Department of Health and Human Services. (Web)

Centers for Disease Control and Prevention. 2014a. *Underlying Cause of Death: 1999–2010*. CDC WONDER Online Database. (Web)

Centers for Disease Control and Prevention. 2014b. *Injury Prevention and Control: Adverse Childhood Experiences (ACE) Study*. (Web)

Centers for Disease Control and Prevention. 2014c. *Health, United States, 2013: Table 5. Nonmarital Childbearing, by Detailed Race and Hispanic Origin of Mother, and Maternal Age: United States, Selected Years 1970–2012*. (Web)

Chakrabarti, V. 2013. *A Country of Cities: A Manifesto for an Urban America*. New York: Metropolis Books.

Chan, S. 2015. "No End in Sight to Tide of Migrants Entering Europe, UN Says." *New York Times*: Sept. 25. (Web)

Chang, D. 2008. *Comparison of Crash Fatalities by Sex and Age Group*. Washington, DC: National Highway Traffic Safety Administration. (Web)

Chauvet, L., F. Gubert, M. Mercier, and S. Mesplé-Somps. 2013. "Do Return Migrants Transfer Political Norms to Their Origin Country? Evidence from Mali." Paris: DIAL–IRD, Université Paris-Dauphine. (Web)

Chen Guidi, and Chuntao Wu. 2006. *Will the Boat Sink the Water? The Life of China's Peasants*. New York: Public Affairs.

Chida Y., A. Steptoe, and L. Powell. 2009. "Religiosity/Spirituality and Mortality: A Systematic Quantitative Review." *Psychotherapy and Psychosomatics* 78: 81–90.

China Daily. 2010a. "China Plans Draft Immigration Law." May 22. (Web)

China Daily. 2010b. "Illegal Immigration from Vietnam Surges in S[outh] China." Apr. 11. (Web)

China Daily. 2014. "Smoother Green Card Application Process in China." (Web)

China Health and Nutrition Survey. 2013. *Project Description*. (Web)

Christakis, N., and J. Fowler. 2007. "The Spread of Obesity in a Large Social Network over 32 Years." *New England Journal of Medicine* 357: 370–9.

Clark, C. 1967. *Population Growth and Land Use*. New York: St Martin's Press.

Clarke, C., T. Miller, E. Chang, et al. 2010. "Racial and Social Class Gradients in Life Expectancy in Contemporary California." *Social Science & Medicine* 70: 1373–80.

Cleland, J. 2014. "Education and Future Fertility Trends, with Special Reference to Mid-Transitional Countries." New York: Population Division, United Nations. (Web)

Coale, A., and S. Watkins (eds). 1986. *The Decline of Fertility in Europe*. Princeton, NJ: Princeton University Press.

Cockburn, P. 2015. *The Jihadis Return: ISIS and the New Sunni Uprising*. New York: OR Books.

Coggan, P. 2012. "Economic Growth: Taking Lessons from Japan." *The Economist*: Mar. 28. (Web)

Collier, P. 2013. *Exodus: How Migration Is Changing Our World*. New York: Oxford University Press.

Commission on the Social Determinants of Health. 2008. *Closing the Gap in a Generation: Health Equity through Action on the Social Determinants of Health*. Geneva: World Health Organization. (Web)

Condon, P. 2006. "Minnesota Leads Nation in Somali Immigrants." *Minnesota Public Radio*: Feb. 17. (Web)

Conteh, J. 2013. "How African-Americans and African Immigrants Differ: The Rift between African-Americans and Recent African Immigrants to the United States." *The Globalist*: Nov. 16. (http://www.theglobalist.com/african-americans-african-immigrants-differ/).

Conyers, D. 1993. *Guidelines on Social Analysis for Rural Area Development Planning*. Rome: Economic and Social Policy Department, Food and Agriculture Organization of the United Nations. (Web)

Copen, C., K. Daniels, and W. Mosher. 2013. "First Premarital Cohabitation in the United States: 2006–2010 National Survey of Family Growth." *National Health Statistics Reports* 64: 1–16. (Web)

Cordain, L. 1999. "Cereal Grains: Humanity's Double-Edged Sword." Pp. 19–73 in A. Simopoulos (ed.), *Evolutionary Aspects of Nutrition and Health, Diet, Exercise, Genetics, and Chronic Disease*. Basel: Karger.

Coulmas, F. 2007. *Population Decline and Ageing in Japan: The Social Consequences*. New York: Routledge.

Council on Foreign Relations. 2013. *Child Marriage*. (Web)

Covre-Sussai, M. 2013. "Cohabitation in Latin America and Developed Countries: A Cross-National Perspective." *International Journal of Humanities and Social Science* 3: 29–43.

Cure Alzheimer's Fund. 2014. *Alzheimer's Genome Project*. (Web)

Curtin, S., S. Ventura, and G. Martinez. 2014. "Recent Declines in Nonmarital Childbearing in the United States." *NCHS Data Brief* 162: 1–7. (Web)

Dahl, M., and O. Sorenson. 2010. "The Migration of Technical Workers." *Journal of Urban Economics* 67: 33–45.

Darboe, K. 2003. "New Immigrants in Minnesota: The Somali Immigration and Assimilation." *Journal of Developing Societies* 19: 458–72.

Das Gupta, M., A. Ebenstein, and E. Sharygin. 2010. *China's Marriage Market and Upcoming Challenges for Elderly Men.* Policy Research Working Paper (World Bank), No. 5351. (Web)

Davis, K. 1945. "The World Demographic Transition." *Annals of the American Academy of Political and Social Science* 271: 1–11.

Davis, M. 2006. *Planet of Slums.* New York: Verso.

Dayton-Johnson, J., A. Pfeiffer, K. Schutettler, and J. Schwinn. 2009. "Migration and Employment." Washington, DC: OECD Development Centre. (Web)

Dearden, L. 2015. "6 Charts and a Map That Show Where Europe's Refugees Are Coming From – And the Perilous Journeys They Are Taking: Record Numbers of People Fleeing War, Persecution and Poverty Are Entering the EU." *Independent*: Sept. 2. (Web)

Dedieu, J.J., L. Chauvet, F. Gubert, et al. 2013. "The 'Battles' of Paris and New York: An Analysis of the Transnational Electoral Behaviour of Senegalese Immigrants in France and New York." *Revue Française de Science Politique* 63: 865–92. (Web)

Demeny, P. 2005. "Policy Challenges of Europe's Demographic Changes: From Past Perspectives to Future Prospects." Pp. 1–9 in M. Macura, A. MacDonald, and W. Haug (eds), *The New Demographic Regime: Population Challenges and Policy Responses.* New York: United Nations.

Demographia. 2014. *World Urban Areas.* 10th edn. (Web)

DeNavas-Walt, C., and B. Proctor. 2014. *Income and Poverty in the United States: 2013.* (Web)

Diamond, J. 1997. *Guns, Germs, and Steel: The Fates of Human Societies.* New York: W.W. Norton.

Diamond, J. 2005. *Collapse: How Societies Choose to Fail or Succeed.* New York: Penguin Books.

Diamond, J. 2012. *The World Until Yesterday: What Can We Learn from Traditional Societies?* New York: Viking.

Dietz, B. 2002. "East–West Migration Patterns in an Enlarging Europe: The German Case." *Global Review of Ethnopolitics* 2: 29–43. (Web)

Docquier, F., and H. Rapoport. 2012. "Globalization, Brain Drain, and Development." *Journal of Economic Literature* 50: 681–730.

Douglas, R. 2012. "The Expulsion of the Germans: The Largest Forced Migration in History." *Huffington Post*, June 29. (Web)

Douglas, R. 2013. *Orderly and Humane: The Expulsion of the Germans after the Second World War.* New Haven, CT: Yale University Press.

Dugger, C. 2007. "In Africa, Prosperity from Seeds Falls Short." *New York Times*: Oct. 10. (Web)

Dunbar, E. 2010. "Comparing the Somali Experience in Minnesota to Other Immigrant Groups." *Minnesota Public Radio*: Jan. 22. (Web)

Dustmann, C., T. Frattini, and I. Preston. 2013. "The Effects of Immigration along the Distribution of Wages." *Review of Economic Studies* 80: 145–73.

Economist, The. 2011. "Costing the Count." June 2. (Web)

Economist, The. 2015. "Not Our Thing: Turnout among Hispanics is Low, But They Are Well Worth Wooing." Mar. 14. (Web)

Edin, K., and M. Kefalas. 2005. *Promises I Can Keep: Why Poor Women Put Motherhood Before Marriage.* Berkeley: University of California Press.

Ehrlich, P., and A. Ehrlich. 2005. *One with Nineveh: Politics, Consumption, and the Human Future.* Washington, DC: Island Press.

Elliott, D., A. Olesen, A. Nathan, et al. 2013. "The End of China's One-Child Policy?" *The Atlantic*: Mar. 15. (Web)

Eltis, D., and D. Richardson. 2010. *Atlas of the Transatlantic Slave Trade.* New Haven, CT: Yale University Press.

Ember, C., and M. Ember. 1992. "Resource Unpredictability, Mistrust, and War: A Cross-Cultural Study." *Journal of Conflict Resolution* 36: 242–62.

Emery, K. 2013. "Mobility and Mortality: Migration in a Black Death Cemetery." *Bones Don't Lie* (Jan. 24). (Web)

European Commission. 2013. *Climate Change, Environmental Degradation, and Migration.* Brussels: European Commission. (Staff Working Document, 2013:138, final). (Web)

European Commission. 2015. *Irregular Immigration.* (Web)

Eveleigh, D. 2003. *Bogs, Baths, and Basins: The Story of Domestic Sanitation.* Stroud: Sutton Publishing.

FAO. 2014a. "Help Eliminate Hunger, Food Insecurity and Malnutrition." (Web)

FAO. 2014b. *Hunger Portal.* (Web)

FAO. 2014c. *The State of Food Insecurity in the World.* (Web)

Farrimond, H. 2012. "Beyond the Caveman: Rethinking Masculinity in Relation to Men's Help-Seeking." *Health* 16: 208–25.

FBI. 2014. *Crime in the United States 2012: Table 33, Ten-Year Arrest Trends.* (Web)

Feng, W., Y. Cai, and B. Gu. 2012. "Population, Policy, and Politics: How Will History Judge China's One-Child Policy?" *Population and Development Review* 38: 115–29.

Feng, X., D. Poston Jr, and X. Wand. 2014. "China's One-Child Policy and the Changing Family." *Journal of Comparative Family Studies* 45: 17–29.

Ferris, E. 2014. *Ten Years after Humanitarian Reform: How Have IDPs Fared?* Washington, DC: Brookings Institution. (Web)

Fetter, B. 1997. "The Epidemiologic Transition." *Health Transition Review* 7: 235–56.

Fetzer, J. 2000. *Public Attitudes toward Immigration in the United States, France, and Germany.* New York: Cambridge University Press.

Fincher, L. 2014. *Leftover Women: The Resurgence of Gender Inequality in China.* New York: Zed Books.

Fisher, M. 2014. *Migration: A World History.* New York: Oxford University Press.

Foley, J. 2014. "A Five-Step Plan to Feed the World." *National Geographic* 295: 27–59.

Fong, V. 2004. *Only Hope – Coming of Age under China's One-Child Policy.* Stanford, CA: Stanford University Press.

Foreman, K., and R. Monger. 2014. *Nonimmigrant Admissions to the United States: 2013.* Washington, DC: Office of Immigration Statistics. (Web)

Frankel, N. 2009. *The Atlantic Slave Trade and Slavery in America.* (Web)

Freedom House. 2014a. *Freedom in the World 2014.* Washington, DC: Freedom House. (Web)

Freedom House. 2014b. *Freedom in the World 2014 Methodology.* Washington, DC: Freedom House. (Web)

Frey, W. 2014. *Diversity Explosion: How New Racial Demographics Are Remaking America.* Washington, DC: Brookings Institution.

Frison, E., J. Cherfas, and T. Hodgkin. 2011. "Agricultural Biodiversity Is Essential for a Sustainable Improvement in Food and Nutrition Security." *Sustainability* 3: 238–53.

Froy, F., and L. Pyne. 2011. *Ensuring Labour Market Success for Ethnic Minority and Immigrant Youth.* OECD Local Economic and Employment Development (LEED) Working Papers. (Web)

Gaines, S. Jr, W. Marelich, K. Bledsoe, et al. 1997. "Links between Race/Ethnicity and Cultural Values as Mediated by Racial/Ethnic Identity and Moderated by Gender." *Journal of Personality and Social Psychology* 72: 1460–76.

Gallo, L., F. Penedo, K. Espinosa de los Monteros, and W. Arguelles. 2009. "Resiliency in the Face of Disadvantage: Do Hispanic Cultural Characteristics Protect Health Outcomes?" *Journal of Personality* 77: 1707–46.

Gallup. 2015a. *Immigration.* Washington, DC: Gallup, Inc. (Web)

Gallup. 2015b. *Islamophobia: Understanding Anti-Muslim Sentiment in the West.* Washington, DC: Gallup, Inc. (Web)

Gans, H. 1982. *The Urban Villagers: Group and Class in the Life of Italian Americans.* Updated and expanded edn. New York: Free Press.

Gaud, W. 1968. "The Green Revolution: Accomplishments and Apprehensions." Washington, DC: Society for International Development. Paper presentation (Mar. 8). (Web)

Gauthier, A. 2005 "Policy Challenges of Europe's Demographic Changes: From Past Perspectives to Future Prospects." Pp. 95–110 in M. Macura, A. MacDonald, and W. Haug (eds), *The New Demographic Regime: Population Challenges and Policy Responses.* New York: United Nations.

Geiger, J. 2003. "Racial and Ethnic Disparities in Diagnosis and Treatment: A Review of the Evidence and a Consideration of Causes." Pp. 417–54 in B. Smedley, A. Stith, and A. Nelson (eds), *Unequal Treatment: Confronting Racial and Ethnic Disparities in Health Care.* Washington, DC: National Academies Press. (Web)

Gelatt, J. 2005. "Schengen and the Free Movement of People across Europe." Washington, DC: Migration Policy Institute. (Web)

General Social Survey. 2012. (Web)

Gillis, J. 2014. "Panel's Warning on Climate Risk: Worse Is Yet to Come." *New York Times*: Mar. 30. (Web)

Giovino, G., S. Mirza, J. Samet, et al. 2012 "Tobacco Use in 3 billion Individuals from 16 Countries: An Analysis of Nationally Representative Cross-Sectional Household Surveys." *Lancet* 380: 668–79.

Glaeser, E., and J. Vigdor. 2012. *The End of the Segregated Century: Racial Separation in America's Neighborhoods, 1890–2010.* New York: Manhattan Institute for Policy Research. Civic Report No. 66 (Jan.). (Web)

Global Footprint Network. 2015. *Footprint Basics: Introduction.* (Web)

Goldscheider, C. 1999. "Religious Values, Dependencies, and Fertility: Evidence and Implications from Israel." Pp. 310–30 in R. Leete (ed.), *Dynamics of Values in Fertility Change.* New York: Oxford University Press.

Gonzalez-Barrera, A., and J. Krogstad. 2014. "US Deportations of Immigrants Reach Record High in 2013." Washington, DC: Pew Research Center. (Web)

Groen, J., and A. Polivka. 2008. "Hurricane Katrina Evacuees: Who They Are, Where They Are, and How They Are Faring." *Monthly Labor Review* 131 (March): 32–51.

Gu Baochang, Feng Wang, Zhigang Guo, and Erli Zhang. 2007. "China's Local and National Fertility Policies at the End of the Twentieth Century." *Population and Development Review* 33: 129–47.

Gupte, M., and K. Jadhav. 2014. "The Concept of Reverse Brain Drain and Its Relevance to India." *International Monthly Refereed Journal of Research in Management & Technology* 3: 83–7. (Web)

Guttentag, M., and P. Secord. 1983. *Too Many Women? The Sex Ratio Question.* Beverly Hills, CA: Sage.

Haimei, S. 2011. *Inflow of International Immigrants Challenges China's Migration Policy.* Washington, DC: Brookings Institution. (Web)

Hardy, T., and T. Tollefsbol. 2011. "Epigenetic Diet: Impact on the Epigenome and Cancer." *Epigenomics* 3: 503–18.

Harris, G. 2014. "Poor Sanitation in India May Afflict Well-Fed Children with Malnutrition." *New York Times*: July 13. (Web)

Harris, M. 1979. *Cultural Materialism: The Struggle for a Science of Culture.* New York: Vintage.

Harris, M. 1991. *Cannibals and Kings: Origins of Cultures.* New York: Vintage.

Harris, M., and O. Johnson. 2007. *Cultural Anthropology.* 7th edn. Boston: Pearson Education.

Haskins, R. 2007. *Immigration: Wages, Education, and Mobility.* Washington, DC: Economic Mobility Project. (Web)

Haub, C. 2013. "United Nations Raises Projected World Population." Washington, DC: Population Reference Bureau. (Web)

Haupt, A., T. Kane, and C. Haub. 2011. *PRB's Population Handbook.* 6th edn. Washington, DC: Population Reference Bureau. (Web)

Hayward M., T. Miles, E. Crimmins, and Y. Yang. 2000. "The Significance of Socioeconomic Status in Explaining the Racial Gap in Chronic Health Conditions." *American Sociological Review* 65: 910–30.

Heath, A., C. Rothon, and E. Kilpi. 2008. "The Second Generation in Western Europe: Education, Unemployment, and Occupational Attainment." *Annual Review of Sociology* 34: 211–35.

HelpAge International. 2016. *Global Agewatch Index.* (Web)

Hemenway, D. 2009. *While We Were Sleeping: Success Stories in Injury and Violence Prevention.* Berkeley: University of California Press.

Hesser, L. 2006. *The Man Who Fed the World: Nobel Peace Prize Laureate Norman Borlaug and His Battle to End World Hunger.* Dallas: Durban House.

Hirschman, C. 2005. "Population and Society: Historical Trends and Future Prospects." Pp. 381–401 in C. Calhoun, C. Rojek, and B. Turner (eds), *The Sage Handbook of Sociology.* Thousand Oaks, CA: Sage.

Hoem, J. 2008. "The Impact of Public Policies on European Fertility." *Demographic Research* 19: 249–60.

Homedes, N. 1996. *The Disability-Adjusted Life Year (DALY): Definition, Measurement and Potential Use.* Human Capital Development Working Papers (World Bank), No. 68. (Web)

Hooghe, M., and T. de Vroome. 2013. "The Perception of Ethnic Diversity and Anti-Immigrant Sentiments: A Multi-Level Analysis of Local Communities in Belgium." *Ethnic and Racial Studies* 38: 38–56.

Horton, J., and L. Horton. 2006. *Slavery and the Making of America.* New York: Oxford University Press.

Hudson, V., and A. den Boer. 2004. *Bare Branches: The Security Implications of Asia's Surplus Male Population.* Cambridge, MA: MIT Press.

Human Rights Watch. 2013. *This Old Man Can Feed Us, You Will Marry Him: Child and Forced Marriage in South Sudan.* New York: Human Rights Watch. (Web)

Ihrke, D. 2014. *Reason for Moving: 2012 to 2013: Population Characteristics.* Washington, DC: US Census Bureau. P20-547, June. (Web)

Immunization Action Coalition. 2014. *Vaccine Timeline.* (Web)

Inglehart, R. 2000. "Globalization and Postmodern Values." *The Washington Quarterly* 23: 215–28. (Web)

Institute for Policy Studies. 2014. *Inequality and Health.* (Web)

Institute for Safe Families. 2013. *Findings from the Philadelphia Urban Ace Survey.* (Web)

Internal Revenue Service. 2014. *Questions and Answers for the Additional Medicare Tax.* (Web)

International Health Partnership. 2014. *Aligning for Better Results.* (Web)

International Organization for Migration. 2015. *Migration, Climate Change and the Environment.* (Web)

IPCC. 2012. *Summary for Policymakers in Managing the Risks of Extreme Events and Disasters to Advance Climate Change Adaptation: A Special Report of Working Groups I and II of the Intergovernmental Panel on Climate Change.* New York: Cambridge University Press. (Web)

IPCC. 2015. *Fifth Assessment Report.* (Web)

Jacobsen, L., M. Mather, and G. Dupuis. 2012. *Household Change in the United States.* Washington, DC: Population Reference Bureau. (Web)

Japanese General Social Survey. 2005. "APPCCNUM: Ideal Number of Children." Ann Arbor: ICPSR. (Web)

Jarvandi, S., Y. Yan, and M. Schootman. 2012. "Income Disparity and Risk of Death: The Importance of Health Behaviors and Other Mediating Factors." *PLOS ONE* 7: 1–11.

Johnston, W. 2015. "Historical Abortion Statistics, Japan." *Johnston's Archive: Abortion Statistics and Other Data.* (Web)

Jolly, S., and G. DiGiusto. 2014. "Xenophobia and Immigrant Contact: French Public Attitudes toward Immigration." *Social Science Journal* 51: 464–73.

Jones, L. 2015. "More Indians Who Moved to the US Decide to Return Home." *National Public Radio*: Mar. 13. (Web)

Kane, E. 1995. "Education and Beliefs about Gender Inequality." *Social Problems* 42: 74–90.

Kaplan, D. 2000. "The Darker Side of the Original Affluent Society." *Journal of Anthropological Research* 56: 301–24.

Katsiasficas, C. 2014. *Political Participation of Immigrants in the EU: Challenges and Tools*. Athens: Bridging Europe. EU Migration Policy Working Paper, No. 11. (Web)

Keim, S., A. Klärner, and L. Bernardi. 2013. "Tie Strength and Family Formation: Which Personal Relationships Are Influential?" *Personal Relationships* 20: 462–78.

Kendall, E., J. Montgomery, J. Evans, et al. 2013. "Mobility, Mortality, and the Middle Ages: Identification of Migrant Individuals in a 14th Century Black Death Cemetery Population." *American Journal of Physical Anthropology* 150: 210–22.

Khatiwada, I., A. Sum, and T. Barnicle. 2006. *New Foreign Immigrant Workers and the Labor Market in the US: The Contributions of New Immigrant Workers to Labor Force and Employment Growth and Their Impact on Native Born Workers, 2000 to 2005*. Washington, DC: National Center for Education and the Economy. (Web)

Kim, S., and C. Brown. 2014. "How Immigration Reform Died." *Politico*: June 27. (Web)

King, R., R. Skeldon, and J. Vullinetari. 2008. "Internal and International Migration: Bridging the Theoretical Divide." St Anne's College, Oxford: International Migration, Integration and Social Cohesion Conference. Paper presentation (July 1). (Web)

Kinter, H. 2008. "The Life Table." Pp. 341–70 in J. Siegel and D. Swanson (eds), *The Methods and Materials of Demography*. Bingley: Emerald Group Publishing.

Kirk, D. 1996. "Demographic Transition Theory." *Population Studies* 50: 361–87.

Kluge, F., E. Zagheni, E. Loichinger, and T. Vogt. 2014. "The Advantages of Demographic Change after the Wave: Fewer and Older, but Healthier, Greener, and More Productive?" *PLOS One* 9: 1–11. (Web)

Kolar, F., and B. Ostadal. 2013. "Sex Differences in Cardiovascular Function." *Acta Physiologica* 207: 584–7.

Koop, C., C. Pearson, and M. Schwartz (eds). 2002. *Critical Issues in Global Health*. San Francisco: Josey-Bass.

Kottman, M. 2010. "Mumbai Slums." Disciples Church Blog (Calvary Chapel Leatherhead). (Web)

Koumplilova, M. 2014. "New Somali Refugee Arrivals in Minnesota Are Increasing." *Minneapolis Star-Tribune*: Nov. 1. (Web)

Kramer, S. 2013. *The Other Population Crisis: What Governments Can Do about Falling Birth Rates*. Washington, DC: Woodrow Wilson Center.

Kret, M., and B. De Gelder. 2012. "A Review of Sex Differences in Processing Emotional Signals." *Neuropsychologia* 50: 1211–21.

Krogstad, J. 2014. "Asian America Vote Turnout Lags Behind Other Groups: Some Non-Voters Say They're 'Too Busy'." Pew Research Center. (Web)

Krogstad, J., and M. Keegan. 2014. "15 States with the Highest Share of Immigrants in Their Population." Pew Research Center. (Web)

Krogstad, J., and M. Lopez. 2014. "Hispanic Nativity Shift." Pew Research Center. (Web)

Kunst, A., and J. Mackenbach. 1994. "The Size of Mortality Differences Associated with Educational Level in Nine Industrialized Countries." *American Journal of Public Health* 84: 932–7. (Web)

Lacey, L., and I. Speizer. 2015. *Population Analysis for Planners*. Washington, DC: US Agency for International Development (USAID). (Web)

Lancet. 2014. "Global Burden of Diseases, Injuries, and Risk Factors Study 2013." (Web)

Lawrence, F. 2011. "Alarm as Corporate Giants Target Developing Countries: Diabetes, Obesity and Heart Disease Rates Are Soaring in Developing Countries, as Multinationals Find New Ways of Selling Processed Food to the Poor." *Guardian*: Nov. 23. (Web)

Lee, R. 1968. "What Do Hunters Do for a Living, or How to Make Out on Scarce Resources." Pp. 30–43 in R. Lee and I. DeVore (eds), *Man the Hunter*. Chicago: Aldine.

Leete, R. (ed.). 1999. *Dynamics of Values in Fertility Change*. New York: Oxford University Press.

Lehrer, E. 2000. "Religion as a Determinant of Entry into Cohabitation and Marriage." Pp. 227–52 in L. Waite (ed.), *The Ties That Bind: Perspectives on Marriage and Cohabitation*. Hawthorne, NY: Aldine de Gruyter.

Leitenberg, M. 2006. *Deaths in Wars and Conflicts in the 20th Century*. 3rd edn. Ithaca, NY: Cornell University Peace Studies Program, Occasional Paper No. 29. (Web)

Lesthaeghe, R. 2010. *The Unfolding Story of the Second Demographic Transition*. Report 10-696. Ann Arbor, MI: Population Studies Center.

Lewis, R. 2013. "Eight Years after Hurricane Katrina, Many Evacuees Yet to Return." *Aljazeera America*: Aug. 29. (Web)

Liberia Institute of Statistics and Geo-Information Services. 2008. *Liberia Demographic and Health Survey 2007: Key Findings*. Calverton, MD: Macro International. (Web)

Lister, C. 2014. "The 'Real' Jabhat al-Nusra Appears to Be Emerging." *The World Post*: Oct. 7. (Web)

Locoh, T. 2009. "Family Structure and Fertility Trends in Intermediate-Fertility Countries of West Africa." Pp.165–81 in *Completing the Fertility Transition (Special Issues Nos. 48/49)*. New York: United Nations.

Lopez, M., and P. Taylor. 2012 "Latino Votes in the 2012 Election." Washington, DC: Pew Research Center. (Web)

Lozano-Ascencio, F., B. Roberts, and F. Bean. 1999. "The Interconnections of Internal and International Migration: The Case of the United States and

Mexico." Pp. 138–61 in L. Pries (ed.), *Migration and Transnational Social Spaces*. Brookfield, VT: Ashgate Publishing.

Luthra, R., and R. Waldinger. 2013. "Intergenerational Mobility." Pp. 169–205 in D. Card and S. Raphael (eds), *Immigration, Poverty, and Socioeconomic Mobility*. New York: Russell Sage.

Lutz, W., and S. Scherbov. 2008. *Exploratory Extension of IIASA's World Population Projections: Scenarios to 2300*. Laxenburg: International Institute for Applied Systems Analysis. (Web)

Macartney, S., A. Bishaw, and K. Fonteno. 2013. *Poverty Rates for Selected Detailed Race and Hispanic Groups by State and Place: 2007–2011*. American Community Survey Briefs, US Census Department. (Web)

McCartney, G., L. Mahmood, A. Leyland, G. Batty, and K. Hunt. 2011. "Contribution of Smoking-Related and Alcohol-Related Deaths to the Gender Gap in Mortality: Evidence from 30 European Countries." *Tobacco Control* 20: 166–8.

MacDonald, J., and L. MacDonald. 1964. "Chain Migration, Ethnic Neighborhood Formation, and Social Networks." *The Milbank Memorial Fund Quarterly* 42: 82–97.

McKeown, T. 1976. *The Modern Rise of Population*. New York: Academic Press.

Makun, P., and S. Wilson. 2011. *Population Distribution and Change: 2000 to 2010*. March: C2010BR-01. Washington, DC: United States Census Bureau. (Web)

Malthus, T. 1798. *An Essay on the Principle of Population*. (Web)

Manning, P. 1990. *Slavery and African Life*. Cambridge: Cambridge University Press.

Manning. R. 2014. "Hidden Downsides of the Green Revolution: Biodiversity Loss and Diseases of Civilization." *Mother Jones*: June/July. (Web)

Marin, G. and B. Marin. 1991. *Research with Hispanic Populations*. Newbury Park, CA: Sage.

Marmot, M. 2004. *The Status Syndrome: How Social Standing Affects Our Health and Longevity*. New York: Holt.

Marmot, M., and D. Smith. 1989. "Why Are the Japanese Living Longer?" *British Medical Journal* 299: 1547–51.

Marsh, V. 2012. "China to Overhaul 'Threatening' One-Child Slogans." *BBC News*: Feb. 27. (Web)

Martin, J., B. Hamilton, S. Ventura, et al. 2012. "Births: Final Data for 2010." *National Vital Statistics Reports* 61: 1–72. (Web)

Martinez, G., K. Daniels, and A. Chandra. 2012. "Fertility of Men and Women Aged 15–44 Years in the United States: National Survey of Family Growth, 2006–2010." *National Health Statistics Reports* 51: 1–29.

Marx, K. 1867. *Capital*, Volume 1. New York: Vintage Books, 1977.

Massey, D., and N. Denton. 1998. *American Apartheid: Segregation and the Making of the Underclass*. Cambridge, MA: Harvard University Press.

Massey, D., J. Arango, G. Hugo, et al. 1998. *Worlds in Motion: Understanding International Migration at the end of the Millennium*. New York: Clarendon.

Melillo, J., T. Richmond, and G. Yohe (eds). 2014. *Climate Change Impacts in the United States: The Third National Climate Assessment.* Washington, DC: US Government Printing Office. (Web)

Miles, T. 2014 "UN Says 13.6 Million Displaced by Wars in Iraq and Syria." *Reuters:* Nov. 11. (Web)

Min, S., X. Zhang, F. Zwiers, and G. Hegerl. 2011. "Human Contribution to More-Intense Precipitation Extremes." *Nature* 470: 378–81.

Minneapolis Foundation. 2004. *Immigration in Minnesota: Discovering Common Ground.* Minneapolis: The Minneapolis Foundation. (Web)

Minnesota Historical Society (2015). "Somali-Americans in Minnesota: Overview." St Paul, MN: Minnesota Historical Society. (Web)

Mokdad, A., J. Marks, D. Stroup, and J. Gerberding. 2004. "Actual Causes of Deaths in the United States, 2000." *Journal of the American Medical Association* 291: 1238–45.

Mokdad, A., J. Marks, D. Stroup, and J. Gerberding. 2005. "Correction: Actual Causes of Deaths in the United States, 2000." *Journal of the American Medical Association* 293: 293–4.

Mokomane, Z. 2014. *Anti-Poverty Family-Focused Policies in Developing Countries.* Pretoria: Human Sciences Research Council. (Web)

Monger, R., and J. Yankay. 2014. *US Lawful Permanent Residents: 2013.* Washington, DC: Office of Immigration Statistics. (Web)

Monshipouri, M. 2014. *Democratic Uprisings in the New Middle East: Youth, Technology, Human Rights, and US Foreign Policy.* Boulder, CO: Paradigm Publishers.

Morehouse, C., and M. Blomfeld. 2011. *Irregular Migration in Europe.* Washington, DC: Transatlantic Council on Migration.

Mosher, S. 2008. *Population Control: Real Costs, Illusory Benefits.* New Brunswick, NJ: Transaction Publishers.

Motel, S., and E. Patten. 2013. *Statistical Portrait of the Foreign-Born Population in the United States, 2011.* Pew Research Center. (Web)

Murdock, D. 1998. "The Greatest Story Never Told: Everyday America's Racial Harmony." *The American Enterprise* Nov./Dec.: 24–6. (Web)

Murphy, S., J. Xu, and K. Kocahek. 2013. "Deaths: Final Data for 2010." *National Vital Statistics Reports* 61: 1–118. (Web)

Murray, C., S. Kulkarni, C. Michaud, et al. 2006. "Eight Americas: Investigating Mortality Disparities across Races, Counties, and Race-Counties in the United States." *PLOS Medicine* 3: 13–24. (Web)

Musick K., P. England, S. Edgington, and N. Kangas. 2009. "Education Differences in Intended and Unintended Fertility." *Social Forces* 88: 543–72.

Myers, N. 2002. "Environmental Refugees: A Growing Phenomenon of the 21st Century." *Philosophical Transactions of the Royal Society of London* 357: 609–13. (Web)

Nam, C., and S. Philliber. 1984. *Population: A Basic Orientation* 2nd edn. Englewood Cliffs, NJ: Prentice-Hall.

NASA. 1996. "Atmospheric Aerosols: What Are They, and Why Are They So Important?" Hampton, VA: Langley Research Center (FS-1996-08-11-LaRC). (Web)

National Center for Health Statistics. 2003a. "US Standard Certificate of Live Birth." (Web)

National Center for Health Statistics. 2003b. "US Standard Certificate of Death." (Web)

National Center for Health Statistics. 2008. *Health, United States, 2007, with Chartbook on Trends in the Health of Americans.* (Web)

National Center for Health Statistics. 2012. *Health, United States, 2011: With Special Feature on Socioeconomic Status and Health.* (Web)

National Geographic. 2014a. *The Human Journey: Migration Routes.* (Web)

National Geographic. 2014b. *The Genographic Project: Behind the Science.* (Web)

National Institutes of Health. 2012. "An Overview of the Human Genome Project: What Was the Human Genome Project?" (Web)

National Institutes of Health. 2014. "Human Genome Project: Specific Genetic Disorders." (Web)

National Science Foundation. 2005. "New Clues Add 40,000 Years to Age of Human Species." Press Release 05-024 (Feb. 16). (Web)

Newport, F., and J. Wilke. 2013. "Hispanic Immigrants to US More Like than Native-Born To Be Independent." Washington, DC: Gallup, Inc. (Web)

Nielsen. 2015. *SiteReports.* (Web)

Norris, F. 2013. "Population Growth Forecast from the UN May Be Too High." *New York Times*: Sept. 20. (Web)

Notestein, F. 1945. "Population: The Long View." Pp. 36–57 in T. Schultz (ed.), *Food for the World.* Chicago: University of Chicago Press.

NOVA. 2004. *World in the Balance: The Population Paradox.* (Web)

Nugent, W. 1992. *Crossings: The Great Transatlantic Migrations, 1870–1914.* Bloomington: Indiana University Press.

Nunn, N. 2007. *The Long-Term Effects of Africa's Slave Trades.* Cambridge, MA: National Bureau of Economic Research. Working Paper 13367. (Web)

OECD. 2009. *Comparative Child Well-Being across the OECD.* (Web)

OECD. 2011. *The Future of Families to 2030: A Synthesis Report.* Paris: OECD Publications. (Web)

OECD. 2013. *Health at a Glance 2013: OECD Indicators.* (Web)

OECD. 2014. *PISA 2012 Results in Focus: What 15-Year-Olds Know and What They Can Do with What They Know.* (Web)

Office for National Statistics. 2013. *Annual Population Survey (APS).* (Web)

Office of Refugee Settlement. 2015. *Refugee Arrival Data.* Washington, DC: US Department of Health and Human Services. (Web)

Office of the Registrar General & Census Commissioner. 2013a. "Census of India, 2011: Household Schedule." (Web)

Office of the Registrar General & Census Commissioner. 2013b. "Sample Registration." (Web)

Oksuzyan, A., K. Juel, J. Vaupel, and K. Christensen. 2008. "Men: Good Health and High Mortality – Sex Differences in Health and Aging." *Aging: Clinical and Experimental Research* 20: 91–102.

Olesen, A. 2011. "Experts Challenge China's 1 Child Population Claim." Boston. com: Oct. 27. (Web)

Olshansky, S., and A. Ault. 1986. "The Fourth Stage of the Epidemiologic Transition: The Age of Delayed Degenerative Diseases." *Milbank Quarterly* 64: 355–91.

Orr, A. 2011. "Americans Broadly Oppose Raising Retirement Age or Reducing Benefits." *Economic Policy Institute*: Jan. 24. (Web)

Oskin, B. 2013. "Africa's Worst Drought Tied to West's Pollution." LiveScience. com: June 7. (Web)

Paajanen, T., N. Oksala, P. Kuukasjärvi, and P. Karhunen. 2010. "Short Stature Is Associated with Coronary Heart Disease: A Systematic Review of the Literature and a Meta-Analysis." *European Heart Journal* 31: 1802–9.

Pakenham, T. 1992. *The Scramble for Africa: White Man's Conquest of the Dark Continent from 1876 to 1912*. New York: Avon Books.

Pall, P., T. Aina, D. Stone, et al. 2011. "Anthropogenic Greenhouse Gas Contribution to Flood Risk in England and Wales in Autumn 2000." *Nature* 470: 382–3.

Parser, J. 2015. "DAPA and DACA: What Happened to President Obama's Executive Action?" *National Law Review*: July 29. (Web)

Passell, J., G. Livingston, and D. Cohn. 2012. *Explaining Why Minority Births Now Outnumber White Births*. Washington, DC: Pew Research Center. (Web)

Patten, E., and M. Lopez. 2013. "Are Unauthorized Immigrants Overwhelmingly Democrats?" Washington, DC: Pew Research Center. (Web)

Pearce, F. 2010. *The Coming Population Crash*. Boston: Beacon.

Pearce, F. 2014. "Japan's Ageing Population Could Actually Be Good News." *New Scientist*: Jan. 7. (Web)

Pearce, J. and K. Witten (eds). 2010. *Geographies of Obesity: Environmental Understandings of the Obesity Epidemic*. Burlington, VT: Ashgate.

Peeke, P. 2014. "Epigenetic Transformation — You Are What Your Grandparents Ate." TEDxLowerEastSide. (Web)

Penninx, R. 2005. "Integration of Migrants: Economic, Social, Cultural and Political Dimensions." Pp. 137–52 in M. Macura, A. MacDonald, and W. Haug (eds), *The New Demographic Regime: Population Challenges and Policy Responses*. New York: United Nations. (Web)

Pesticide Action Network Asia and the Pacific. 2007. *The Great Rice Robbery – A Handbook on the Impact of IRRI in Asia*. Penang: Pesticide Action Network Asia and the Pacific. (Web)

Peters, E. and C. Dush (eds). 2009. *Marriage and Family: Perspectives and Complexities*. New York: Columbia University Press.

Peterson, T., P. Stott, and S. Herring (eds). 2012. *Explaining Extreme Events of 2011 from a Climate Perspective*. Boston: American Meteorological Society. (Web)

Pew Research Center. 2013a. *Changing Patterns of Global Migration and Remittances: More Migrants in US and Other Wealth Countries; More Money to Middle-Income Countries*. (Web)

Pew Research Center. 2013b. *Second Generation Americans: Detailed Demographic Tables*. (Web)

Pew Research Center. 2013c. *Second-Generation Americans: A Portrait of the Adult Children of Immigrants*. (Web)

Pew Research Center. 2013d. *The Rise of Asian Americans*. (Web)

Pew Research Center. 2014a. "Chapter 4. Population Change in the US and the World from 1950 to 2050." (Web)

Pew Research Center. 2014b. *Five facts about Illegal Immigration in the US* (Web)

Pew Research Center. 2014c. "How Obama's Executive Action Will Impact Immigrants, by Birth Country." (Web)

Pew Research Center. 2016. *Immigration*. (Web)

Pfeiffer, E. 2012. "China to Soften Its One-Child Policy Slogans, But Not the Law Itself." *Yahoo News*: Feb. 28. (Web)

Phelan, J., B. Link, and P. Tehranifar. 2010. "Social Conditions as Fundamental Causes of Health Inequalities: Theory, Evidence, and Policy Implications." *Journal of Health and Social Behavior* 51: S28–40.

Philipov, D., Z. Spéder, and F. Billari. 2006. "Soon, Later, or Ever? The Impact of Anomie and Social Capital on Fertility Intentions in Bulgaria (2002) and Hungary (2001)." *Population Studies* 60: 289–308.

Pink, S., T. Leopold, and H. Engelhardt. 2014. "Does Childbearing Spread among Colleagues? Fertility and Social Interaction at the Workplace." *Advances in Life Course Research* 21: 113–22.

Pollard, K., and W. O'Hare. 1999. *America's Racial and Ethnic Minorities*. Washington, DC: Population Reference Bureau. (Web)

Pongu, R. 2013. "Why Is Infant Mortality Higher in Boys Than in Girls? A New Hypothesis Based on Preconception Environment and Evidence from a Large Sample of Twins." *Demography* 50: 421–44.

Population Connection. 2013. "World Population Video" (online version). (Web)

Population Connection. 2015. "Wildlife and Natural Resources." (Web)

Population Reference Bureau. 2009. "Birth Rates Rising in Many Low Birth-Rate Countries." (Web)

Population Reference Bureau. 2011a. "Uganda: At the Beginning of the Demographic Transition." (Web)

Population Reference Bureau. 2011b. "Guatemala: Beyond the Early Phase of the Demographic Transition" (Web)

Population Reference Bureau. 2011c. "India: On the Path to Replacement-Level Fertility?" (Web)

Population Reference Bureau. 2011d. "Germany: Beyond the Demographic Transition's End." (Web)

Population Reference Bureau. 2012. *2011 World Population Data Sheet: The World at 7 Billion*. (Web)

Population Reference Bureau. 2014. *2013 World Population Data Sheet*. (Web)

Population Reference Bureau. 2015. *2014 World Population Data Sheet*. (Web)

Population Reference Bureau. 2016. "Human Population: Future Growth" ("lesson plans" article). (Web)

Portez, L., J. Cubanski, and T. Neuman. 2011. *Medicare Spending and Financing: A Primer*. Menlo Park, CA: Kaiser Family Foundation. (Web)

Posner, R. 2012. "Why Did Asian Americans Mostly Vote for President Obama? Democrats Court Them, Republicans May Alienate Them." *Slate*: Nov. 26. (Web)

Poston, D., and L. Bouvier. 2010. *Population and Society: An Introduction to Demography*. New York: Cambridge University Press.

Pries, L. 1999. "New Migration in Transnational Spaces." Pp. 1–35 in L. Pries (ed.), *Migration and Transnational Social Spaces*. Brookfield, VT: Ashgate Publishing.

Public Radio International. 2013. "China Past Due: One-Child Policy." *PRI.org*: Apr. 15. (Web)

Public Radio International. 2014. "Immigration and Development, with Amartya Sen." (Web)

Randers, J. 2012. *2052: A Global Forecast for the Next Forty Years*. White River Junction, VT: Chelsea Green Publishing.

Rantac, J. 2014. "Syrian Refugees in Turkey: Defusing the Powder-Keg." London: openDemocracy (May 21). (Web)

Rauh, A. 2013. "Successful Black Immigrants Narrow Black-White Achievement." Chicago: Department of Economics, University of Chicago. Working Paper (Oct. 15). (Web)

Ravenstein, E. 1885. "The Laws of Migration." *Journal of the Statistical Society* 48: 167–235.

Ravenstein, E. 1889. "The Laws of Migration: Second Paper." *Journal of the Royal Statistical Society* 52: 241–305.

Razzell, P. 1974. "An Interpretation of the Modern Rise of Population in Europe – A Critique." *Population Studies* 28: 5–17.

Remington, N. 2008. *African Immigrants in Minnesota*. Minneapolis: Institute for Agriculture and Trade Policy. (Web)

Reuters. 2015a. "German Police Arrest Two Suspected Members of Islamic State." Jan. 22. (Web)

Reuters. 2015b. "Trial of Woman Charged with Supporting Islamic State Starts in Germany." Jan. 21. (Web)

Rimer, S., and K. Arenson. 2004. "Top Colleges Take More Blacks, but Which Ones?" *New York Times*: June 24. (Web)

Roble, A., and D. Rutledge. 2008. *The Somali Diaspora: A Journey Away*. Minneapolis: University of Minnesota Press.

Román, E. 2013. *Those Damned Immigrants: American's Hysteria over Undocumented Immigration*. New York: New York University Press.

Rosling, H. 2010a. "Population Growth Explained with IKEA Boxes." *Gapminder*. (Web)

Rosling, H. 2010b. "Reducing Child Mortality – A Moral and Environmental Imperative." *Gapminder* (Web).

Rosling, H. 2012. "Religions and Babies." *Gapminder*. (Web)

Royal Society. 2012. *People and the Planet*. London: The Science Policy Centre, The Royal Society. (Web)

Ruark, E., and M. Graham. 2011. *Immigration, Poverty and Low-Wage Earners: The Harmful Effect of Unskilled Immigrants on American Workers*. Washington, DC: Federation for American Immigration Reform. (Web)

Rubalcava, L., G. Teruel, D. Thomas, and N. Goldman. 2008. "The Healthy Migrant Effect: New Findings from the Mexican Family Life Survey." *American Journal of Public Health* 98: 78–84.

Ruedin, D. 2011. *The Role of Social Capital in the Political Participation of Immigrants: Evidence from Agent-Based Modelling*. Neuchâtel: Swiss Forum for Migration and Population Studies, Université de Neuchâtel (Discussion Paper SFM 27). (Web)

Ryder, N. 1959. "Fertility." Pp. 400–36 in P. Hauser and O. Duncan (eds), *The Study of Population*. Chicago: University of Chicago Press.

Rydgren, J. 2008. "Immigration Sceptics, Xenophobes or Racists? Radical Right-Wing Voting in Six West European Countries." *European Journal of Political Research* 47: 737–65.

Sabin, P. 2013. *The Bet: Paul Ehrlich, Julian Simon, and Our Gamble over Earth's Future*. New Haven, CT: Yale University Press.

Sale, P. 2011. *Our Dying Planet: An Ecologist's View of the Crisis We Face*. Berkeley: University of California Press.

Samaras, T. 2002. "Height, Body Size, and Longevity: Is Smaller Better for the Human Body?" *Western Journal of Medicine* 176: 206–8.

Sanger-Katz, M. 2015. "Income Inequality: It's Also Bad for Your Health." *New York Times*: Mar. 30. (Web)

Schiller, N., L. Basch, and C. Blanc. 1999. "From Immigrant to Transmigrant: Theorizing Transnational Migration." Pp. 73–105 in L. Pries (ed.), *Migration and Transnational Social Spaces*. Brookfield, VT: Ashgate Publishing.

Schnall, P., P. Landsbergis, C. Pieper, et al. 1992. "The Impact of Anticipation of Job Loss on Psychological Distress and Worksite Blood Pressure." *American Journal of Industrial Medicine* 21: 417–32.

Schoen, C., R. Osborn, D. Squires, et al. 2011. "New 2011 Survey of Patients with Complex Care Needs in Eleven Countries Finds That Care Is Often Poorly Coordinated." *Health Affairs* 30: 437–48.

Schultz, P. 1994. "Marital Status and Fertility in the United States: Welfare and Labor Market Effects." *Journal of Human Resources* 29: 637–69.

Schultz, R. 2014. *Technology versus Ecology: Human Superiority and the Ongoing Conflict with Nature*. Hershey, PA: Information Science Reference.

Scommegna, P. 2014. *Family, Friends Help Shape Childbearing Choices*. Washington, DC: Population Reference Bureau.

Semple, K. 2012. "Many US Immigrants' Children Seek American Dream Abroad." *New York Times*: Apr. 15. (Web)

Sessoms, G. 2015. "The Importance of Demographics to Marketing." *Houston Chronicle*: Apr. 4. (Web)

Shan, J. 2014. "China to Improve Population Forecasting." Beijing: National Health and Family Planning Commission. (Web)

Shane, S. 2015. "From Minneapolis to ISIS: An American's Path to Jihad." *New York Times*: Mar. 21. (Web)

Sherman, I. 2007. *Twelve Diseases that Changed Our World*. Washington, DC: ASM Press.

Shetty, P., and J. Schmidhuber. 2011. *Nutrition, Lifestyle, Obesity and Chronic Disease* (Expert Paper No. 2011/3). New York: United Nations. (Web)

Siegel, J., and D. Swanson (eds). 2007. *The Methods and Materials of Demography*. 2nd edn. Bingley: Emerald Group Publishing.

Simon, J. 1981. *The Ultimate Resource*. Princeton, NJ: Princeton University Press.

Simons, C. 2013. *The Devouring Dragon: How China's Rise Threatens Our Natural World*. New York: St Martin's Press.

Sinding, S. 2007. "Overview and Perspective." Pp. 1–12 in R. Freedman and A. Hermalin (eds), *The Global Family Planning Revolution: Three Decades of Population Policies and Programs*. Washington, DC: World Bank.

Skeldon, R. 2013. *Global Migration: Demographic Aspects and Its Relevance for Development*. New York: United Nations.

Smedley, B., A. Stith, and A. Nelson (eds). 2003. *Unequal Treatment: Confronting Racial and Ethnic Disparities in Health Care*. Washington, DC: National Academies Press. (Web)

Smith, C. 1992. *The Great Hunger: Ireland: 1845–1849*. New York: Penguin.

Smith, H. 1991. *The World's Religions: Our Great Wisdom Traditions*. San Francisco: HarperCollins.

Social Security Administration. 2013. *The 2013 Annual Report of the Board of Trustees of the Federal Old-Age and Survivors Insurance and Federal Disability Insurance Trust Funds*. (Web)

Social Security Administration. 2014a. *Retirement Planner: Benefits by Year of Birth*. (Web)

Social Security Administration. 2014b. "Table 2.A3 – Annual Maximum Taxable Earnings and Contribution Rates, 1937–2006." (Web)

Social Security Administration. 2014c. "Automatic Determinations in Recent Years." (Web)

Social Security Administration. 2015. *Life Tables for the United States Social Security Area 1900–2100*. (Web)

Stein, P., S. Willen, and M. Pavetic. 2014. "Couples' Fertility Decision-Making." *Demographic Research* 30: 1697–732. (Web)

Stevens, P. 2004. *Diseases of Poverty and the 10/90 Gap*. London: International Policy Network (Web)

Stix, G. 2007. "A Malignant Flame: Understanding Chronic Inflammation, which Contributes to Heart Disease, Alzheimer's and a Variety of Other Ailments, May Be a Key to Unlocking the Mysteries of Cancer." *Scientific American* 297: 60–7.

Stockburger, D. 2013. *Introductory Statistics: Concepts, Models, and Applications*. 3rd edn. (Web)

Strauss, D. 2015. "Poll: 57% of GOPers Support Making Christianity the National Religion." *Talking Points Memo*: Feb. 24. (Web)

Sundhaussen, H. 2010. *European History Online: Forced Ethnic Migration*. Mainz: Leibniz Institute of European History. (Web)

Tammen, S., S. Frisco, and S. Choi. 2013. "Epigenetics: The Link between Nature and Nurture." *Molecular Aspects of Medicine* 34: 753–64.

Taubes, G. 2011. *Why We Get Fat: And What to Do About It*. New York: Knopf.

Tax Policy Center. 2014. "Historical Social Security Tax Rates." (Web)

Telles, E. 2006. *Race in Another America: The Significance of Skin Color in Brazil*. Princeton: Princeton University Press.

Telles, E. 2012. "The Overlapping Concepts of Race and Colour in Latin America." *Ethnic and Racial Studies* 35: 1163–8.

Temple-Raston, D. 2015. "For Somalis in Minneapolis, Jihadi Recruiting is a Recurring Nightmare." National Public Radio: Feb. 15. (Web)

Thomas, H. 1997. *The Slave Trade: The Story of the Atlantic Slave Trade: 1440–1870.* New York: Simon & Schuster.

Thompson, W. 1929. "Population." *American Journal of Sociology* 34: 959–75.

Thomson, E. 1997. "Couple Childbearing Desires, Intentions, and Births." *Demography* 34: 343–54.

Tolson, G., J. Barnes, G. Gay, and J. Kowaleski. 1991. "The 1989 Revision of the US Standard Certificates and Reports." *Vital and Health Statistics* 4: 1–34 (June). (Web)

Toppo, G., and P. Overberg. 2014. "Diversity in the Classroom: Sides Square off in Minnesota." *USA Today*: Nov. 25. (Web)

Tropp, L., and T. Pettigrew. 2010. "Reducing Ethnocentrism and Prejudice through Intergroup Contact: Summarizing Results from a Meta-Analysis Review." Pp. 104–10 in G. Carter (ed.), *Empirical Approaches to Sociology.* 5th edn. Boston: Allyn & Bacon.

Uchino, B. 2004. *Social Support and Physical Health: Understanding the Health Consequences of Relationships.* New Haven, CT: Yale University Press.

Unger, N. 2006. "Interaction of Ozone and Sulfate in Air Pollution and Climate Change." Goddard Institute for Space Studies, National Aeronautics and Space Administration. *Science Briefs*: March. (Web)

UNHCR. 2014. "First Somali Refugees in Kenya Decide to Return Home as Part of a New Pilot Project." Dec. 8. (Web)

UNHCR. 2015a. *2015 UNHCR Country Operations Profile – Syrian Arab Republic.* (Web)

UNHCR. 2015b. *2015 UNHCR Country Operations Profile – Somalia.* (Web)

United Nations. 1970. *Methods of Measuring Internal Migration.* (Web)

United Nations. 1983. *Manual X: Indirect Techniques for Demographic Estimation.* (Web)

United Nations. 2000. *Agricultural Production and Productivity in Developing Countries.* (Web)

United Nations. 2002. *World Population Aging: 1950–2050.* (Web)

United Nations. 2008. United Nations Expert Group Meeting on Population Distribution, Urbanization, Internal Migration and Development. UN/POP/EGM-URB/2008/01. (Web)

United Nations. 2010. *World Urbanization Prospects: The 2009 Revision Population Database, Definition of Major Areas and Regions.* (Web)

United Nations. 2011a. *Human Development Report 2011.* New York: Palgrave Macmillan.

United Nations. 2011b. *World Population Prospects: The 2010 Revision, Volume II – Demographic Profiles.* (Web)

United Nations. 2012a. "Statistics and Indicators on Women and Men: Table 3B – Marriage." (Web)

United Nations. 2012b. *The State of the World's Children.* "Total Fertility Rate (TFR)." (Web)

United Nations. 2012c. *World Urbanization Prospects: The 2011 Revision.* (Web)

United Nations. 2012d. *Changing Levels and Trends in Mortality: The Role of Patterns of Death by Cause.* (Web)

United Nations. 2012e. *Resilient People, Resilient Planet.* (Web)

United Nations. 2012f. *Marrying Too Young: End Child Marriage.* (Web)

United Nations. 2013a. *Least Developed Countries.* (Web)

United Nations. 2013b. *Principles and Recommendations for a Vital Statistics System, Revision 3* (Final Draft, Apr.). (Web)

United Nations. 2013c. *World Population Prospects: The 2012 Revision, Volume 1 – Comprehensive Tables.* (Web)

United Nations. 2013d. *World Population Prospects: The 2012 Revision, Excel Tables – Mortality Data.* (Web)

United Nations. 2013e. *Levels and Trends in Child Mortality: Report 2013.* (Web)

United Nations. 2013f. *Outcome Document of the Special Event to Follow up Efforts Made towards Achieving the Millennium Development Goals.* Oct. 1. (Web)

United Nations. 2013g. *Demographic Yearbook, 2012.* (Web)

United Nations. 2013h. *World Population Policies 2013.* (Web)

United Nations. 2013i. *World Population Prospects: The 2012 Revision, Excel Tables – Fertility Data* (Web)

United Nations. 2013j. *World Fertility Report 2012.* (Web)

United Nations. 2013k. *World Population Ageing 2013.* (Web)

United Nations. 2014a. *World Urbanization Prospects: The 2014 Revision.* (Web)

United Nations. 2014b. *State of the World's Children, 2012: Table 2 – Nutrition.* (Web)

United Nations. 2014c. *Slum Profile in Human Settlements.* (Web)

United Nations. 2014d. *Millennium Development Indicators: World and Regional Groupings.* (Web)

United Nations. 2014e. *The State of Food Insecurity in the World 2013.* (Web)

United Nations. 2014f. *Breaking the Silence on Open Defecation.* (Web)

United Nations. 2014g. *The Millennium Development Goals Report 2014.* (Web)

United Nations. 2014h. *Totality Fertility Rate.* (Web)

United Nations. 2014i. *World Marriage Data – 2012.* (Web)

United Nations. 2014j. *Dependency Ratio.* (Web)

United Nations. 2014k. *Population of Urban Agglomerations with 300,000 Inhabitants or More in 2014, by Country, 1950–2030. [Excel] File 12.* (Web)

United Nations. 2014l. "More than 191,000 People Killed in Syria with 'No end in Sight' – UN." (Web)

United Nations. 2015a. *Zero Draft of the Outcome Document for the UN Summit to Adopt the Post-2015 Development Agenda – Transforming Our World: The 2030 Agenda for Global Action.* June 2. (Web)

United Nations. 2015b. *The Millennium Development Goals Report 2015.* (Web)

United Nations. 2015c. *International Migrant Stock: By Age and Sex, 2013 Revision.* (Web)

United Nations. 2016a. *World Urbanization Prospects: The 2015 Revision – Age Composition, Population by Age Groups, Male (XLS).* (Web)

United Nations. 2016b. *World Urbanization Prospects: The 2015 Revision – Age Composition, Population by Age Groups, Female (XLS).* (Web)

United Nations. 2016c. *UN Women.* (Web)

US Census Bureau. 2010a. *Official 2010 Census Form.* (Web)

US Census Bureau. 2010b. *2010 Census Urban and Rural Classification and Urban Area Criteria.* (Web)

US Census Bureau. 2012a. "Census Bureau Releases Estimates of Undercount and Overcount in the 2010 Census." Newsroom Archive: May 22.

US Census Bureau. 2012b. "Figure 1 – Median Age at First Marriage by Sex: 1890 to 2010." (Web)

US Census Bureau. 2013a. *American Community Survey: Information Guide.* (Web)

US Census Bureau. 2013b. *Current Population Survey Annual Social and Economic Supplement.* (Web)

US Census Bureau. 2013c. *World Population, 1950–2050.* (Web)

US Census Bureau. 2013d. *World Population: Historical Estimates.* (Web)

US Census Bureau. 2013e. *Total Ancestry Reported: Minnesota.* (Web)

US Census Bureau. 2014a. *State and County Quick Facts.* (Web)

US Census Bureau. 2014b. *CPS Historical Time Series Tables: Educational Attainment.* (Web)

US Census Bureau. 2014c. *Families and Living Arrangements: Living Arrangements of Children.* (Web)

US Census Bureau. 2014d. *Natality Information: Live Births.* (Web)

US Census Bureau. 2014e. *Mortality: Underlying Causes of Death.* (Web)

US Census Bureau. 2015a. *Geographical Mobility: 2012 to 2013, Table 1.* (Web)

US Census Bureau. 2015b. *The 2012 Statistical Abstract – Births, Deaths, Marriages, & Divorces.* (Web)

US Census Bureau. 2016a. *International Programs: International Data Base.* (Web)

US Census Bureau. 2016b. *US and World Population Clock.* (Web)

US Department of Health and Human Services. 2014a. "Enrollment in the Health Insurance Marketplace Totals over 8 million People, More than 4.8 million Additional Medicaid/CHIP Enrollments." (Web)

US Department of Health and Human Services. 2014b. "Medicaid & CHIP: March 2014 Monthly Applications, Eligibility Determinations, and Enrollment Report." (Web)

US Department of Health and Human Services. 2014c. *Social Determinants of Health.* (Web)

US Department of Homeland Security. 2014. *Yearbook of Immigration Statistics: 2013.* (Web)

US Department of State. 2004. "One-Child Policy in China: Arthur E. Dewey, Assistant Secretary for Population, Refugees and Migration, Testimony before the House International Relations Committee." Dec. 14. (Web)

US Department of State. 2014. *Independent States in the World*. (Web)

USAID. 2015. *Demographic and Health Surveys*. (Web)

Ushakov, D. (ed.). 2015. *Urbanization and Migration as Factors Affecting Global Economic Development*. Hershey, PA: Information Science Reference.

van de Kaa, D. 2004. "Is the Second Demographic Transition a Useful Research Concept? Questions and Answers." *Vienna Yearbook of Population Research* 2: 4–10.

van de Walle, E., and J. Knodel. 1980. "Europe's Fertility Transition: New Evidence and Lessons for Today's Developing World." *Population Bulletin* 34: 1–45.

Veevers, J. 1975. "The Moral Careers of Voluntarily Childless Wives: Notes on the Defense of a Variant World View." *The Family Coordinator* 4: 473–87.

Vespa, J., J. Lewis, and R. Kreide. 2013. *America's Families and Living Arrangements: 2012*. Washington, DC: US Census Bureau. (Web)

Voyages Database. 2009. *Voyages: The Trans-Atlantic Slave Trade Database*. (Web)

Wallerstein, E. 1980. *The Modern World System II: Mercantilism and the Consolidation of the European World-Economy, 1600–1750*. New York: Academic Press.

Wang, H., L. Dwyer-Lindgren, K. Lofgren, et al. 2012. "Age-Specific and Sex-Specific Mortality in 187 Countries, 1970–2010: A Systematic Analysis for the Global Burden of Disease Study 2010." *The Lancet* 380: 2071–94.

Waters, M. 2001. *Black Identities: West Indian Dreams and American Realities*. Cambridge, MA: Harvard University Press.

Watkins, S. 1991. *From Provinces into Nations: Demographic Integration in Western Europe, 1870–1960*. Princeton, NJ: Princeton University Press.

Watkins, S., and A. Danzi. 1995. "Women's Gossip and Social Change: Childbirth and Fertility Control among Italian and Jewish Women in the United States, 1920–1940." *Gender & Society* 9: 469–90.

Weeks, J. 2012. *Population: An Introduction to Concepts and Issues*. 11th edn. Boston: Cengage Learning.

Weeks, J. 2016. *Population: An Introduction to Concepts and Issues*. 12th edn. Boston: Cengage Learning.

Weinstein, J., and V. Pillai. 2001. *Demography: The Science of Population*. Boston: Allyn & Bacon.

Weiss J., and S. Wagner. 1998. "What Explains the Negative Consequences of Adverse Childhood Experiences on Adult Health? Insights from Cognitive and Neuroscience Research." *American Journal of Preventive Medicine* 14: 356–60.

Wendt, C., M. Mischke, M. Pfeifer, N. Reibling, et al. 2011. "Cost Barriers Reduce Confidence in Receiving Medical Care When Seriously Ill." *International Journal of Clinical Practice* 65: 115–17.

Whatley, M., and J. Batalova. 2013. *Indian Immigrants in the United States*. Washington, DC: Migration Policy Institute. (Web)

Wherry, L., and K. Finegold. 2004. "Marriage Promotion and the Living Arrangements of Black, Hispanic, and White Children." *Assessing the New Federalism* B-61: 1–8.

White, T. 2006. *China's Longest Campaign: Birth Planning in the People's Republic, 1949–2005*. Ithaca, NY: Cornell University Press.

Wikimedia Commons. 2015. *Net Migration World.png*. (Web)

Wilcox, W. 2008. *Then Comes Marriage: Religion, Race, and Marriage in Urban America*. Waco, TX: Baylor Institutes for Studies of Religion. (Web)

Wilcox, W., A. Cherlin, J. Uecker, and M. Messel. 2012. "No Money, No Honey, No Church: The Deinstitutionalization of Religious Life among the White Working Class." Pp. 227–50 in L. Keister, J. McCarthy, and R. Finke (eds), *Research in the Sociology of Work*, Vol. 23. Bingley: Emerald Group Publishing.

Wilkinson, R., and K. Pickett. 2009. *The Spirit Level: Why Greater Equality Makes Societies Stronger*. New York: Bloomsbury.

Williams, D.C. 2012. *Global Urban Growth: A Reference Handbook*. Santa Barbara: ABC-CLIO.

Williams, D.R., and C. Collins. 1995. "US Socioeconomic and Racial Differences in Health: Patterns and Explanations." *Annual Review of Sociology* 21: 349–86.

Williams, D.R., and M. Sternthal. 2010. "Understanding Racial-Ethnic Disparities in Health: Sociological Contributions." *Journal of Health and Social Behavior* 51: 515–27.

Williams, D.R., R. Haile, and D. González. 2007. "The Mental Health of Black Caribbean Immigrants: Results from the National Survey of American Life." *American Journal of Public Health* 97: 52–9.

Wilson, C. (ed.). 1985. *Roland Pressat – The Dictionary of Demography*. New York: Basil Blackwell.

Wilson, E. 2014. *The Meaning of Human Existence*. New York: Liveright Publishing.

Wise, J. 2013. "About That Overpopulation Problem: Research Suggests We May Actually Face a *Declining* World Population in the Coming Years." Slate. com: Jan. 9. (Web)

Woolf, S., and L. Aron (eds). 2013. *US Health in International Perspective: Shorter Lives, Poorer Health*. Washington, DC: National Academies Press.

World Bank. 2013. *World Development Indicators, 2013*. (Web)

World Bank. 2014a. *World Development Indicators, 2014*. (Web)

World Bank. 2014b. *The Disability-Adjusted Life Year (DALY) Definition, Measurement and Potential Use (English)*. (Web)

World Bank. 2014c. "World Bank Presents Views on Post-2015 Framework for MDGs." (Web)

World Bank. 2014d. "Age at First Marriage – Female by Country." (Web)

World Bank. 2015. "Battle-Related Deaths (Number of People)." (Web)

World Factbook, The. 2013. Washington, DC: Central Intelligence Agency. (Web)

World Factbook, The. 2014. Washington, DC: Central Intelligence Agency. (Web)

World Factbook, The. 2015. Washington, DC: Central Intelligence Agency. (Web)

World Health Organization. 2011a. *Global Status Report on Noncommunicable Diseases 2010*. (Web)

World Health Organization. 2011b. *Noncommunicable Diseases – Country Profiles 2011: Who Global Report*. (Web)

World Health Organization. 2014a. *Joint UNICEF – WHO – The World Bank Child Malnutrition Database*. (Web)

World Health Organization. 2014b. *Global Health Observatory Data Repository*. (Web)

World Health Organization. 2014c. *WHO/UNICEF Joint Monitoring Programme for Water Supply and Sanitation*. (Web)

World Health Organization. 2014d. "Health Transition." (Web)

World Health Organization. 2014e. *Health Statistics and Information Systems: Statistics*. (Web)

World Health Organization. 2014f. *World Health Statistics 2014*. (Web)

World Health Organization. 2014g. *Noncommunicable Diseases: Fact Sheet*. (Web)

World Health Organization. 2014h. *Burden of Disease: Disease and Injury Country Estimates*. (Web)

World Health Organization. 2014i. *Burden of Disease: Age Standardized Disability Adjusted Life Year – DALY – Rates (per 100,000 Population) 2012*. (Web)

World Health Organization. 2014j. *Social Determinants of Health*. (Web)

World Health Organization. 2016. *Women's Health*. (Web)

Worldwatch Institute. 2013. *State of the World 2013: Is Sustainability Still Possible?* Washington, DC: Island Press.

Worldwatch Institute. 2014. *State of the World 2014: Governing for Sustainability*. Washington, DC: Island Press.

Wrigley, E. 1969. *Population and History*. New York: McGraw-Hill.

Wrong, D. 1990. *Population and Society*. New York: McGraw-Hill.

Wyatt, C. 2015. "Paris Attack Highlights Europe's Struggle with Islamism." BBC News: Jan. 7. (Web)

Xienhuanet.com. 2012. "New Law Targets Foreigners' Illegal Presence." June 30. (Web)

Yew, L. 2012. "Warning Bell for Developed Countries: Declining Birth Rates." *Forbes*: Apr. 25. (Web)

Yonetani, M., et al. 2014. *Global Overview 2014: People Displaced by Disasters*. Geneva: Internal Displacement Monitoring Centre, Norwegian Refugee Council. (Web)

Yuen, L. 2009. "Somali-American Professors Angered over Repeated Searches." Minnesota Public Radio: Aug. 24. (Web)

Yuen, L., and S. Aslanian. 2013. "Minnesota Pipeline to al-Shabab." Minnesota Public Radio: Sept. 25. (Web)

Yusuf, A. 2012. *Somalis in Minnesota*. Minneapolis: Minnesota Historical Society Press.

Zhang, D. 2014. "China Looks to Relax Green Card Policy." (Web)

Zhang, J. 2012. "Proposal to Push Retirement Age to 65." China.org.cn: July 2. (Web)

Zlotnick, H. 2003. *The Global Dimensions of Female Migration*. Washington, DC: Migration Policy Institute. (Web)

Zuo, M. 2014. "China Will 'Inevitably' Raise Retirement Age, Says Labour Ministry." *South China Morning Post*: Jan. 25. (Web)

Zwerdling, D. 2009a. "India's Farming 'Revolution' Heading for Collapse." National Public Radio: Apr. 13. (Web)

Zwerdling, D. 2009b. "'Green Revolution' Trapping India's Farmers in Debt." National Public Radio: Apr. 14. (Web)

Index